I am for the writers. All of them. The rich, the famous, the talented, the new writers and the old. The poor and the unknown writers. The writers who have won Academy Awards and have stars buried in the cement cemetery of Hollywood Boulevard. And the unrewarded writers. The unheralded, the unwanted writers too. I am for all writers: writer-directors, writer-producers, and the "and" writers (those whose names came second or third). All the damned and blessed writers wherever you are . . . even the dead writers.

—Richard Brooks, writer/director

The writer is the only absolutely essential element of Hollywood, and he must never find out.

—Irving G. Thalberg, legendary studio boss

If I had the influence I would use it to help everyone, just one time even, say that the emperor is naked, that craziness is craziness and that bad taste is beneath their contempt. I'd get them to tell someone they've sold their souls to what they really think of them . . . that they are completely unprincipled, untalented . . . to do that one single thing that affirms some kind of justice or standards . . . I wish I had that influence. I'd feel like I really made a difference . . .

—Anonymous

THIS BUSINESS OF SCREENWRITING

HOW TO PROTECT YOURSELF AS A SCREENWRITER

Ron Suppa, Esq.

lone eagle™
PUBLISHING COMPANY
Los Angeles

LONE EAGLE PUBLISHING COMPANY, LLC™
2337 Roscomare Road, Suite Nine
Los Angeles, CA 90077-1851
Tel: 800-FILMBKS • Toll Free Fax: 888-FILMBKS
www.loneeagle.com and www.eaglei.com

Printed in the United States of America

Cover design by ADVANTAGE, London, T: +44 20 7613 3933
Book design by Carla Green
Edited by Janna Wong Healy

Library of Congress Cataloging-in-Publication Data applied for.

WGA forms courtesy of Writers Guild of America, west, Inc., 700 West Third Street, Los Angeles, CA 90048, (323) 951-4000

Lone Eagle books may be purchased in bulk at special discounts for promotional or educational purposes. Special editions can be created to specifications. Inquiries for sales and distribution, textbook adoption, foreign language translation, editorial, and rights and permissions inquiries should be addressed to: Jeff Black, Lone Eagle Publishing, 2337 Roscomare Road, Suite Nine, Los Angeles, CA 90077 or send e-mail to: info@loneeagle.com

Distributed to the trade by National Book Network, 800-462-6420

Lone Eagle Publishing Company is a registered trademark.

to Lisa and Nicolas,

and to Grace,
with love and appreciation

CONTENTS

ACKNOWLEDGMENTS

How does anyone come to write a book? In my case, this book would not have been written had it not been for two people who have never met each other—Dr. Linda Venis and Erik Bauer.

For the past 12 years I have been privileged to teach screenwriting in the largest and most comprehensive adult education program in the world, the Writers Program at UCLA Extension. Dr. Venis, the program's talented, resourceful and innovative director, gathered a handful of teachers one fine spring weekend and took our show on the road. At the opening symposium in Chicago, I was asked to deliver a short lecture on the business aspects of screenwriting. One of the students present at that lecture, Erik Bauer, would later edit and publish a writer's journal. Sometime later, he contacted me and asked if I would contribute a regular column. "Don't sugarcoat it," he said, and I did not. It was in those columns—and with Erik's unfailing guidance and encouragement—that the subject matter of this book was first explored. For their inexhaustible good nature and their steadfast support through the years, I am forever indebted and beholden to Erik and to Dr. Venis; and, I am ever thankful for their friendship.

My heartfelt appreciation also to Janna Healy for her unerring editorial acumen, and to Carla Green and Jeff Black for all their support and hard work in preparing this text for publication.

Finally, to my publisher, Joan Singleton, an especially warm encomium is due for believing this author could find the light through the murky eccentricities of the most celebrated and misunderstood business in the world.

AUTHOR'S NOTES

"Becoming a writer is not a career decision, like becoming a doctor or a policeman. You don't choose it so much as get chosen, and once you accept the fact that you're not fit for anything else, you have to be prepared to walk a long, hard road for the rest of your days."

Novelist Paul Auster wasn't targeting screenwriters in particular when he wrote this, but he may as well have been. As a career, screenwriting is one of the toughest—but the potential rewards are great. Informed that copies of his scripts were selling for $100 on the black market, screenwriter Joe Eszterhas (*Flashdance, Basic Instinct, Showgirls*) responded: "I guess they're bought by guys who want to figure out how the hell you can be paid millions of dollars for a few week's work."[1]

Compared to other forms of writing, screenwriting has always been at the top of the salary heap. Even famed writers such as William Faulkner, F. Scott Fitzgerald, Bertolt Brecht, Gore Vidal and Norman Mailer have answered the financial—if not the artistic—call of Hollywood. In 1926, Herman Mankiewicz, co-author of *Citizen Kane* with Orson Welles, lured Chicago newsman Ben Hecht to Los Angeles with the following cable: "Will you accept $300 per week to work for Paramount Pictures? All expenses paid. The $300 is peanuts. Millions are to be grabbed out here and your only competition is idiots. Don't let this get around."[2]

Of course it did get around and today, more than ever, busloads of screenwriting wanna-bes are descending on Hollywood, not only for the money, but also for the glory. Critical recognition has finally caught up with the notion that films are written, that they are conceived in the mind of a writer. Until recently, this has been a fairly well-kept secret; the spotlight focused on the director, the star, sometimes the producer, but rarely the writer. Well, the secret

---

[1, 2] Both from an article by William Cash, *London Times, Saturday Review*, Oct. 24, 1992.

is out. Not only in Los Angeles, but in Boston, Chicago, Miami and Washington, D.C., writing a screenplay has quietly become the new American Dream.

Over the years, I have worn many hats—entertainment lawyer, film company executive, producer, director, screenwriter, script consultant, teacher. I have read at least 5,000 screenplays and had the good fortune to know, in some small way, over 3,000 writers. As both a buyer and seller of screen stories, I have become convinced that all jobs in the film business come down to one: finding a screenplay that can attract talent and, ultimately, an audience.

Those hoping to tap into the unprecedented opportunities for screenwriters are faced with an explosion of books, classes and seminars designed to arm them with at least a basic knowledge of the art and craft of screenwriting. And that is how it should be—art before business. It stands to reason that you can sell something only if you have something to sell. Yet the writer's work is necessarily incomplete until it is read, purchased, produced and released in the marketplace.

Director Steven Spielberg echoed this sentiment: "Most of my life has been spent in the dark watching movies. Movies have been the literature of my life. And I think in our romance with technology and our excitement at exploring all the possibilities of film and video, I think that we have partially lost something that we now have to reclaim. I think it's time to renew our romance with the word."[3]

And as you are probably aware, the marketplace is changing. New markets created by the electronic age, the expansion of cable and network television and the rebirth of the independent film have opened wide Hollywood's once closely-guarded gates. In my work with the New Members Committee of the Writers Guild of America, west, I have witnessed over fifty new memberships granted in a single month. All these new Hollywood players wrote well enough to sell to or be hired by Guild signatory production companies, but the methods by which each found his way to these companies—through the sometimes mystifying maze of agents, attorneys, producers and studio executives—varied as widely as their personality, age, and ethnic background.

I wrote this book as a survival guide to help all writers through that maze. There is no reason for any writer, even those living far from Hollywood, to feel left out of this opportunity. For anyone who has persevered and written a screenplay or teleplay, whose

---

[3] A speech before the WGA, recorded in *Words,* documentary short by Chuck Workman.

good work is left to wither unseen in a desk drawer or under a pile of magazines, it is my hope this book will expand your contacts and your resolve.

In the end, I hope the reader will come to believe as I do that selling a screenplay is not all that mystifying, holy, or pedantic a subject. It couldn't be; agents do it all the time.

Caveat

Throughout this book, I have borrowed freely from 25 years of personal experience in the film business to convey a taste of what the real world of professional screenwriting is like and to help even the neophyte writer compete on an insider level in that world. Yet clearly, one person's experience will differ from someone else's and no two sets of circumstances or facts are ever exactly alike. *For this reason, nothing in this book is intended nor should be construed as doctrine or legal advice.* There are exceptions and qualifications to all legal principles and it is not my intention to fully explore the complex subtleties of those principles in these pages.

Chapter 1
THE SCREENWRITER'S LIFE

WHY WE WRITE

Novelist John Barth has said "a writer knows he's a writer."

A writer is not something you strive to be—it is something you are. I have a baseball cap with the word "writer" on the brim; it defines me. I don't write all the time, nor do I always want to, but I will always write. If you, too, must write (or explode!), if you are nothing if you are not a writer, if you would do it for free, then we are brothers.

Novels, short stories, poetry, plays, screenplays, movies of the week, episodic television—each has different challenges and rewards. But whatever the medium, the desire for the writer is the same: to communicate, to inform, to move people to laughter or tears, to set them dreaming, to touch them with your personal vision of the world.

Certainly, if you have no talent you can still write. There are plenty of untalented authors—just check any airport book rack. But, while I regard the untalented author with benign amusement, I regard the talented hack—the writer whose heart and soul is not consumed with the power of dreams, the violent struggles of poverty, the cancer of racism, the loneliness of old age, the cosmic point to all this *life*—as a menace to society and I hold him in contempt of mankind. However, if you have talent, then good for you. But, remember: talent is not always enough. If you have nothing to say, your best writing is a waste of time and the lessons in this book are academic.

The "business" of screenwriting may give the impression of being only about money, deals and commerce, but selling your work should be a prerequisite to reaching an audience, not an end in itself. The world demands more from its scribes than the worship of naked commerce. Ours is a higher calling. To paraphrase Shelley in his poem Mont Blanc, ". . . it is your charge to interpret the human experience, to feel it deeply, and to make it deeply felt."

1

Shelley was writing about a mountain in France, a mountain to which people come to view, to ski or hike its peaks and to fish in its streams. But the poet reserved a special place for the artist. He found in the silence and solitude of that great natural wonder, "a voice . . . not understood by all," a passionate voice to which only the artist, the poet, the writer, "the wise and great and good" among us, could bear witness. And he held that to be our duty, our challenge, our very *raison d'être*—whether we presume to speak for that mountain, for a battered single mother in an urban ghetto, for a crippled Vietnam vet or for a couple of quirky strangers who meet by chance and fall in love.

In a recent address to a PEN[1] conference in Prague, Václav Havel echoed Shelley when he said: "[Writers] are people whose profession, indeed whose very vocation, is to perceive far more profoundly than others the general context of things, to feel a general sense of responsibility for the world and to articulate publicly this inner experience." Armed with only his poetry to throw "a sharp light on the misery of the contemporary human soul," Václav Havel went from dissident writer to President of the Czech Republic. Havel knows that all writers are political writers: they cannot sit on the fence, they must take sides, make judgments as to what is moral or immoral, good or evil. Then, consciously or unconsciously, audiences or readers will evaluate every act of every character according to their own moral or ethical scale.

These days, some people believe the world is going to hell in a hand basket. The good news is that writers don't have to take it lying down. As writers, we have the prerogative to challenge authority, inspire rebellion, sway public opinion, arouse emotion and motivate change. Our words have the power to disturb and disrupt or perhaps just to deliver a few good belly laughs. Our reward, and that of our audience, is the enlarged sense of life which is the ultimate gift of art.

In that regard, I offer an excerpt from the remarks of screenwriter Phil Alden Robinson (*Field of Dreams*), made at the hearings against film colorization, held in Los Angeles in January, 1990, before members of the U.S. House of Representatives:

> When we begin to write a motion picture, life stops. We write for months and months, draft after draft, and then

2

when we're finally done . . . we re-write for months and months; changing, questioning, doubting, discovering, experimenting, honing, throwing things out and putting them back. After about 10 or 12 drafts, we put a title page on it that says First Draft. We think it's pretty good. We show it to a friend who tells us it stinks. We know he's right. So we do six or eight more drafts and put a new title page on it. It still says First Draft.

After a few more of those we finally get the nerve to turn one in to the studio. They read it. Pretty soon, we get to enjoy the helpful suggestions of studio executives who may or may not have a clue what we're trying to do . . . so we do five or six more drafts, slap on a title page that says Second Draft and turn it in. Now the suggestions come not just from studio executives, but from their assistants, their friends, their mothers, their friends' mothers, and their children. Actually, the children give pretty good notes.

After a very long time, if we're really, really lucky, we then get notes from a director who may have a completely different vision of the movie . . . from actors who feel that their character wouldn't say this or do that . . . we find that scenes we labored over for months cannot be filmed, or are completely changed during production, or are cut out entirely during editing . . . and yet we endure all this. We endure it for one reason—it's not the money, and it's certainly not the glamour; it's for that slim wisp of a hope that at the end of all the pain and angst and self-doubt and pride swallowing and politicking and fighting and accommodating and tap dancing and seven-day weeks and 14-hour days and sleepless nights—that at the end of it all—after years of all that—a MOVIE is made, a movie that somehow miraculously reflects that original vision you had long, long ago sitting by yourself with the blank piece of paper.

And maybe all over America and all over the world people will sit in dark rooms and watch something that existed only in your head. And they'll be moved, or entertained, or enlightened, or touched . . . and a part of it will stay with them and become a piece of their memories, a piece of their life. And this movie that you imagined, and that is the product of so many people working so hard for so long, this movie that against all odds turned out pretty good, this movie that bears your name, will outlive you. You will have succeeded in leaving something behind with the power to touch people. Something that says I was here. And I tried. And this is what I did when I was here . . . To have even a chance of accomplishing that is the prime reason we create.

3

PREPARING FOR A WRITING CAREER

Most everyone these days secretly thinks himself a writer, or more precisely, he could be a writer if only . . . he could type, spell or use a computer. Makes a nice daydream, but WGA award-winning writer Burt Prelutsky (*A Small Killing, Homeward Bound*), after 30 years of slogging away in the trenches, sees it a bit differently: "Only write if you absolutely have to. It is a very difficult way to make a living, so if you have any choice in the matter, get into some other racket."

On the other hand, if you say, "what else am I going to do? I've no training, no profession, like to stay indoors when it rains and have an unnatural love of silk pajamas," maybe screenwriting will work for you. But here's a news flash: success as a writer requires the same commitment, hard work and other professional courtesies you would devote to a career in any other profession, be it law, medicine or making sandals on Hollywood Boulevard.

Like all arts, writing is a way of life, not an isolated effort. You may have talent; you may have one great inspirational story that burns to be told. But latent talent and one screenplay does not a career make. Writers build a body of work by maintaining a *daily routine*, not unlike that of any standard nine-to-five job.

. . . .

4

Consider this advice posted on the Writers Guild electronic bulletin board by Phil Alden Robinson in a message to a fellow writer on the subject of "How I Write:"

As for what my day consists of, here's my writing routine. And I highly recommend it.

I don't get up too early (as I don't want to be groggy on a day when I'm writing), feed the dog, exercise (good for clearing the head before writing), shower, eat a good breakfast (very important to prepare you for writing), read the newspapers (sharpens your mind), make some phone calls and do all the assorted little things around the house that have piled up to get them out of the way so they don't give you an excuse later for not writing.

Then it's time for lunch. I go out and eat, finding that getting out of the house is a good way to clear the mind for writing. Lunch invariably leads to an errand or two, maybe a little shopping or something, sometimes even involving the purchase of necessary items without which one cannot write, such as three-hole punch paper, or a book that you need for research or background.

When you get home, there's mail to answer, and phone calls to return, all of which are very important to get out of the way so they don't impede your writing. By late afternoon, you're faced with a dilemma: start writing now, only to have to interrupt it for dinner, thus losing valuable momentum and focus . . . or put it off until after dinner. I highly recommend you not start at this point. Most people are not at their peak in the late afternoons, and there's nothing worse than getting a head of steam going only to cut it off prematurely. So now's a good time for catching up on magazines, some of which might actually contain a nugget that inspires or informs your work.

After dinner, you realize there's a movie you've been putting off seeing, and let's be brutally honest here: How can we be so presumptuous as to write movies if we're not seeing them? It is absolutely crucial that we learn from our peers, profit from their mistakes, experience what the audience likes and dislikes.

Okay. The movie lets out at 10, and home you go. Now, finally, there are no more distractions, all the possible procrastinations are gone, you're primed and inspired to start writing. But here's the thing. If you start writing now, you'll be up until 2 or 3 in the morning, and that's going to screw up tomorrow something fierce, so go right to bed.

The next morning, be sure not to get up too early, as you don't want to be groggy on a day when you're writing . . . (et cetera, et cetera, et cetera).

I do this for weeks on end until I feel so guilty and fraudulent that I drop everything, turn off the phones and do nothing but write from morning til night until I'm done.

. . . .

May I suggest an alternative method? Here are a dozen steps you might take to prepare yourself, not just to write, but for *a writer's life*:

➤ *Get out of your bathrobe and get dressed.*
This advice, once given to me by author Tommy Thompson, may be the most crucial of all. Real writers view their work as a job, not a hobby. You may enjoy writing in a flannel shirt, but don't demean your work by coming to your computer before you've brushed your teeth.

5

➤ *Take the time to develop your craft.*
College can take four years, a law degree three more. How much time are you willing to invest in your professional career as a writer? Two hours a day? Four? A writer friend of mine makes a contract with herself and pays herself a small salary (into the cookie jar) for the time she spends writing.

Writing, like skiing, requires "time on the slopes" to get you over the inevitable plateaus. Consider your other responsibilities, then find a block of time that matches the extent of your commitment, the same as you might do for an exercise program. Set a realistic schedule, maybe two or three hours a day, three or four days a week. And be prepared to stick with it. Be ready to stare at a blank page, to type up recipes or lists of baseball players—anything to keep

Screenwriter John Milius (*Apocalypse Now*) claims this legendary formula brought him success: he devoted one hour a day, at exactly 5 p.m., to his writing; he did this 365 days a year.

you glued to your word processor until the characters that inhabit your unconscious mind begin to speak to you and demand their place in the universe.

Remember, if you hope to earn, say, $120,000 for an original feature film screenplay (Writers Guild minimum is around $80,000), that equals *$1,000 per page, white space and all.* Even if it took a full week to write each and every single page, wouldn't that be fair pay for an honest day's work?

➤ *Find a time and a place to write.*

Woody Allen believes that "eighty percent of success is just showing up." Be prepared to be there, *somewhere*, primed and ready to work. All writers don't write all the time, but all writers do *eventually* write.

Be aware that the duties of life can drown the fire in your belly. In England, there is a saying, "the death of the artist is the pram in the hall." Try to arrange your work schedule to avoid distractions or to keep away from those who will not respect the seriousness of your time alone with the blank page. Understand that most people will not have an inkling what it is you *really* do. (They might be wondering when you're going to get a real job.) It is up to *you* to demand respect and understanding for your very real job. (Okay, jobs are supposed to *pay* something; their mothers should have taught them that it's rude to ask people how much they earn.)

Lord Byron, upon the third interruption of his work by his half-sister Augusta, left this note for her on her dresser:[2]

> I am trying to write. I doubt you understand what is involved. Use your imagination if you can. I write. I create. I conjure up visions from inside my mind and set them down on paper, in rhyme. I know all my friends think it is merely a gift, a hobby. I feel the muse upon me and I sit down and dash off a few lines which everyone is anxious to read. Do you really suppose it is as simple as that? Do you really suppose I would enjoy the success I do by merely indulging a hobby? . . . It is not a heaven-sent messenger who turns my thoughts into verse. *I* have to do that. *I* have to take a nebulous idea, delightful to dream about as I lie half-awake in bed, and turn it into some sense, some *words*.

➤ *Behave like a writer.*

Do all the things on a daily basis that are part of your art. If you head off to the beach, consider it a "writer's holiday." Use it as precious ruminating time. Always carry pen and paper or a tape recorder with you, the way a photographer carries a camera. We all have moments of inspiration, but writers jot them down.

2 Nicole, Christopher. *The Secret Memoirs of Lord Byron.*

To have that light bulb flash in your head, you must work to heighten your powers of observation. Examine your life and the people and things around you; there's a rich mother lode there to mine. If you're reclusive, force yourself to get out more! Befriend another writer; they always have time for lunch. Make and nurture business contacts. *Listen* to people. Go to a museum, take in a play, walk to work, shoot some hoops. The human condition cannot be lost on you, nor can the charms of nature, history, politics, religion, sports, the arts, the sciences or the fantastic.

➤ *See movies.*

See the good ones and the bad ones and learn the difference. Which movies moved you to tears or laughter or set you to dreaming? Which made your heart ache from wishing *you* had written them? These are likely to promote the same themes you will pursue most successfully as a writer.

➤ *Read the "how-to" books on writing.*

Read them all—there are some good ones out there. While you're at it, take screenwriting classes offered in your area. Attend the seminars on the business. Think of this as career training. There may be repetition, but if you pick up one new tip that improves your work, you've made a smart investment.

7

➤ *Read "The Trades."*

Daily Variety, Hollywood Reporter. It won't hurt to include others, such as *Entertainment Weekly, Screen International, Premiere.* Learn the business, the players, the jargon. Know where executives are working and what agendas they are currently espousing for their companies. Allow *the biz* to seep into your daily habits, as if by osmosis. It's vital to your career to know what agencies are hot, what players are needed to get "a package" into production and who is at which studio this month.

➤ *Read screenplays.*

It doesn't matter whether they're produced or unproduced. Most local film commissions have screenplays on file, as do many university libraries (especially those with film programs). Many screenplays are published and available at the bookstore. A number of classic and current screenplays can be purchased through the Internet. (Some online sites like Drew's Script-O-Rama [www.script-o-rama.com] post current TV and movie scripts that can be downloaded for free.) If you have access to the Academy of Motion Picture Arts and Sciences Margaret Herrick Library or the Writers Guild Library, you can read screenplays or teleplays simply by posting your driver's license.

Another tip is to rent the video and then watch it while you read the script (preferably the writer's version, without scene numbers and in screenplay format) and see how the words eventually translate onto the screen.

➤ *Read good fiction.*
Notice how several of these steps suggest that you "READ." Writers must first be readers. The great authors and the classic works are our teachers. Milan Kundera[3] said that a writer must go beyond himself, beyond the boundaries of his own experience, and seek out "the possibilities of life in the trap the world has become" (himself borrowing from Kafka). Books take you out of your world and open up a universe of thematic and situational possibilities; they also help you discover your own unique style and voice.

➤ *Grant yourself the freedom to fail.*
Your first steps are bound to be shaky. Accept the fact there's a learning curve. (Van Gogh did not sell a painting in his lifetime.) It takes time to find your voice; it will also take time to find your audience. The difference between the successful writer and the failed writer is that the successful writer has *failed more often.*

➤ *Never stop writing.*
8

Do a page a day, every day for the rest of your life. When you've finished one script, start another. Better still, write at least three before showing the first to anyone of consequence. Rejection won't stop you if you're halfway through your next opus. Writer's block? That's a tired excuse from one tired of life.

Playwright John MacNicholas, in his unpublished play *Dumas,* gives us this wonderful exchange between Alexandre Dumas (*The Three Musketeers*) and his son, also Alexandre (*Camille*):

```
                     Son
          I have nothing to write about.


                    Father
          I believe you're acquainted
          with - let's see - Love?
          Beauty? Death? Those subjects
          have sold well for several
          thousand years.


                     Son
          I don't know how to start.
```

---

[3] Kundera, Milan. *The Unbearable Lightness of Being,* Harper + Row, New York, 1984.

```
              Father
Dip the pen into ink, cover the
page with words.


               Son
But form, incidents, the style -


              Father
- Just start. Farmers in
Normandy say if the horse is
blind, you load the wagon and
go to market anyway.
```

➢ *Don't write like a great man, just write.*
This advice, given to me by a one-armed poet who can write all of
us under the table, means that you shouldn't fall into the trap of
believing that everything you write must be brilliant. Allow the
artist in you to create before the critic in you destroys. On the other
hand, *never* submit your work until it is ready. That means it should
be written, polished and rewritten again—until it is truly your best
work. The movie business isn't known for giving a lot of second
chances.

Forget about the fairytales of overnight, multi-million dollar script
sales that you read about in the trades. Success takes luck, timing,
talent and a lot of sweat. But if the very prospect of all that effort is
anathema to you, you may be headed down a wrong-way street to
begin with. Because for your work to breathe, to have life on the
page, you must have passion for it. Like Burt Prelutsky, you do it
because you have to. And cheer up. As Somerset Maugham said,
"Writing may not be a good living, but it's a good life!"

9

12-STEP PROGRAM FOR A WRITER'S LIFE:
- **Get out of your bathrobe and get dressed.**
- **Take the time to develop your craft.**
- **Find a time and a place to write.**
- **Behave like a writer.**
- **See movies.**
- **Read the how-to books.**
- **Read the trades.**
- **Read screenplays.**
- **Read good fiction.**
- **Grant yourself the freedom to fail.**
- **Never stop writing.**
- **Don't write like a great man, just write.**

WHAT'S L.A. GOT TO DO WITH IT?

No doubt, it is not inspiration, but perspiration, that makes a writer. But can it also be location?

First, a little perspective. In the beginning, comes the work. Then, comes the peer group validation of the work. Only then should travel plans or moving vans be considered. Nonetheless, the question most frequently asked by writers in screenwriting seminars around the country is: Is it absolutely necessary that I move to Los Angeles to have a career as a screen or television writer?

Unlike *Jeopardy*, there is no one right answer to this question (or question to this answer, if you will). On the one hand, if you have yet to sell a feature screenplay or win an assignment for a television series, don't worry yet about moving to Los Angeles. Or, if you decide to write for news agencies, industrials, commercials or regional television, for example, you may never have to travel. (Neighborhood reputations can, and often do, lead to national exposure.) Furthermore, once you are established as an "A" list feature screenwriter, you can plug your laptop into the arctic tundra if you so choose and no one will object.

On the other hand, while an active screenwriting community as outlined above extends far beyond the borders of Los Angeles, *most* screenwriters and virtually all television writers work and reside in "Hollywood," the generic area popularly referred to by the worldwide media that can, in reality, encompass all of Southern California. If you want a career in film, cable or network television and if you want it sooner rather than later, there is no escaping the fact that Los Angeles is where the action is.

"Across America and beyond," according to journalist Richard Rodriquez, "men and women are gathering their bags and their suitcases, closing the family house, leaving behind common memory and heading for the great city to work. They head for Los Angeles."

Certainly, Los Angeles is where the Industry lives and breathes. It's where "the business" is headquartered and the creative meetings are held: where stars and starmakers bump into one another at restaurants and film premiers. It's also where film and television writers are represented, interviewed, hired and, importantly, it's where they work. As critics quickly point out, it may be this very insular nature of the Hollywood writing community that contributes to the current state of entertainment, which is dominated by formulaic storylines.

In reaction to this, many novels are purchased by producers in search of a diverse viewpoint. But, as if to second-guess their own good instincts, most screenplays based on those novels are written by writers working in Los Angeles. Similarly, television production

10

is increasingly being located outside Hollywood to escape the charmless skyline and studio sets, the sameness of the ambiance and weather. But again, the writers for those shows rarely board a plane; *Northern Exposure* may have been filmed entirely on location in Washington State, but its writer/producers toiled at their computers in an industrial park in West Los Angeles.

Consider this: it's a people business. Executives like face-to-face meetings; they like to stay close to the creators of their projects. To maintain those all-important relationships—which translate into employment and careers—writers must do more than pick up the phone or send a fax. An occasional dinner party must be attended, a round of golf or set of tennis played, a holiday or child's birthday celebrated together. Perhaps, in a perfect world, one could live in a cabin in Montana and write for *Touched by an Angel* but, on top of all the other odds working against a new writer, do you wish to *increase* your chances of success or *lower* them?

I realize this is a sensitive issue. Few writers want to give up lifelong friendships, family ties and green spaces to pursue a risky entry into a business located in a far-off city, based only on their passion to tell a story. I couldn't agree more. I live in Los Angeles, but occasionally I too opt out for a breath of fresh air.

. . . .

In 1988, my father died reaching for a glass of ice water. After that, the year evaporated—disappeared— along with his laugh, and I was ripe for a change of atmosphere. When I came across an ad in *Daily Variety* for a house trade in England ("a flat in Regent's Park and a country house in Surrey, plus two cars, for appropriate Westside accommodation"), I notified my agent, prepaid my Guild dues and hopped a taxi to LAX.

In London, I was greeted by a freezing rain. I lugged my bags up five flights of stairs and was greeted by four dank rooms overlooking the park. I didn't know a soul; the phone never rang and there was no one to meet for lunch (besides it was too cold and wet to go out). So, noting that every wall in the flat was lined with books, I read voraciously, devouring everything from Flaubert and Sarte to Jane Austen and the Brontës.

Even the collected works of Lenin. I talked my way into a five-year pass to the Round Reading Room of the British Library where, under the spell of its huge dome, I was rendered speechless with reverence for the power of words. I occasionally occupied the same seat at which Karl Marx or Bernard Shaw had labored at creations that would endure countless lifetimes.

I worked and networked. I wrote poems, short stories, even started a serious work of historical fiction. On Sundays, I played baseball in Regent's Park with stringers from Reuters and NBC and *60 Minutes*. And yes, I eventually met with executives from most of the British film companies and the BBC. I did have lunch with producers and directors, and I parlayed whatever Hollywood cachet I imported into a temporary membership at the Groucho Club in Soho where journalists, literary and film giants from all over Europe gathered to trade tales of their writing adventures. It was arguably the best year of my life.

But I didn't write any screenplays. No television either. No one offered. Nowhere but in Hollywood is it more true: out of sight, out of mind.

. . . .

There were many such times—long vacations if you will—when my agency lost contact and patience with me: if I couldn't meet face-to-face with series showrunners or schmooze over coffee in the commissary with studio executives, how could my agents be expected to generate any heat for my career? It was always difficult after I returned to Los Angeles to plug myself back into the Hollywood system and regain anything near the industry entree I had previously enjoyed.

Nonetheless, despite the importance of establishing a presence in Hollywood, I still believe that it is probably best not to change your life and uproot your family for what, at the start, is only a *chance* at making a career as a screenwriter. But, that doesn't mean you should compromise your dreams. After all, we live in a world of faxes, e-mails and frequent flyer miles. Write that spec feature or sample television episode and send it across the continent. If it leads to phenomenal success, you can have a career and still live in Wyoming. Many screenwriting careers flourish in cities far away from Hollywood.

But here's the catch: Most writers with long distance careers are established *feature* writers who have been granted long deadlines and who have developed isolated writing routines. Moreover, even they must maintain strong Hollywood representation and a willingness to come to town at the drop of a hat for meetings and story conferences.

Television writers, particularly those in episodic TV, will have a harder time maintaining a flexible location. While there are stories of showrunners who manage a bicoastal existence, I know of not a single writer working in series television who lives beyond local commuting distance to the show. There will be meetings you'll have to attend, notes dispensed which require immediate script revision; the whole world of series television sometimes seems to be conducted in a state of perpetual panic by a staff facing impossible deadlines on a daily basis. Simply put, it is not a long-distance gig.

If you don't want to move, once you have a couple of good screenplays or teleplays under your belt, a practical plan might be to circulate your work in your local film community. Atlanta, Chicago, Miami, San Francisco, Vancouver and Toronto, to name a few, have become busy production locations. And local film commissions (probably in or near your city) have lists of film activities within their jurisdictions and names of local personnel who have worked on the productions. These are all good contacts for your career.

Moreover, virtually every major U.S. city has at least one good literary agency with arms stretched out to Hollywood. Contact these agencies first, if only because they likely will be more accessible to local talent. Contacting a smaller agency can also garner a new writer a valuable (and, free) first read; whether or not this leads to representation, most writers will appreciate a professional appraisal of their work.

Once you've received comments on your work, rewritten the piece to iron out the kinks and given it another polish, *then* make phone calls and send query letters and faxes to Los Angeles contacts. Follow up by announcing your intention to be in the L.A. area for a few days (think of it as a working vacation) to see if you can prompt agents or producers to meet with you. Many will be considerate of your effort and time.

But become an invited guest before you pack your bags for a long stay. And then, many screenplays later, when your talent is self-evident, perhaps you can make the mountain come to Mohammed.

For television writers, a good time to go to L.A. is during "pilot season," or when a new show is staffing up. An agent will be invaluable to you for opening doors and setting meetings. Or, on your own, you can get contact information for all shows by calling the Writers Guild and speaking with someone who edits the "TV Market" list. In fact, you can even stop by the Guild in person. Like the Automobile Club, the Guild has experience, information and forms to offer; they may even suggest a good restaurant.

13

Chapter 2

THE SCREENWRITER'S SALES TOOLS: FROM CONCEPT TO SCRIPT

By now, you've decided the writer's life is for you: you have worked out your immediate living arrangements and travel plans; your desire is strong and the rewards are self-evident. But trust me on this—as one sage wrote, "there is many a slip betwixt the cup and the lip." Or, as Woody Allen put it in his film *Crimes and Misdemeanors* (as uttered by Alan Alda's character Lester, a hardened film producer), "This is the real world. They don't pay off on high aspirations. You've got to deliver."

The question is: "Deliver what to whom?"

The answer is: A full-length, original feature screenplay is the *sine qua non* for entry into the "promised land" of feature films; for television, at least two "spec" writing samples must precede any contact with a prospective employer. There are no shortcuts for the new writer—*no ideas, concepts, treatments or outlines will do.*

Books or seminars which tell you otherwise are fudging the facts to make you feel better. Still, you wonder, what about those stories in the trades of writers spinning yarns and tossing off one-liners for big bucks and Hollywood superstardom? Isn't there something short of that full first draft that will get you into the club? Well, no, but what follows are valuable *screenwriter tools* that serve an essential purpose in both the scripting and the marketing of ideas.

THE CONCEPT
An idea for a film, also referred to as a "concept," is as ethereal as the vacuum in outer space. It is not a tangible intellectual property; it is not protectable by copyright and it is *not sellable*, at least for the novice writer, until fleshed out with plot, characters and dramatic structure. Nonetheless, the idea *is*, however half-baked, the basic raw material out of which movies are made.

Some early ideas are so dumb that they seem hardly worth a second thought. Yet, study the history of good ideas, urges Arthur VanGundy, Professor of Communication at the University of

Oklahoma, and the most powerful appear to come from puttering around with the seemingly ridiculous. The real point, per VanGundy, is to allow yourself to be wildly imaginative, without censure; to brainstorm. Some ideas may prove unworkable, but others may be like caterpillars that hatch into beautiful butterflies.

On the other hand, some ideas seem ready-made for the movies the moment they are hatched. The oft bandied-about term "high-concept" is no more than studio lingo for a film premise easily grasped or summarized in a single sentence, an idea so exciting it seems to levitate off the page. Some examples of high-concept films are:

- *Die Hard*—An off-duty New York cop must single-handedly battle terrorists in an L.A. high-rise and rescue innocent hostages, including his wife
- *Splash*—A young man finally finds the woman of his dreams, only she's a fish.
- *Beverly Hills Cop*—A mission to solve his best friend's murder leads a street-wise black cop from Detroit to squeaky-clean Beverly Hills.

These films don't require a lot of explanation; they scream "commerciality" and boast great lead roles for actors. But even weakly-conceived high-concept movies—those short on plot credibility, characters or dialogue, but which strain to accommodate tie-ins with fast food restaurants and toymakers (dare I say, *Twister* or *Independence Day*)—still require a strong dramatic structure that builds to a high emotional impact.

THE PITCH

These days, the trades seem to carry almost daily reports of yet another high-powered Hollywood executive going into a feeding frenzy over a verbal "pitch," resulting in a wildly extravagant sum paid to the author to develop the project. This may lead new writers to wonder why they must agonize alone at their desk over character arcs and structure when, apparently, this new breed of executive views his time as too valuable to actually read, preferring to have writers present their story ideas (and why they should be filmed) in a pleasant chat over cafe lattes in an air-conditioned suite. This is the mystery and the allure of the infamous "pitch meeting."

The Pitch Meeting

What could be a more civilized way to do business? The writer meets the executive, shakes hands, and presents his proposed story and himself in a brief, entertaining performance. But while I don't wish to dash your hopes of winning lucrative development deals without actually having to write a screenplay, sorry, this method is generally reserved for recognized talent only. That means writers

16

with a track record of produced work or a solid reputation as a writer who "delivers."

Still, a talented few new writers may get in the door—if they have a hot writing sample (preferably, a feature film) and a strong contact behind them (like an agent) to set up the meeting. Development executives who find a fresh writing style or a deft handling of a particular genre are often eager to meet new talent. Perhaps you will be right for a pet project they're hot to develop or you have the bombshell answer to the key question: "So, what else have you got?."

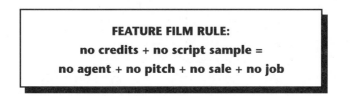

FEATURE FILM RULE:

no credits + no script sample =

no agent + no pitch + no sale + no job

On the other hand, in television, the pitch meeting is the lifeblood of the business. This is not necessarily good news for a new writer, however. Producers and executives know that to option or buy a completed teleplay can be an expensive and futile waste of time and money, especially for telefilms (also known as "movies of the Week," or "MOW's") where there are so few buyers and limited venues. It is simply good business sense, now ingrained into practice, to develop the concept in-house with established writers practiced in the techniques of writing to strict act breaks for commercials and tailoring their work to stars packaged into the show for the demonstrable viewer loyalty they carry with them.

For series television, however, fresh blood is always in short supply. Even new writers may be awarded freelance slots and eventual staff positions if they are able to display a fertile imagination, a wealth of ideas and an infectuous enthusiasm in their pitch meeting. But new writers armed only with story ideas won't be invited to pitch: Two spec episodes of a currently running television series which demonstrate writing talent and a grasp of the essence of the show are the minimum entry requirements.

Writers invited to pitch a Movie of the Week or a pilot for a new series, or those brought in to develop a miniseries (sometimes parceled out in parts to various writers), usually are seasoned television veterans with long track records. Or, they are writers who may be attached to producers or star acting talent with whom the network or cable company would like to be involved or with whom they already have programming commitments and a working relationship. However, sometimes a new writer may find himself in this position; make the most of this rare opportunity. While it is unlikely that any kind of arrangement will be approved for your long term involvement with the very show you have conceived, don't despair; one idea does not a career make. Negotiate the best credit you can, make every attempt to include future writing assignments into your deal and trust that the success of the show will alert everyone in the business to your talent and potential and future work will follow.

Finally, if you think writing is the career for you because of your shy, reserved personality, think again. The writer brought in to pitch must coherently organize a storyline and bring it to life before a sometimes distracted executive who has possibly heard every story ever written. If you hesitate, repeat yourself, can't adjust to interruptions or feedback without losing your composure or your momentum, you may need to find yourself a writing partner, someone who can play off your best moments with enthusiasm, clarity and convincing salesmanship.

If you do have a writing partner, be in agreement; complement each other's rifts and moves; don't argue or contradict each other. (The buyer of your pitch wants to feel secure; he wants to feel that he's a part of a well-oiled team, a member of the gang that backs each other up, not the one in which members stab each other in the back.)

Preparing To Pitch

At its best, pitching can be an electrifying experience; more often, it's frustrating, humiliating and downright bizarre. (Some very respected writers find themselves twisting balloons and wearing arrows through their heads to get their points across.) In other words, this is not an ordinary job interview.

Arrive on time, stay relaxed, have both short and long versions totally rehearsed. Be ready to dazzle, entertain, listen, adapt any story to new suggestions and always have an answer to the question, "So, what else have you got?" Also, be polite to everyone you meet with (and their entire staff) and show genuine gratitude for their time.

It also helps to realize that the person(s) you are pitching to is both the buyer and the seller of concepts. Once you have convinced that person, he in turn must convince someone else of your story's merits—by pitching it, of course. So what the executive wants is something fresh,

I was once told by a Vice President at a major network that my concept was such a natural for television, she was shocked that it wasn't already on TV—but she couldn't buy it because television wasn't doing it already!

new and exciting, yet as familiar and comfortable as an old shoe. "It's just like X, only in this show . . ." Television programmers shy away from taking risks. They know that audiences have only a few lines in *TV Guide* and a few minutes of on-air promos to grasp the show's concept and decide whether or not to watch.

Some development executives and story editors hear as many as 1,000 pitches a year. So think of your pitch as a TV commercial—you've got a few precious minutes to sell your wares. Therefore, keep it short and simple. But, that doesn't mean you have to be too brief or too businesslike, either. A few sincere pleasantries exchanged before you launch into your pitch is expected. Remember: to turn your pitch meeting into a job and a career, try to be someone they'll want to hire because they like your enthusiasm, attitude, grasp of the show, or even because you'll be fun to hang out with!

Should you get a pitch meeting, here are my **Ten Rules of Pitch Meetings**:

1. *Go in prepared.* Practice until you know your pitch cold. Know the show, its running characters, their relationships and the setting they're in. And, of course, know all there is to know about your story.
2. *Go in loaded.* Use props if you need to, but always give them a good show. For a television series pitch, five or six storylines are expected. Feature or MOW pitching is usually limited to one, more highly-developed, concept.
3. *Start simple.* Have a strong, clear, single-line premise and give a brief overview of story and characters. The decision to buy or pass is usually made within the first two minutes. Use these to focus on memorable scenes, the big, plot-twisting moments.
4. *Be prepared to perform.* Deliver your pitch with passion, clarity and confidence. Be enthusiastic and animated, but don't overdo it. The point is to keep them awake, not to frighten them.
5. *Keep it short.* Five to ten minutes for a TV series show, shorter if you see their eyes begin to glaze over, and never more than 15 minutes, even if you're on a roll; 15 minutes or longer for a feature or MOW is usually expected. In every case, never tell everything you know about your story; keep the imagination engaged.
6. *Play to your audience.* Adapt to the tone of the group. When possible, take the lead, but keep it light and cheerful.
7. *Listen.* Don't take offense at questions. Invite them into the pitching process. Be flexible and open to suggestions. Take notes and don't be afraid to ask for help.
8. *Know when to stop.* If you pay attention, you'll see the signals. It's an art to know when to walk away before you're asked to leave.

9. *Leave as little behind as possible.* A page or two, at the most, to refresh their memories. Remember that most pitches take on new identities, as new ideas are grafted onto the original idea, so don't have your concept so etched in stone that it differs from the one the executive thought he bought.

10. *Smile and say, "Thank you."* If they like you, they'll want to find a way to work with you.

And then, leave. Avoid the long goodbye. If they've already accepted working with you, why hang around and give them time to question their judgment?

TEN RULES OF PITCH MEETINGS

1. **Go in prepared.**
2. **Go in loaded.**
3. **Start simple.**
4. **Be prepared to perform.**
5. **Keep it short.**
6. **Play to your audience.**
7. **Listen.**
8. **Know when to stop.**
9. **Leave as little behind as possible.**
10. **Smile and say thank you.**

THE BEAT OUTLINE AND THE TREATMENT

How does one begin a journey? By taking the first step. This bit of wisdom is the inspiration for most books or methods on screenwriting. Professionals know that the hardest hurdle of all, especially when facing a seemingly monumental task, is getting started. Witness Syd Field's early tome, *Screenplay*[1]; its great achievement was in breaking down those large, foreboding 120 pages of screenplay into smaller bits. (Readers of the book learned that most screenplays contain three "acts"; that it is easier to begin an act than a screenplay; easier to write a 10-page opening than 30 pages, and so on.)

Outlines or treatments are writing tools which accomplish the same thing. A "beat outline" lays out the story, scene-by-scene, in simple sentences or short paragraphs. A "treatment" is the narrative of a film story, usually between 5 and 20 pages in length (al-

---

[1] Field, Syd. *Screenplay: The Foundations of Screenwriting.* Dell Publishing Co., New York, 1979, 1982.

though writers have been known to develop treatments that are half the length of their screenplays). As we will see, both are essential development tools for any screenwriter.

Outlines and treatments focus on the scene-by-scene construction of the story; they refine the narrative structure and chart character growth. Line-by-line, or in a brief narrative, they are easy to follow, easy to change and rearrange. The writer is free to create and discard scenes (a crucial step in the creative process) before committing them to the apparent permanency of a screenplay.

By way of example, here is a three act feature film beat outline of key plot-developing scenes from Ernest Lehman's classic *North By Northwest*, directed by Alfred Hitchcock and starring Cary Grant as Roger Thornhill.

> Act I (Setting Up the Dramatic Situation - wherein, to quote Gore Vidal, we put the protagonist "up a tree").

> Midtown Manhattan, the tempo of Madison Avenue, streets swarming with smartly dressed people. V.O. "Would it not be strange, in a city of seven million people, if one man were *never* mistaken for another . . ."

> ROGER THORNHILL, tall, lean, faultlessly dressed, and far too original to be wearing the grey flannel uniform of his kind, meets business associates for lunch. When he rises to send a telegram to his mother, LICHT and VALERIAN mistake him for "George Kaplan." They hustle him into a waiting car at gunpoint, refusing to tell him where he's being taken.

> Thornhill is taken to the Townsend estate where PHILLIP VANDAMM, posing as Mr. Townsend, also assumes he's Kaplan. Vandamm accuses him of lying and grills him on how much he knows of "our arrangements." Upon Thornhill's denials, LEONARD, Valerian and Licht force a fifth of bourbon into him.

> Valerian and Licht put the drunk Thornhill behind the wheel of a moving car on a winding mountain road. Thornhill manages to steer the car until he is followed by a police cruiser and arrested.

> Thornhill, his mother, lawyer and two cops, return to the Townsend mansion to verify his story. A woman assumed to be Mrs. Townsend contends that Thornhill attended a party the night before and drove away drunk. She says her husband is addressing the UN today. As the party leaves, they are watched by Valerian posing as a gardener.

21

Thornhill and his mother manage to gain access to the real George Kaplan's room at the Plaza Hotel, where they find a newspaper picture of Vandamm.

Thornhill, posing as Kaplan, goes to the UN looking for "Townsend." The Townsend he finds is not the man from the mansion. Valerian watches from b.g. As Thornhill shows the real Townsend the newspaper photo, Townsend gasps and falls into Thornhill with a knife in his back. Thornhill grabs for him and is photographed holding the knife above the dead man.

Act II (Progressive Complications - wherein we "throw stones at him.")

A group of CIA men view the same photo on the front page of the newspaper. They regret Thornhill is mistaken for Kaplan but, "there's nothing we can do for him without endangering Number One."

Thornhill boards a train for Chicago, eluding police with the help of EVE KENDALL, who hides him in her sleeping compartment. But she also sends a note via the porter to Vandamm: "What do I do with him in the morning?"

In Chicago, Eve arranges for Thornhill to met Kaplan, but instead Thornhill is attacked by a crop duster in a cornfield. He returns to find Eve with Vandamm. He follows them to an art auction where Vandamm picks up a statue filled with microfilm. Thornhill confronts him, but when Leonard and Valerian prevent his escape, he causes a scene and is arrested.

In the police car, he confesses that he is a wanted murderer, but instead of taking him to jail, the police deliver him to the airport, where he is met by the PROFESSOR, the head of the CIA.

Thornhill learns that Vandamm is an international smuggler of secrets, that Eve is actually a CIA agent and that his relationship with her has endangered her life.

To convince Vandamm that "Kaplan" is no longer a threat, the Professor stages Thornhill's "death" at Mt. Rushmore by having Eve shoot him with blanks.

Thornhill and Eve meet afterwards and confess their love for each other—but Eve must leave the country with Vandamm that night, never to return. They kiss goodbye as the Professor leads him away.

Act III (Conclusion - wherein we "get him back down")

Thornhill escapes the Professor's protective custody and goes to Vandamm's house to try and keep Eve from leaving. He discovers that Leonard and Valerian know she's a spy and intend to kill her.

Thornhill manages to get Eve and the statue away, but they are pursued on foot through the woods until they emerge on the top of Mt. Rushmore. Trying to climb down the treacherous slope, they are attacked by Valerian and Leonard until a CIA sharpshooter kills Leonard. Thornhill must still rescue Eve from the precipice where she has fallen, pulling her up until—

Eve lands beside him in the upper berth of a moving train.

In truth, few writers really like outlines or treatments—they're boring and they usually do not have enough witty repartee to keep the writer amused. But the fact is that almost *all successful screenwriters will admit to spending more time on the outline or treatment stage of their writing process than on the actual screenplay.*

Established writers may find a treatment/outline to be a potent *selling tool* as well, useful in accompanying a verbal pitch, for example. Many step deals often get started by a required treatment or outline stage so that the producer can work with the writer to iron out story problems before they become fixed in the cement of the screenplay. However, the treatment/outline is an entirely different animal from a screenplay—in format, content and tone—and neither the outline nor the treatment alone has a chance of launching your writing career. Producers simply are unable, or unwilling, to

Industry-savvy director Monte Hellman, who plows through two scripts a day in search of viable screen material, throws away treatments he receives. He comments, "Whatever a treatment tells me about a story is too often muddled and lost in the costly and time-consuming process of getting it into a coherent screenplay. Why should I risk that when there is a plethora of full screenplays to consider?"

23

decipher screenwriting talent or the big-screen worthiness of your story on the basis of a treatment or outline alone.

Make no mistake, in an industry overwhelmed with books, screenplays and other written materials, producers may ask a new writer for a treatment or a synopsis (a condensed version of a story, told objectively, not dramatically as in a treatment). But, usually, it will be requested *in addition to* a full screenplay. (Should you submit one, brevity is best; at the least, it will force them to read your script to get the complete story.) No doubt, this makes the producer's work easier, but is it to your advantage? After all, in relatively few pages, you must convey the uniqueness of your characters and the full scope of your story in a different format. If you fail, the reader will pass on the treatment and avoid reading your fully realized dramatic screenplay. If the reader likes the treatment, he will then read the screenplay anyway (thus, you get two chances to be rejected!). This might not be the ticket you were hoping for to your screenwriting career.

Don't be seduced into thinking your treatment can make money—the Art Buchwald way. Buchwald sold a treatment to Paramount Pictures but later had to sue the studio to prove that his treatment was the inspiration for the Eddie Murphy film *Coming to America*. According to former Paramount Creative Executive David Kirkpatrick, the studio optioned only one treatment in the ten years he was there—Buchwald's. And that was only because of Buchwald's formidable reputation as a writer and the attachment of a producer with whom Paramount had interest in doing future business.

THE "SPEC" SCREENPLAY

In showbiz lingo, a "spec" script is a screenplay written with the hope (the speculation) that someone will buy it. Born of the writer's passion and created without any guarantee that it will be sold, a spec script, written by seasoned pros and novices alike, is undertaken with the hope that someone—someday—will appreciate its merits and step forward with a bonafide purchase offer. A spec screenplay is also the preferred method that a new writer takes to break into the film business.

In fact, there was a boom period for spec sales (which has since peaked) around 1994. Back then, the studios were snapping up anything! Producers looking for a quick road to blockbuster riches were scheduling meetings in 20-minute increments, just long enough to hear the one-line high concepts that would surely be the catalyst for the next summer's worldwide box-office smash. But as those same high-rollers learned the hard way, high-concept premises do not always produce good or successful films. As a result, the studios were left with well-marketed, highly-publicized and totally unproducable screenplays, for which they paid sinful sums. One such script, "The

Cheese Stands Alone," riding a P.R. wave of legendary proportions, sold in a bidding war. Years later, it is yet unproduced. After that, bidding wars were almost overnight confined to novels or genre work from dependable A-List screenwriters.

But, just as quickly, there has been another turnaround: the doldrums seem to have been shaken out of the spec marketplace. Based on stories in the trades, spec scripts are pouring out of word processors and flowing directly into development. Agents are setting up scripts for big "coming out" parties, getting overnight reads and orchestrating furious bidding wars. Expensive spec sales are back in the headlines. For the screenwriter, the spec screenplay no longer "sleeps with the fishes."

As an unsold writer, only *you* know that you have original, exciting ideas and the talent to transform them into riveting stories for the screen. The spec script serves as the writer's calling card. It is designed to get your talent noticed and get you meetings, even if your first few screenplays don't actually sell.

What are buyers looking for in a spec script today? Some buyers will tell you they want nothing more than "a good story." Some are in search of a particular genre or a vehicle for a particular talent, be it star or director. Others are more specific—they want "passion" in the writing or "dialogue that levitates off the page." Whatever they say, all buyers are after the same thing: a surefire hit. But, be forewarned—one thing is certain: no one screenplay will please every buyer.

25

. . . .

At a conference on spec selling at the Writers Guild of America, West, William Morris agent Alan Gasmer espoused at length on the virtues of movie concepts which could be reduced to one powerful, easily grasped, easily repeatable, sentence. It's all about marketing, he explained, and studios getting audiences into the theater. He added, studios do this with a visual effects extravaganza that features a main character attractive to a male star. The fact that 18 of the top 20 highest grossing films of all time are visual effects-laden films aimed at males (i.e.,the *Star Wars* trilogy and prequel, *Raiders of the Lost Ark* and its sequels, *Independence Day*) is not lost on these executives. Gasmer was forthcoming with his opinion that no current female star is considered strong enough to "open" a movie (even after the success of *Thelma & Louise*). As for family-oriented material, Gasmer pointed out the obvious: currently, there are no strong 14-year-old stars. Studio lingo for a "family movie" is *Men in Black* (which made more money for Sony Pictures than any film in that studio's history) or *Independence Day*, or any other PG-13 film.

A story that is compelling in image and character and that provides a catharsis of emotions (but which does not meet the above criteria) may be limited to the independent market—an arduous journey in which the writer must essentially package and find financing for his own work.

. . . .

Many agents prefer to hear their clients' stories first. For example, it is not unusual for a writer to want to cash in on a box-office trend with a new twist on a hot genre. A plugged-in agent will gently remind the writer that he may be jumping on a ship that has already sailed. (Why waste time developing an idea that is outdated or oversold.) But, you may be wondering, the agent as creative censor? Consider this: agents earn their commission by knowing the current state of the entertainment industry. No matter how competitive the agencies and studio executives may appear to be, in reality, they breakfast together, party together, sleep together and trade positions like baseball cards. With e-mail, it takes only the click of a mouse for every development executive in town to know the details of every other one's reading list.

Make no mistake: for the novice screenwriter, shortcuts should not be taken. High-concept one-liners, treatments and verbal pitches are selling tools for the writer who is already a known quantity, whose track record commands recognition and respect in the marketplace. (Even then, such writers are usually limited to pitching ideas in the genre in which they've already staked out a reputation.)

There is a famous story floating around about an executive at a major studio who was livid that he had lost out on a high-concept comedy (eventually made by DreamWorks SKG) because he was in the restroom when the agent phoned for final bids.

For the unknown writer, a full-length, original feature screenplay is still the only remaining key with which to unlock a screenwriting career. The spec screenplay doubles as the writer's resume, especially in an industry in which most work is "on assignment" (and assignments are handed out only to writers with a track record or viable script samples). With your spec screenplay, you will have a product for sale and a "brochure" for the main product in your warehouse—YOU!

To be a successful representation of your talent, it is generally agreed that a spec screenplay should be bold and risky, about a highly personal subject and featuring characters you know intimately. (It is rumored that George Lucas' troubled relationship with his father, combined with his boyhood refuge at Saturday matinee serials, gave birth to the *Star Wars* films. Notice how the main character is named "Luke" and that Vader recalls the German word "Vater," which

26

means "father.") The technical aspects of screenwriting, including solid dramatic structure and clean screen format, can be learned. What sells is your unique point of view—your fears, your fantasies, your passions. And for the pure joy of writing about your dreams (or your nightmares), all you risk is your time.

The spec script also maintains your creative integrity. As you'll discover when you are hired to write a script (based on your idea or someone else's), you will be writing under the supervision of an employer and your creative instincts will be "guided" by well-intended, but often infuriating, "story notes." Your screenplay will then become what is known as a "work for hire."

This is why spec writing isn't for new writers only. Even seasoned veterans will forego a guaranteed "work-for-hire" paycheck (along with the "helpful suggestions" of producers and studio executives) in exchange for the freedom to quietly develop their next screenplay in the privacy of their own thoughts.

Spec writing also allows writers to create stories in different genres from that in which they are pigeonholed. And, on the sale of original material, spec writers who are members of the Writers Guild will retain a small portion of rights, known as "separated rights" (e.g. novelization and publication rights) and are accorded, per Writers Guild rules, first crack at the rewriting of their work. Freedom is the by-word here.

Under the 1976 Copyright Act, all written work done under contract or "on assignment" essentially belongs to the employer. In fact, not only is the employer considered the owner of the work ("the owner of all the rights comprised in the copyright": 17 U.S.C. ¶ 201 [1976]), but the law actually goes so far as to consider the studio or other employer the author of the work written for hire. Is it therefore any wonder that the studios feel free to change, revise, rewrite and alter the material written for them on assignment?

27

. . . .

Spec writing too often translates (in the new writer's mind) as "free" writing; the thought of writing for free can be the death of good work, passion and self-worth. Instead, consider it as one way of having dominion over yourself and your work. No one has to give you permission to write (un-like acting or directing, for example). What you write has future value and you own it completely. As an added kicker, whenever a spec script sells, it has potential for spawning a bidding war, which almost always commands the highest purchase price.

. . . .

There is a downside to spec writing. Of course, the most obvious is that there is no paycheck attached to your work. And, truth be told, most first, probably second, and even third spec scripts by a new writer may not sell. There are thousands of unsold spec scripts lining the shelves of story departments in every studio in town. Only a fraction (under 5%) of the scripts sold—those put into development and which have time and money and often teams of good writers working on them—ever get made.

On the other hand, good work usually finds a champion. A screenplay needs only one buyer. If you are driven to write, fear of failure should not enter into the equation.

In poker, there's a saying: scared cards can't win. The film business rewards its players, not those who quit at the first sign of rejection. Screenwriter Michael Tolkin (*The Player*), while a guest speaker at a UCLA Extension seminar, put it succinctly: "If you write something that no one has ever read before and it's good, stick with it, you'll get it made."

In 1998, there were 38,608 script registrations at the Writers Guild of America, West. Considering there are only 8,000 Guild members and more than a third of those are retired or "emeritus" members, most of these scripts were by newcomers. The truth is, many try but few succeed at making a consistent living as a screenwriter. Success is a combination of luck, patience, talent and timing. But, why dwell on the odds? Some of the world's most successful people achieved success because they were too naïve or too oblivious to know or care about the odds against them. Paul Allen, one of the founders of Microsoft has said, "If I knew how impossible what I was trying to do was, I would've never started."

THE "SPEC" TELEPLAY

Submitting your work for television involves a slightly different approach than for features. Television networks rarely buy completed works—they buy concepts, primarily on the strength of a pitch meeting. Networks then develop those concepts using writers selected from lists of "network-approved" writers, ranked according to their history of ratings success, organized by genre (comedy, action, romance, etc.) and listed by the writer's contract price and availability. So, how does the novice writer get to pitch or get on that approved writer list? First comes the work—writers must have track records or writing samples appropriate for the market in which they hope to sell. If you score a pitch meeting in collaboration with a seasoned producer with whom the network enjoys a long and fruitful relationship, and if the executives are hot for your idea, you will be hired to develop that idea only if the network is convinced that you can handle the assignment—and this happens only via your existing, powerful writing sample.

But, let's start with the basics. If you're going to write for television, you must watch TV! Shunning the medium won't get you far in a world comprised of people who eat, breathe and sleep television. It's foolish for a writer to attempt writing a spec episode of a TV series if that writer has rarely seen the show and demonstrates no grasp of the specific character tics and running plotlines of the series.

For MOWs or miniseries, the writer should research the general parameters of what the networks are buying. MOWs, for example, have recently favored true stories (docudramas) or issue-oriented themes centering on a woman's challenge or dilemma. Even with the recent trend toward "epic" programming (movies based on best-selling books or classic novels) and tabloid topics, women-in-peril dramas continue to be MOW staples.

If you have such a concept in the works and/or have obtained the rights to a true story (see Chapter 9), and even with a reputable agent in tow, do not go directly to the networks. The preferred method is to seek a producer or a studio with a network track record who has produced projects similar to yours who can then champion your project.

. . . .

Most television series writing is done by the show's staff writers, who receive extra pay for episodes they write, as well as career boosts if their episodes should win awards. (When I confronted a writer-producer of a top-ranked series about the uncanny resemblance of several recent episodes to storylines I had pitched him months earlier, he said, in a rare moment of candor, "Why should we give *you* the Mercedes?") Yet, even the stingiest producers are faced with heavy workloads and are forced to parcel out one or two free-lance writing jobs per season via pitch meetings. Your spec script (two or three samples are better than one) showcases your ability to write in either the dramatic or sitcom mode; it will illustrate your knack for getting to the heart of any dramatic or comedic truth; and will indicate your grasp of the individual voices for the show's continuing characters.

. . . .

While it is sound policy to submit a sample script to a show of the same format (a sitcom to a sitcom; a drama to a drama), it is not necessary to submit a sample script of a particular show to that same show (i.e., a sample of *Friends* to the producers of *Friends*). While a rare few producers, like *Frasier*, strongly prefer to read samples only of their show, current wisdom is that submitting your sample episode to that specific series may be the worst place for it. Why? Because the showrunners are way ahead of you; storylines have been tacked to their corkboard for months. It is hard to surprise a staff that spends its every waking hour writing or hearing pitches about their own show. While your spec episode is absolutely necessary to get you that pitch opportunity—which could lead to employment—it will rarely, if ever, be purchased outright.

Series producers read to find talent, not story ideas. It stands to reason, then, that a *Just Shoot Me* could easily be sent to *Friends* or any other half-hour sitcom. The same holds true for hour dramas (an episode of *Chicago Hope* could easily be submitted to *ER* and vice-versa).

It is, however, a good idea to write an episode for a show you know has a future. Even as a sample sent to other shows, a script from a canceled show dates your work; it is then not considered a valid or current representation of your writing abilities.

A good writing sample, an enthusiastic approach and bull-headed (but charming) persistence can bring you assignments and also a staff position. Why? The burn-out factor. Writers invest long hours trying to be original week after week, season after season. Successful shows need new blood. The sheer pressure of writing yet another exciting or funny show for those well-known and much-loved characters can deplete energy and imagination. That's why there is always room for the ambitious, hard-working writer to break in, to do the grunt work and to move up the ranks to producer and, eventually, that lofty position of "showrunner" (the head writer/executive producer on the show).

Check a current issue of *Written By* for the names and phone numbers of television series contact people. Most accept submissions from agents only but don't let that discourage you; a little dogged ingenuity can open doors. Try obtaining a copy of the show's bible (general guidelines, requirements and format) or a script from a produced episode. Also, tape at least four or five episodes of the show and study them, to gain a grasp of the characters, setting, theme and structure.

Caveat for Guild members:

Any writer may labor for himself, but spec writing in the employ of or at the direction of another is strictly prohibited and applicable Guild minimums must be met. Prohibited spec writing includes any services for which payment is contingent upon the acceptance or approval of the material ("Write it; if I like it, I'll pay for it"). Also, pursuant to the "second meeting" rule, television producers or network executives may not request a second meeting without entering into a "story commitment"—if the first meeting concerned the writer's original idea. Nor may they meet with the writer a third time without entering into a binding obligation.

ADAPTATIONS

While the terror of the blank page is somewhat mollified in the adaptation process (characters, settings and plot are predetermined), imagination and artistry are no less a requirement. Screenwriters must be brutal in culling or redesigning those aspects of the work that will not play for the particular medium of film. For example, some plays offer as few as two characters and serve their plot needs within one set, while film begs to use the full scope of the medium. So, scenes may need to be opened up, more diverse locations written in and action substituted for long speeches. Conversely, the sprawling novel may require characters to be combined, entire subplots lost and new material written to fit in its place. For example, the novel, *The Godfather*, by Mario Puzo, was too rich for even one epic film; it found a formidable sequel in whole chapters discarded from the first film.

The mantra of the adapter is cut, cut, cut. And the screenwriter may be vilified for it. Novelists, critics and loyal readers may understand that their beloved work must undergo a substantial transformation on the way to film, but they are often no less vituperative toward the result. Some will not argue the process (as co-screenwriter of the adaption of his own novel, *The Prince of Tides*, Pat Conroy had little about which to complain), while others like Richard Russo, author of *Nobody's Fool*, may find that his sprawling novel was no better served by a faithful adaptation and the presence of Paul Newman; writer/director Robert Benton adhered slavishly to the text, but to my mind, at least, the subtle charm of the characters and setting were strangled in the tight two-hour format of film.

Should you set out to adapt a novel, play, true story or other material for the screen, you will first need to secure the rights. This subject is dealt with in detail in Chapter 9. Of course, you don't need anyone's permission to write your screen version of any published or produced work— but you can't sell it without the rights to the original material (this is known as delivering a "clear chain of title"). Unless, that is, you sell it to someone who already owns those rights. Such legalities notwithstanding, you can always use your work as a writing sample to showcase your talent at adapting plot, characters and dialogue.

31

OTHER MEDIA

There are many ways to have your point of view reach an audience. Your particular writing talent may be in exploring the inner discourses of the mind, the murky world of dreams and thoughts. You may shy away from "action" writing, aspiring instead to the direct connection that language itself can make between your heart and mind and that of an audience. You may like the freedom of moving back and forth in time or the power of a beautifully-turned phrase and not wish to be so constricted in the format or length of your work. Why not, then, write a novel?

Hollywood has always had a love affair with the publishing world. Not only do books come pre-approved by editors and publishers with as tough a set of writing and marketing criteria as any film studio, but they also come with a pre-sold audience of loyal readers. As a bonus, novels usually offer strong, well-structured stories and vivid, three-dimensional characters. And, your reward as a novelist? If the rights to your book are sold to a studio or producer, you'll likely receive a celebrity stature rarely achieved as a screenwriter, as well as a lucrative deal for the screen rights. Best-selling authors may even be paid for unfinished works. And many novelists are paid to write the screen adaptations of their screenplays. (Not that everyone jumps for joy at the prospect: one novelist recently described the process as being like "a cannibal eating his own foot.")

WRITER'S SALES TOOLS:
• **Concept**
• **Pitch**
• **Beat Outline**
• **Treatment**
• **Spec Screenplay**
• **Spec Teleplay**
• **Adaptations**
• **Other Media**

If dialogue is your strong point and you have little need for either the vast mindscape of the novel or the expansive physical arenas possible in film, perhaps you will find greater satisfaction and more immediate gratification in writing for the stage.

Once you have established your voice in one medium, you can transfer that voice to the screen. Neil Simon and David Mamet are playwrights who have forged successful screenwriting careers. Indeed, Mamet is one of the few screenwriters (William Goldman is another) who stipulates that the words he writes shall be altered by him alone. While common for playwrights, this is unprecedented creative power for a screenwriter.

Find the medium that best suits your writing talents and the needs of your story. That may be the single most important creative decision you make as a writer.

Chapter 3
THE MARKETABLE SCREENPLAY, PART ONE: THE HOLLYWOOD FILM

"NOW PLAYING AT A THEATER NEAR YOU"

New writers may feel overwhelmed by all the rules pronounced in the avalanche of screenwriting primers or in the almost religious fervor of screenwriting seminars. Put your ear to the ground and you may hear "The Seven Steps," "The 12 Stages," "The 22 Building Blocks," "The 30 Stations," etc. Aristotle introduced the basics centuries ago: a story must have a beginning, a middle and an end. Others after him have added "not necessarily in that order." So is there really that much to know before you can write (and sell) a screenplay? Well, yes and no.

All art has form. It's a waste of time to argue whether or not there are or should be "rules" for writers (or for any other form of art, for that matter). The passion to write may be the only prerequisite a writer needs. But, there *are* storytelling standards that any development executive in the film business will expect your script to meet: **strong characters involved in a crucial central conflict that is solidly structured to deliver a satisfying emotional experience to an audience.**

Moreover, in a world that accepts Hollywood movies as among America's most influential and desirable cultural exports, films today must be able to play as well in Bangkok as in Burbank. They must convey story points and basic human emotions through powerful images and not simply through words. It stands to reason, then, that the universal appeal of your work has a great deal to do with its marketability.

Finally, never forget that your primary goal as a writer is to appeal to a series of readers or executives whose task it is to find and develop viable screen stories. These executives must then convey the merits of your story to senior executives who wield the power to "green light" a movie (send it from development to production).

These executives may see their careers being made or broken by the audience (the final arbiter of the true worth of your story). And, the audience has expectations of its own.

It is up to you to deliver the best writing of which you are capable. While it is not the purview of this book to reiterate the advice of countless good works on the art and craft of screenwriting, here are some of the more important ingredients that seem to make up any recipe for a marketable screenplay:

➤ *Themes from your heart.*

Milan Kundera says, "Whenever a novel abandons its themes and settles for just telling the story, it goes flat."[1] A theme can be as simple as the triumph of good vs evil (as in *Star Wars*); it can be as obvious as the film's title (*Sense & Sensibility*, which offers a theme of reason vs passion); or, it can be as complex as finding heroism in the face of failure (as in *Saving Private Ryan* or *Apollo 13*). Whatever the theme, your work must have a point of view, whether it be derived from your heartfelt passion or your keen perception. As a writer, you must eschew the safe middle ground; you must take sides.

Ancient Zen philosophy tells us that one cannot always hit a target by aiming at it. You may not be certain what theme will emerge from your story, but, as a writer, you must never forget that you are both a student and teacher of human behavior. Don't limit your work to your knowledge or experience; write about what piques your curiosity and what drives you to learn and experience—a powerful theme will follow.

> **It almost doesn't matter if the side you take is not the most popular one. In *Das Boot*, the main character is a German submarine commander during World War II. The author's strong POV presented this character as simply another human soul caught up in the horror of war. As a result, the audience found itself rooting for the Germans to escape detection from the Allies and win!**

➤ *A viable premise.*

A solid premise, like a thumbnail sketch of the plot, helps the writer stay focused on the story he sets out to tell and keeps him from veering off into different directions.

---

[1] Kundera, Milan. *The Art of the Novel*, first published in English translation in the U.S.A. by Grove Press, Inc., New York, 1988.

34

> *The Verdict* offers an example: "An alcoholic lawyer has one last chance to gain his self-respect: by winning justice for his comatose client." This sentence supplies the main character, his problems and his chance for redemption.

The premise differs from theme in that it concentrates on the story dynamics rather than on the sentiment the author wishes to convey. Let's take, for example, *The Music Box*, the drama written by Joe Ezsterhas which starred Jessica Lange. The theme might be described as, "the conflicts a woman faces when someone she loves and trusts has his most basic morality questioned." On the other hand, the premise would be, "In 1990, a criminal attorney must defend her father who is accused of Nazi war crimes."

William Faulkner described the basics of any story as "a likable character, facing seemingly insurmountable odds, toward a worthy goal." A premise invariably states or implies those crucial story elements, while it also suggests the inciting incident which kicks off the story by pitting an unstoppable character against an immovable force. (Sometimes called a story hook, this incident or event upsets the balance of life for the main character and forces him into unavoidable action.) A solid premise also implies a central conflict that is sufficiently credible to allow for the suspension of our disbelief, yet one that is also unique, visual, fresh, the product of an original voice and compelling enough to hold the audience in their seats for two hours in the dark.

➤ A recognizable genre.

This does not mean that you should create a piece of formulaic writing. "Genre" simply implies a story that offers a clear theme (good vs evil; truth; honor; heroism; passion, etc.) and a strong central character within a recognizable story format. Genre also translates to time-tested audience appeal and identifiable characters which attract stars.

The conventional genres are:
- Action-Adventure (*Die Hard, Raiders of the Lost Ark, Lethal Weapon*);
- Comedy (*The Waterboy, National Lampoon's Animal House*);
- Drama (*The English Patient, Lawrence of Arabia*); this category is often subdivided into Family, Period, Legal, Epic Historical, Coming of Age, War, etc.
- Film Noir (*Sunset Boulevard, Body Heat*)

35

- Gangster (*The Godfather, Scarface, Bugsy*)
- Horror (*Alien, Scream*);
- Mystery (*Chinatown, Basic Instinct*);
- Romantic Comedy (*Sleepless in Seattle, When Harry Met Sally . . .*)
- Sci-Fi (*The X-Files; Star Trek* films);
- Thriller (*Silence of the Lambs, Psycho*);
- Western (*Red River, The Searchers*).

Most films are mixed-genres (e.g., *Titanic* would be an adventure-love story). In these mixed- genre films, the main plot often is carried by the controlling genre while the subplot carries the thematic genre (e.g. *Witness*, a mystery-love story). And, just because a genre script may be less risky for the marketplace doesn't mean that it shouldn't take risks and explore new boundaries. Instead, understand that audience expectations are ingrained over thousands of hours of storytelling; use that to your advantage and allow the conventions of a genre to set up your story and then give a twist in plot or character to surprise an audience that expects the usual thing. Examples of this include *The Shining, Pulp Fiction, Unforgiven, Platoon.*

> ➢ *A great opening.*

Busy story departments plow through the hundreds of submissions they receive per week the way we might clean out our garage—anything that can be tossed, must be tossed. If you are a successful, known quantity (on par with David Mamet, William Goldman or Alvin Sargent, for example) the executives will grant you some latitude and read your entire screenplay to see how it develops. But, the new writer has maybe 10 to 20 pages (tops) to grab the reader with clever dialogue, fleshed-out characters that actors want to play and a plot that screams "blockbuster." Accomplishing this takes a strong, motivated setup that forces the reader to turn the page.

A good opening should introduce your main character in a fresh, interesting way. It should hint at a possible hole in his life that needs to be filled. And then it should begin the conflict by engaging the story hook. Just as the screenplay may be one long metaphor for your theme, the opening (which establishes that theme in context) may be thought of as a metaphor for your screenplay.

Remember the powerful opening image of *The Godfather*? Against a black screen, an Italian man seeks a desperate favor to avenge his daughter's disgrace—from the only source of justice he can count on, a man whose very way of life threatens everything he respects in the America he loves. This is an opening that forces the reader to keep reading.

➢ *A clear goal.*

Before writing the first page, every writer must know the last. The writer must also know what it is he is trying to accomplish. Only then can you determine what your main character must accomplish. The goal must be specific, clearly identifiable, as crucial to your character as life and death and not subject to compromise. It is in the striving toward such a goal that true depth of character is gained. Ernest Hemingway, struggling against his own demons, acknowledged that, "The world may break us, but afterward many are stronger at the broken places." In fact, this is the very essence of the film hero. James Allen, the 19th Century English author, put it this way, in his pithy but enduring classic, *As A Man Thinketh*:

> A man should conceive of a legitimate purpose in his heart, and set out to accomplish it . . . He should make this purpose his supreme duty, and should devote himself to its attainment . . . Even if he fails again and again to accomplish his purpose (as he necessarily must until weakness is overcome), the *strength of character gained* will be the measure of his *true* success, and this will form a new starting point for future power and triumph.[2]

➢ *Characters we care about.*

37

If you examine your response to most great films, you will find that you have a strong concern for the characters as *people*. Actors find the truth in their characters by creating a world of inner motivations for the decisions demanded by the script. Similarly, a writer must imagine himself in his character's shoes, from birth onward, and understand his character's fears and desires, successes and failures, disappointments and dreams, values and ideals. Only then can the writer depict human, identifiable and memorable characters acting and reacting with emotional accuracy.

RULE:
Write parts actors want to play. Characters should be multidimensional, motivated and vulnerable. They should be engaged in risky human behavior and be faced with life-altering challenges.

---

2   Allen, James. *As A Man Thinketh*. Running Press, Philadelphia, 1989.

A writer must also walk in the shoes of his audience, which has its own expectations for characters it cares about. Writer Paddy Chayefsky, in his list of steps for structuring the actions of a main character in a film, asks not only what the character wants, but what the audience wants for him.

EXAMPLE

Imagine a film in which Clint Eastwood is stalked by an escaped murderer he put in jail years before. Imagine also that he is a widower with a five-year-old daughter. Finally, imagine that the writer, reaching that tough second act curtain, decides to have the stalker kill Clint's daughter. He's thinking this will get the audience rooting for Clint's revenge. The writer has just committed the cardinal sin of misreading audience expectations. Screen villans usually lose; we know that. But, after coming to care for the little girl, she is now irreplaceable to the audience and they would emotionally "check out" of the film at the point of her death. Clint's character, unable to save his own daughter, would be rendered powerless—a flaw that could not be redeemed by any kind of revenge killing.

38

➢ *A balanced structure.*

Gustave Flaubert said: "It is not the pearls that make the necklace, but the thread." Wonderful scenes and quirky characters are wasted if the incidents aren't structured along a clear, defining line that lends them purpose and dramatic power. To achieve this, writers design a story as an architect designs a house. Building blocks may be placed in the opening pages (time locks, narration, motifs, taglines and foreshadowing are a few such tools defined in writing primers) to support or make more meaningful the actions in the climax of the film. The goal is a cohesive story which balances the viewer's expectations with the film's final act.

Structure, then, is the dominating principle in a screenplay; it is the bungee cord that prevents scenes from straying too far; it's what keeps springing everything back to point. There is no great mystery to it; if you play an instrument, if you can dance, you know structure. It's an instinctual grasp of rhythm and timing; it hits highs and lows; it never stands still, but it all stands together. And it must work its magic within a fairly set time frame. From the ancient bards who went from town to town selling their stories like so many pots and pans, to the modern multiplex theaters which pack in audiences at two-hour intervals, storytellers have tailored their yarns to audience boredom levels.

. . . .

I once got a sneak peek at the storyboards for an animated feature film. Scenes were typed on 3x5 cards and pinned to a corkboard. At the top of the board was a graph dedicated to the main character. As the story unfolded, the graph charted the character's progress toward his goal, scene by scene. (A character can only rise if he has fallen, but even as he spirals down there is hope, a chance to recover.) Thus, the character arc was formed, which peaks at the film's end, (when the protagonist typically develops into a stronger person, with a greater understanding of himself and thus at a higher place in life).

The lower half of the graph was dedicated to the viewer, who should be on an emotional roller coaster, too. Was he scared, happy, excited, sad? If he was on the edge of his seat too long, he was given a moment to sit back and relax, only to have his emotions rekindled in the next segment of the film. (Hence, the expression, "comic relief.")

. . . .

The viewer puts himself in your hands and he expects to be taken on a skillfully designed thrill ride. He does not need a car chase every ten minutes or even a happy ending, but he does need to be captivated, surprised and entertained. And, he probably would appreciate some kind of ending—a reward of sorts—for having gone along for the ride.

39

> *A strong protagonist spine.*

As Aristotle expressed in *Poetics,* the ordering of the incidents is the first duty of the writer. Those incidents (scenes) are not haphazard, but rather, connected by the motivated actions or unconscious desires of the main character. All drama, in the end, is about the quest of the main character to discover who he is and what he is made of when the chips are down. These actions and desires form the "spine" of the movie and drive it to its conclusion.

John F. Kennedy said that "a man does what he must, in spite of obstacles, pressures and the opinions of mankind, and that is the basis of all human morality." In film (the ultimate morality play), events hap-

Action is not what *happens* to your character, action is what your character *does* about what is happening to him.

pen—sometimes disturbing, often morally ambiguous—which force a character to tap into his deepest reserves to overcome them. He may stumble, he may fall, but as he does he should learn. As he learns, his true character develops and he realizes he is more than what he has allowed himself to become. Thus, his actions not only drive the plot, but also bond the audience with the moral point of view the author wishes to impose.

EXAMPLE

Animated films clearly dramatize this journey toward self-discovery. For, example, in *Aladdin*, the song, "A Diamond in the Rough," tells the audience, via music, exactly what the movie is all about—a true Prince placed by fate in the rags of a pauper. In *The Lion King*, the wise old monkey asks Simba, "Who are you?" Simba responds, "I thought I knew. Now I'm not so sure." The voice of his father later reminds him: "You are more than what you have become. Remember who you are." As with many films, Simba's revelation of his true destiny (and responsibilities as king) is the second major plot-turning point and powers the film into its final act.

➤ *One main character.*

As there is only one author's voice, there should be only one character who carries that voice. Even in ensemble films which contain a series of thematically linked subplots, there is usually one character around whom all the action seems to revolve, such as Kevin Kline's character in Lawrence Kasden's *Grand Canyon* or *The Big Chill*, or, John Travolta's "wandering angel" gangster in *Get Shorty* who served to center the film's swirl of doublecrosses and film allusions.

Even in love stories (*Romeo & Juliet* or *When Harry Met Sally . . .*) and buddy stories (*Butch Cassidy & The Sundance Kid* or *Thelma & Louise*), one character's actions primarily move the plot and it's usually (but not always) the character who exhibits the greatest amount of growth. In *Romeo & Juliet*, Romeo goes to the ball, seeks Juliet on her balcony, slays her cousin Tybalt and is banished for it, actions that force Juliet into her plan; when he finds her "dead," he is the one who takes his life first. In *When Harry Met Sally . . .* , Harry makes love to Sally but is uncomfortable with the aftermath and must reconcile the ideals of love and friendship. In *Butch Cassidy*, Butch is the leader who decides that robbing banks is getting too risky and ultimately opts to move to Bolivia, taking the Sundance Kid along. In *Thelma & Louise*, many people saw Thelma's character (played by Geena Davis) as the main character. But a closer look reveals that Louise (Susan Sarandon) encourages Thelma to make the trip; she shoots the would-be rapist and makes the decision to run due to her fear of not being able to receive justice in a man's world (set up in the backstory); it is Louise who finally decides that true freedom will be obtained by driving off the edge of the cliff. Clearly then, Louise (not Thelma), possessed of both the backstory and the actions which primarily drive the plot, is the main character.

> ## An identifiable opponent.

Faulker tells us that the most powerful stories emerge from "a heart in conflict with itself." In terms of a character's ultimate, inner need, this is accurate. The prejudices of culture or society, the difficulties of a modern, Kafkaesque bureaucracy or even natural calamities such as fire, flood or earthquake can add weight to the burden on a main character's shoulders. But the visual immediacy of film requires a living opponent to personify the struggles taking place within the character's psychic makeup.

A good writer loves his opponent as he does his protagonist and endows that opponent with all the human qualities which will make him believable to an audience; even a villain must be given a heart. Arguably, the most purely evil dramatic character in Shakespeare is Iago from *Othello*. Yet, the actor chosen to play Iago is usually a handsome, charming man. Theater lore tells us that even Shakespeare knew that this evil character had to be made human or the audience would never be able to take him seriously.

> ## Conflict.

"He who would achieve much, must sacrifice much."[3] It is only through great and sustained effort against the forces of true adversity that characters can attain success. To this end, a story requires conflict that can challenge the protagonist's internal resources. Usually kicked off by an inciting incident that upsets the normal balance of life for the main character (for example, when Roger Thornhill is mistaken for "George Kaplan" in *North by Northwest*), the conflict escalates through a series of progressive complications that raise the stakes to life-or-death proportions. The writer teases the audience to the end, when the final battle must be between the main character and the identifiable opponent, a battle representing all that they believe in and all that separates them. This battle rewards the audience with a cathartic experience.

41

Conflict this strong is often played out in the extremes of human behavior—sex and violence—from the ancient storytellers who gave us *Hamlet* and *Medea* to the modern ones who gave us *The Godfather* and *Titanic*. Do not shy away from their use, but beware: some subjects, such as violence toward women, racism or child abuse, may offend audience sensibilities.

> ## The illusion of reality.

A common indication of a work by a new writer is the sense of it all being a little too true-to-life. Conversations sound like they would in the street; people make entrances and exits by saying hello and good-bye; actions are too real. The problem is, if people want to see reality, they need only look around them. The writer

3 Allen, James. *As a Man Thinketh*. Running Press, Philadelphia, 1989.

doesn't transcribe life—he dramatizes it, arranges it to delight, excite or surprise the audience.

The painter Matisse once presented one of his stylized portraits to a lady who exclaimed, "but a woman isn't like that." Matisse replied simply, "It isn't a woman, madame, it's a picture." Likewise, the audience knows it isn't life, it's a story. They make a deal with the filmmakers to suspend disbelief in exchange for the chance to escape reality for two hours.

As writer Ed Zwick said, when asked in an interview in *Playboy* magazine if people tuned in to see real-life problems on his hit TV show, *thirtysomething*:

> It is not reality . . . We are distilling reality the way one reduces sauces. It becomes more potent. We are giving the illusion of reality while using the traditional elements of film: rising action, complication, climax and denouement . . . You're left with a sense of truth and reality, but it's calculated in dramatic terms.

While a good film must convince us that what we are seeing is real and immediate enough to involve us, it is *believability*—not reality—that the audience craves. This means that characters must have the skill and internal and external motivations to render their actions credible in the circumstances in which they have been placed. Not real life, but reel life.

42

> ➤ *Good dialogue.*

Every script needs dialogue that is emotionally-charged, informal, economical and brimming with subtext. It is not always what you say in a film that is important, but what you don't say. In good writing, it is the unspoken emotions underlying the words which convey the deeeper meaning. In *The River,* when Mae and Tom Garvey (Sissy Spacek and Mel Gibson) argue over the dwindling fortunes of their farm, their argument is really over the worsening state of their marriage. But, if either character was to say, "Hey, we have a problem in our marriage. Let's talk about it," it would undercut the drama and, hence, the power of the scene. "On-the-nose" dialogue, as it is known, is to be avoided at all times.

Characters in movies also do not speak as you and I would, they only *seem* to. They cut to the heart of any conversation and never waste words. (Six sentences on screen can seem to be a lengthy speech.) Heroes, in particular, like to act, not talk. Also, give each character his own distinct voice and never have your characters be mouthpieces for your theme, or have them tell us what we're seeing, or worse, what we've already seen!

The voiceover (narration), is also a form of screen dialogue, in this case speaking directly to the viewer. Like the flashback or dream sequence, it is an advanced structural technique which is best used only when it is not needed to advance the plot. Such "story substitutes" directly reveal a character's inner thoughts and feelings and do little to generate conflict. Thus, the audience is disengaged from the visceral experience of film; instead of experiencing the action directly, the voiceover not only tells them what is happening, like the ten o'clock news, but often how they should feel about it!

➤ A visual context.

The setting for your story is also a character. We are all shaped by our environment; likewise, film characters must live in and make full use of their world. Deserts, oceans, mountains and rivers act as crucibles by which characters may learn about themselves in the crossing (for example, see *The African Queen, Apocalypse Now* or *The Mission*). Islands can be used to explore new societies, basic human needs, or political metaphors (*Lord of the Flies, The Man Who Would Be King*). A particular time period can heighten social irony (*Planet of the Apes, The Enemy of The People*.) Homes (*Poltergeist,* The War of the Roses), families (*The Brady Bunch Movie, The Munsters*), small towns and isolated locales (*The Shining, Friday the Thirteenth*), violent weather conditions (*Alive, Twister*), all offer areas to make your story richer.

Use the medium. If you write a film like *Top Gun*, craft scenes that let the audience hear and feel the power of the jets. Avoid static settings like offices, restaurants, cars, apartments and phone booths. Instead, make the background a lively character in your film; have it brimming with all the relevant details that make your characters insiders in their world.

➤ A cathartic ending.

From the inciting incident on, the main character battles down blind paths to a final destination where only three conclusions are possible: win, lose or draw. Audiences want a cathartic release for the investment of their time and emotions. If the writer has done his job well, any ending, even a "surprise" ending, is as inevitable as it is satisfying.

Much was made of the shock ending of *Thelma & Loiuse*, but given the chain of events leading up to it, was any other ending viable? Could the women have surrendered? For the most part, the audience wanted an emotional payoff, not an end scroll telling us that, for example, Thelma got two years of a suspended sentence and Louise returned to waitressing after serving four years for manslaughter. Could they have escaped? Escape would hardly have been credible given a plot which hurdled the two toward a grand precipice at the end of a desert plain with police forces from three states in hot pursuit. Should they have been gunned down? The tone of the movie and the audience's empathy with the characters would have been violated (besides, it was already done in *Bonnie & Clyde*). At its core, Thelma and Louise were characters trapped in a world in which the determinants of law and society were so strong that redemption could only be achieved by rejecting those determinants as false and by having them take charge of their own destinies. Or, this could be looked at as winning by losing, as in *Rocky* or *North Dallas Forty* or . . . *And Justice For All* (as contrasted with losing by winning, as in *The Godfather Part II*.)

Even in films in which the ending is not in doubt, the writer must be aware of the tone of the film and audience expectations. For example, in *The Lion King*, the audience easily could predict that the lion cub, Simba, would grow to adulthood and defeat his evil Uncle Scar in a final battle and thus regain his kingdom. But how? In one scenario, Simba, a healthy, brave young lion, could kill Scar, an old, weak lion (and his uncle, no less). The audience might cheer for the moment, but something would sit uneasily with them: it wouldn't be a fair fight. Instead, Simba judiciously bans Scar from the kingdom. But the writers knew that while this punishment was "humane," the audience would feel deprived of a real catharsis (after all, Scar planned and carried out the murder of Simba's father). So, a final battle ensued in which Scar double-crossed his own gang (the merry but deadly hyenas), rewarded Simba's kindness by tossing hot ashes in his eye, and caused his own demise by unintentionally catapulting himself into his band of revengeful hyenas. This scenario appeased the audience's desire for vengeance while preserving Disney's requisite family values.

➢ *A professional screen style and format.*
Do have scene headings, character cues, proper tab settings, appropriate length, and for teleplays, distinct act breaks. The more reader-friendly the writing style, the better. Paragraph freely. Use short sentences, present tense and active voice.

Don't write camera directions unless they are absolutely necessary to make a story point.

Do capitalize all music, sound effects and character introductions to make them easy to find and follow.

Don't number your scenes (numbers are used for scripts in production) and don't include character lists, casting suggestions, detailed set descriptions or a synopsis.

Do proofread your work for grammatical, spelling or punctuation errors (do not trust your computer's Spell Check). Some readers tell me that three spelling or grammatical errors will eliminate your script from their consideration.

Don't end a page on a slug line or character cue or break sentences from one page to the next. Make sure all pages break correctly.

Do use a title page ([title], "written by" [name], contact information, no date). Use plain, thin, card stock covers that are easy to roll back and bind your script with two or three brads. As the Writers Guild of America likes conformity in the title page, here is the complete approved format (per Article 37 of the Minimum Basic Agreement):

Project Title
by
Name of First Writer(s)

(Based on, if any)
Revisions By
(in order of work performed)

Current Revisions By
(Current writer, date)

Name
Address
Phone of Contact

➤ *Rewrite and polish.*

As all writers know, writing is rewriting, which is the final ingredient to the marketable screenplay. Screenwriter Robert Rodat wrote 11 drafts of *Saving Private Ryan* before presenting it to Paramount for the first round of their "notes." Renowned authors Joan Didion and John Gregory Dunne did 29 rewrites of the Michelle Pfeiffer-Robert Redford vehicle *Up Close and Personal*. Even novelist Vladimir Nabokov (*Lolita*) states, "I have rewritten—often several times—every word I have ever published. My pencils outlast my erasers."

45

Put your "final draft" away for a few weeks to get a fresh perspective. Allow time for feedback from one or two trusted friends. Then, like a good gardener, weed out the beats that don't work, prune excessive dialogue, refine the pacing, scene transitions and point of attack (the true beginning of the story or scene). Here are other rewriting flash points:

- Pull out the dialogue to see if scenes are showing rather than telling. (Strong dialogue can mask a dramatically weak scene. The dynamics of a scene should be clear enough that actors can improvise dialogue as well as you can write it.)
- Check to make sure that flashbacks, dream sequences, montages and/or narration succeed as good story-telling techniques. Make sure they're not crutches which

bolster a weak story. (Hint: if you need such a device, you may have a hole in your story structure.)

- Is the dialogue stiff or do all characters sound alike? (Often, the earliest dialogue has yet to find the voice of your characters.)
- Are scenes or characters repetitious? (Can you eliminate scenes or combine characters?)
- How many words can you cut from every scene? (Hint: cut as many as you can, to the point where, if you cut one more word, the scene would make no sense.)
- Check to make sure the scenes and story do not go on after the drama has played. (Old axiom: better to start a scene too late and end it too soon.)

In general, keep your best story-telling instincts tuned to creative deviations and not to the accepted wisdom. As Quentin Tarantino demonstrated when he twisted the structure in *Pulp Fiction*, there can be variations on even "the beginning, middle and end" rule. Use the general guidelines offered in courses and books to *develop* your instincts as a storyteller, not to replace them.

But, going against generally accepted wisdom is risky and should be undertaken only if you know the prevailing wisdom. For example, most feature scripts are between 105 and 130 pages (translating to approximately one minute of screen time per page). Yours can be longer or shorter, but it should be that much better to justify the length. Also, many readers are bothered by the inclusion of camera angles, musical cues or other elements which distract from the dramatic unfolding of the story, especially when such elements are usually production decisions. Yet it is also true that some older classic screenplays are replete with such instructions. Styles change.

Ask 10 working writers whether they use an outline before beginning to write the first draft and one may say no. Ask 10 others if they write in camera angles and, again, you may find a successful writer who does it all the time. Some writers swear by three acts for a feature and a few say they write best in five.

The whims of the audience change as well. Since it takes most films years to come out of development and into your theater, don't try to anticipate studio wish lists or current trends. (There is also what I call the "law of opposites," which simply means that a star who has just completed a high-tech hit may look for a quiet family drama for his next film or a director who has just returned from six months in the jungle might opt next for an urban drama to be closer to his family.) Instead, start your own trend. Take risks with

46

your work. Appeal to our wildest fantasies. Surprise us. Get personal. Or, as one now-famous writer who struggled for years without a sale put it: "Get away from what you think movies are supposed to be and deal with your own nightmares."

But don't preach. Don't make your work a place for cliches or stereotypes. And, don't shy away from the sex, violence and passion that is inherent in life and, more importantly, the heart of dramatic conflict in film. All the great and terrible truths of the world are too big to fit into our hearts; a writer must carve them into images that move us. It is possible to be both commercial and tell a worthwhile story, even one infused with poetry!

And, whether you are a novice writer or a successful one, don't fall into the trap of writing for the money. Of course, to reach true financial heights as a screenwriter, you must *write movies that people want to see* and that means: good stories, which are entertaining and emotionally involving, and which are well-told.

Finally, never forget: let your audience dream, if just for awhile. (Viewers may want to *see Star Wars*, but they want to *be* Harrison Ford.) And, that's reason enough to post on your corkboard the following advice from screenwriter Larry Ferguson (*The Hunt for Red October*): "The way you get screenplays on the screen is you write parts actors want to play." That's the ultimate test of a truly marketable screenplay.

RECIPE FOR A MARKETABLE SCREENPLAY:

- **Themes from your heart.**
- **A viable premise.**
- **A recognizable genre.**
- **A great opening.**
- **A clear goal.**
- **Characters we care about.**
- **A balanced structure.**
- **A strong protagonist spine.**
- **One main character.**
- **An identifiable opponent.**
- **Conflict.**
- **Illusion of reality.**
- **Good dialogue.**
- **A visual context.**
- **A cathartic ending.**
- **A professional screen style and format.**
- **Rewrite and polish.**

47

Chapter 4
THE MARKETABLE SCREENPLAY, PART TWO: THE INDEPENDENT FILM

"DOLLARS AND SENSE"

Welcome to the world of low-budget, independent filmmaking, including those staples of the B-movies: formula films and genre movies. *Beach Party* with Annette and Frankie. *The Blob* with Steve McQueen. *I Was a Teenage Frankenstein.* The movies of horror, sex, violence, comedy and oddities that independent giants like Sam Arkoff, Roger Corman and Lew Grade pumped out for decades to feed the appetite of Saturday matinees, drive-ins and an international market starved for American product. They are also known as exploitation films and more than a few of them were brilliant, with quirky points of view, depressingly real storylines or odd characters

"Kiss me, will ya, kid." Those words were whispered to me 20 years ago, over the expanse of a mahogany desk, by a cigar-chomping pro in an expensive but ill-fitting suit. I had just pitched him a tale of international intrigue that was also a love triangle and a story of grifters and gypsies who found themselves in a complex web of deceit and murder and . . . that's when this guy leaned forward, his eyes glazed over, and said it. He wasn't coming on to me; he was giving me advice. Good, sound advice. "Keep it simple, stupid." The KISS method of storytelling.

that shocked the established film industry executives. And some became cult classics, such as *The Little Shop of Horrors, The Rocky Horror Picture Show* and *Eraserhead.*

Fortunately, a modest budget does not always translate into modest achievement. And, independent films now can acquire a different sort of reputation. For example, mainstream successes like Steven Soderbergh's *sex, lies and videotape* and Quentin Tarantino's *Reservoir Dogs* began as independent films and, in fact, were both spawned at the world's most celebrated workshop for independent film and filmmakers, the Sundance Institute (created by actor-director Robert Redford).

. . . .

The Sundance Film Festival, which is held in Park City, Utah, often turns into a feeding frenzy by distributors scrambling to acquire the rights to the unconventional and often very personal work of independent writers and directors. In 1996, during one crazed two-hour period, four super low-budget films found distributors, and one, Lee David Zlotoff's *The Spitfire Grill*, sold to Castle Rock Entertainment for a reported $12 million!

The festival's success has also spawned a nearby competitive off-shoot, Slamdance, which tries to accommodate the growing number of worthy films which don't make it into Sundance. In the past years, the Sundance Festival has received such massive industry attention that there is now talk of moving it to a new venue, such as Salt Lake City, to handle the growing crowds and increasing need for screens.

. . . .

All the attention, of course, has led to a heightened awareness by Hollywood that there is money to be made from independent films. Executives have been quick to set up independent companies within their larger studios to groom the hottest prospects for stardom. Some independent writer-directors, who have roots in low-budget genre films, like Sam Raimi (*Darkman*) and John Sayles (*Return of the Secaucus Seven*), shuttle back and forth between making personal, independent films and studio-made mainstream films. Others, such as seasoned veteran Jim Jarmusch (*Stranger Than Paradise*), call themselves "film outlaws" and shun Hollywood altogether in favor of the control they wish to maintain over their vision.

To be fair, many low-budget entries lack quality. But while they may contain the plotless sex or violence that is often found in major studio films (but without big stars and special effects), they too can find an audience. These are the films that feed the cable stations and line the shelves of the sprawling video stores in your neighborhood (though there is a decreasing demand for straight-to-video films that have not had at least a limited theatrical release).

True independent films—the ones you could finance from the change in your dad's pockets—have turned more than one kid into the toast of Hollywood. The legend is that Robert Rodriguez shot the original version of *El Mariachi* for $7,000; Spike Lee financed his breakthrough film, *She's Gotta Have It*, on loans from friends and advances on credit cards; *The Brothers McMullen*, written by Edward Burns, was shot on weekends over a two-year period while he was still employed as a production assistant on *Entertainment Tonight*. (Burns went on to win the coveted Screenwriter of the Year Award at NATO/ShoWest '96.)

. . . .

50

Somebody has to write these films. Literary agents say that all this activity (there are close to 100 scripts per day registered at the Writers Guild) means more and greater opportunities for writers. After all, script material can't come from the same handful of studio darlings. Or, can it?

Studios are not in business to make low-budget films or to worry excessively about star salaries. They are in business to make money. If it takes money to make money, so be it. But, at the high cost of making these kinds of films, the studios are not anxious to take risks on "new" material or on untried talent that the audience hasn't previously validated and accepted.

For most union screenwriters—not the few who make the big bucks we read about in the trades, but the rest, the 55 percent of over 8,000 WGA members who never report a dime of income in any given year (of the 45 percent who do, the median income is still less than $50,000)—and the countless thousands of non-union screenwriters who churn out those low-budget films, there are worse things than a steady income and a chance to have a forum for their work.

According to the Motion Picture Association of America, in 1997, the average cost of production for a motion picture was $53.5 million. That's a 34.1 percent increase from 1996, in just the negative cost alone. On top of that, distributors spent an estimated average of $22.26 million on advertising campaigns and prints. That equals nearly $76 million per film.

. . . .

Out of 458 films released in the U.S. in 1997, only about one-third were from the "majors." The number of films increased from 420 in 1996, with total box-office gross jumping to over $6.36 billion, which represents a 7.7 percent increase from 1996. But these films were spread over roughly *the same audience*. All the studio films, backed by large marketing campaigns, have not had the effect of making *more* people want to go to the movies.

. . . .

Years after enjoying the "privilege" of working with studio execs, big budgets and superstars, I was lucky enough to be hired to produce a film with a simple script, no stars, a first-time director and a budget of around $1 million (every Friday, I held my breath until the paychecks cleared). However, a funny thing happened: I found myself less stressed than I had been in ages and I was having one hell of a good time! The writer was beside me on the set, working on dialogue with the actors and director. We

THIS BUSINESS OF SCREENWRITING

made the script better and found practical, fast and cheap solutions to problems. Filmmaking had finally become the fun and collaborative gig I had always heard about.

. . . .

Following are 13 guidelines that may convince a low-budget producer that you have what it takes to write a low-budget, cost-conscious film:

> *Character-driven stories.*
Dialogue is cheaper than planes, boats and trains. But don't create too many speaking parts; even low-budget actors have to be fed, housed, trucked, clothed and rehearsed.

> *Limited locations.*
Don't move your story around too much (e.g., drop the airport scene if you can have your characters do it while they're packing their bags). There's a reason why so much art-house fare is set in an isolated cabin in the forest or a haunted house or a deserted amusement park.

> *No complex stunts.*
These require time to block and stage and time costs money. There's little time available for rehearsals and there's even less for filming multiple takes or angles (a master shot and a closeup may be all the coverage a director will get).

> *Day scenes preferable to night.*
Lighting is difficult and time-consuming and dark movies don't go over as well with the mass market.

> *Interior preferable to exterior.*
The director will shoot outside if the light is right, but for an interior scene, the lighting and sound can be controlled.

> *No special effects.*
A space film without money looks tacky (remember *Plan Nine From Outer Space*?); the same is true of those blow-everyone-away in the middle of a crowded street scenes. In fact, banish guns altogether—they require weapons experts onset as well as expensive insurance. Don't forget: special effects are not just computer graphics and explosions; rain or even traffic can be deemed special effects. (Different seasons in the same script can create havoc; in fact, use the blue pencil on any kind of weather you write, besides sunny summer days.)

➤ *No children or pets.*
Your budget will skyrocket if you have scenes with children—their hours are strictly regulated and there's also the cost of a teacher who must be on the set. (Plus, there can be pesky parents hanging around.) The same goes for animals—the horror stories you've heard about getting animals to act on cue are most likely true (see the famous cat-sipping milk scene in *Day for Night*). And animal trainers can be prima donnas, too.

➤ *No period pieces.*
You might incorporate stock footage to give the film scope, but period pieces are a problem unless you have an "in" at a costume house or access to a "wild west" town in the desert which has banished every vestige of the late 20th century.

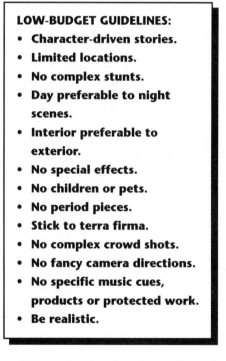

LOW-BUDGET GUIDELINES:
- **Character-driven stories.**
- **Limited locations.**
- **No complex stunts.**
- **Day preferable to night scenes.**
- **Interior preferable to exterior.**
- **No special effects.**
- **No children or pets.**
- **No period pieces.**
- **Stick to terra firma.**
- **No complex crowd shots.**
- **No fancy camera directions.**
- **No specific music cues, products or protected work.**
- **Be realistic.**

➤ *Stick to terra firma.*
That means stay off the water and out of the air. If you don't, you'll regret the insurance rider you'll need. Boats, water stunts, airplanes, helicopters, and blimps are *verboten* to all but the most technically experienced and well-heeled productions.

➤ *No complex crowd shots.*
Don't have the main characters chatting away while jogging in-between traffic and crowds. Extras may work cheaply, but they need proper clothing, makeup and direction (and don't forget the extra fee for Craft Services—that can add another $200 a day in doughnuts!). And police are expensive; save the traffic control for the line to get into your movie.

➤ *No fancy camera directions.*
Let your plot tell the story. Crane shots, dissolves, pans and sweeps, dolly tracks and Steadicams are not cost-effective. Getting "fancy" should mean no more than rubbing a little gel on the lens.

53

➤ *No specific music cues, products or protected work.*
The license fees can break the budget, if proper licenses are even
negotiated. In fact, some wonderful films are still languishing in
studio vaults, deprived of a release date, because the music rights
were never properly licensed for *all media*. In addition, brand name
products and recognizable art or trademarks must be licensed and
even a doctored photo of a celebrity may violate valuable publicity
rights. (Actor Dustin Hoffman recently sued a national magazine
for using a photo of the character he portrayed in *Tootsie*—artfully
displayed in a current designer's dress. A jury awarded him $3 mil-
lion in damages.)

➤ *Be realistic.*
I read one low-budget film in which the opening scene had the main
character dragging his wounded leg up the crest of a hill where he
found himself directly in the path of "a stampede of a thousand
white buffalo!" Unless you want white to be the new color of your
producer's hair, understand your budget limitations and be realistic.

. . . .

That cigar-chomping pro? That was
Sam Arkoff. Undaunted by his gruff
dismissal of my first idea, I pitched
him another one that same day—an
idea I thought would be simple and
inexpensive enough for AIP. It was the
story of a small-time clubfighter who
gets a fluke shot at the heavyweight
title. He wants only to be standing at
the end of the fight and not be "just
another bum from the neighborhood." It was titled *The Italian Stal-
lion* back then, and was later variously
known as *Hell's Kitchen* and *Pepper
Alley*, among other titles. You probably know it best as *Rocky*. Sam
passed on that, too.

Shortly afterward, I made my first
studio deal and was happily en-
sconced in offices at Universal
Studios, nestled snugly between Sly
Stallone and Steven Spielberg. I
promptly forgot all about low budgets and concentrated on making
studio pictures. I thought I'd never
see Sam again.

Then, years later, on one sun-
drenched morning at the Cannes Film
Festival, I was sitting on the terrace
of my hotel, watching the blue water cascade over white rocks and enjoying my breakfast, when my nos-
trils became aware of the wafting
smell of pungent cigar smoke. I
looked over my shoulder and there
was Arkoff, who, without missing a
beat, mumbled in my direction,
"What about that script, kid, huh?
Guess I should've bit on that one."

Right again, Sam.

. . . .

Chapter 5
WRITING TEAMS

Some twenty years ago, Jack Epps, Jr., took a screenwriting class at Michigan State University that was taught by Jim Cash. Even as they came to discover their separate points of view and writing styles, they also found out, as Cash put it, "a third personality that comes together whenever we work." When Epps moved to Los Angeles, Cash stayed behind in East Lansing, but the partnership thrived when they faxed ideas back and forth, worked simultaneously on scenes and drafts via computer modem and commiserated over the exigencies of the writing business by speaker phone. Their collaboration has resulted in such hits as *Top Gun*, *Dick Tracy* and *Turner & Hooch*.

Having a writing partner is a great source of comfort and motivation for many writers because they can avoid facing that blank page alone. In this sense at least, screenwriting enjoys a distinct advantage over most other fields of creative writing, such as writing for novels, short stories or plays (where one is hard-pressed to cite even a few collaborative efforts). Celebrated writing collaborations—e.g., I.A.L. Diamond & Billy Wilder, Ben Hecht & Charles MacArthur, Ruth Gordon & Garson Kanin—have helped to create a long and proud history of team success in cinema writing, a tradition continued by current writing teams like Scott Alexander & Larry Karaszewski (*The People vs. Larry Flynt*), Joel & Ethan Cohen (*Fargo*) and married television writer/producers Andrew Schneider & Diane Frolov (*Northern Exposure* and *Dangerous Minds*).

> **Note here the use of the ampersand when naming the writing partners. Per the Writers Guild, the word "and" is used only for writers who may have worked on the same script, but who are not part of the writing team.**

In the best partnerships, the writers complement each other's strengths. One writer may be better with dialogue while the other works magic with structure. Put those two together and you have a powerful writing team. Some partners write separately and combine their work later. Other teams may work better if one dictates or acts out the scenes while the other translates the words into text (changing it subtly to suit his style as he goes). Another method of team writing is to entrust Act 1 to one writer, Act 2 to the other and hammer out the final act together. Or, the writers may want to go through every beat of the process—from the rough outline to the polished final draft—as a single writing machine.

Particularly when writing comedy, it helps to have someone else in the room laughing. (Or not.) (Think: Lowell Ganz & Babaloo Mandel, who collaborated on *Parenthood*). A partner is also a shoulder to cry on, a cure for writer's block, a critic who cares or sometimes just good company.

For whatever reason two people decide to combine their writing fortunes, no partnership should be entered into lightly. Becoming a writing team is akin to entering into marriage. Partners should grow together, learn to resolve their differences and

Charles Shyer & Nancy Meyers (*Father of the Bride*) told the students in my screenwriting class that they lie across from each other on separate couches and bat ideas back and forth.

be able to put aside their egos for the good of the team. Mutual respect for each other's work, opinions, integrity and creative and business judgment is essential. Trust is crucial. Both partners must be able to handle and benefit from any critical analysis by the other. Compromise cannot be anathema to you. Sooner or later you must agree (or at least agree to disagree) so the work can move forward. It is not always a good idea to become writing partners with your lover or best friend. (A professional working relationship is best at arm's length.) But the two of you should be compatible and like each other enough that you're reasonably assured of staying together. Divorce can be costly. A writing team displays a single creative force to the outside world. If the partners break up, it's probable that neither will have a decent individual writing sample. Both writers likely will need new, individual spec samples and may have to prove their writing talent all over again.

Most importantly, while partners have someone to share the workload, the business side of your work belongs to the team and is subject to team decisions—from creation of the story to the writing of the script and on to the marketing and selling of it.

Before you enter into a writing partnership, here are some questions to ask yourself: How are conflicts over the writing and marketing of the screenplay to be resolved? If one writer comes up with the story and both write the screenplay, how is the income from a sale to be divided? What if one partner wants to sell and the other doesn't like the terms or the buyer—must both participate in script meetings? What if one writer moves on after the first draft and doesn't want to participate in rewrites; can the other do it alone? What if one partner dies before the screenplay has been completed or marketed? Will there be separate compensation for separate work? (A writing team does not get twice the money. The WGA treats two partners as one writer and applicable scale [minimum compensation] is split between them. Presumably, a team can write twice as fast, get twice the jobs and earn twice the money in a given period.)

If you and your partner decide to write as a team, you will want to draw up a Writers Collaboration Agreement which outlines the duties and parameters of your relationship, including a formula for completion of the work, rewriting assignments, ownership and copyright, division of income and expenses, representation, screen credit, etc. Following are common points which this written agreement should address:

57

➤ *The Work.*
In agreeing to collaborate, consider the writing services each will contribute to the final product, a completion date (if warranted) and final ownership of the work. Also consider if the parties' writing services are exclusive to the partnership or if either may work on other spec projects or accept separate employment. This can often affect the candor with which partners share ideas during the writing process.

➤ *Ownership.*
Shall the work be copyrighted or registered in the name of both parties? If so, each should designate the other as his attorney-in-fact to complete such registration.

➤ *Mutuality.*
Shall all decisions, with respect to the completion, representation, sale or other disposition of the work, be in writing? Are all decisions mutual or may one person, in some affairs or at opportune times, act for the team?

➤ *Expenses & Income.*
How shall expenses incurred in connection with the work or its disposition be shared? How shall proceeds flowing from the

exploitation of the work (whether fixed, deferred or contingent, or whether from the sale of rights or licenses in all or any of the various mediums) be divided and paid?

➤ Credit.
How and in what order shall the writers receive credit on the work and on any motion picture based upon the work? Writing teams most often position themselves alphabetically but some grant the coveted first position to the more experienced writer or, perhaps, to the one who came up with the initial concept. Whatever formula your team decides upon, do so in advance to ward off any potential problems.

➤ Interruption of Services.
If one party, for whatever reason, ceases work on the project at any given point, may the other party complete it? If so, must the writer complete it alone or can another partner be engaged? How, then, will the percentage of ownership and possible proceeds from the work be divided?

➤ Disputes & Termination.
May either party terminate the agreement, and if so, how will the work or its disposition be affected? How are disputes in general, with respect to the work or its disposition, to be handled? Should arbitration be mandatory? (The Writers Guild has a mediation arbitration procedure for its members.)

58

➤ Agency.
Shall the work be represented by one agent for both parties? What if each has or ultimately acquires separate representation? The commissions payable and the procedure by which duel agents may represent the work or its authors should be set forth.

➤ Further Writing Services.
Shall (or must) the parties share any offered rewrite assignments? What if one party is unwilling or unavailable to participate in further writing services with respect to the work—shall the other be permitted to undertake such an engagement, and if so, how shall additional compensation be shared? (For example, substantial bonuses are often attached to the purchase price of the original screenplay. But if such film is based not only on the original work but also on a one-party rewrite, should the division of the writing bonus between the partners be altered?)

➤ Other Services.
Will either party be contributing other services to the work (i.e., attaching himself as producer, director or some other creative

capacity)? This could affect the marketability of the work and might raise the question of whether some percentage share in any related compensation is appropriate for the non-attached party.

A short-form Writers Collaboration Agreement, approved for use by members of the Writers Guild of America, addresses many of these concerns and is printed by permission of the Guild at the end of this chapter. Current versions can also be obtained for a nominal fee (currently, $1.00) from the Guild. Attach an SASE and send your request to: WGA West: 7000 West Third Street, Los Angeles, CA 90048-4329; WGA East: 555 West 57th St., New York, N.Y. 10019. However, to fully address the intricacies of the questions above and other perplexing issues which may confront the partnership, consult an entertainment attorney; this might be the first mutual decision the partnership makes.

WRITING TEAM CONTRACTUAL POINTS:
- **The Work**
- **Ownership**
- **Mutuality**
- **Expenses & Income**
- **Credit**
- **Interruption of Services**
- **Disputes & Termination**
- **Agency**
- **Further Writing Services**
- **Other Services**

59

A WORD ABOUT LOAN-OUT COMPANIES

Primarily for tax purposes, writers often choose to incorporate themselves. Usually, the writer is the sole officer and the entire board of directors of his closely-held corporation and he owns all the company's stock (though some writers may have a spouse or other family members on the roster as well). The writer contracts to work exclusively for the corporation (in film business jargon, the corporation is a "loan-out company"), in exchange for a salary and other corporate perks such as a car, retirement plan, insurance and so on. The loan-out company then proceeds to "lend and furnish" the writer's services to anyone interested in employing the writer.

Advantages to this arrangement include receiving payment for services rendered without taxes being deducted by the employer and the ability to spread income over two personal tax years. Disadvantages include the loss of normal employer contributions, such as state unemployment insurance (though some employers may be convinced to reimburse the loan-out company for contributions actually paid to the government). Still, the most highly prized feature of any corporation—limited liability—will usually not apply to the writer with a loan-out company. Any savvy employer will require the writer to personally contract his services to the employer (in what is known as an inducement letter), as well as execute a second agreement between the employer and the loan-out company which contracts to "cause the writer to commence his services" to the employer (known as a *lending agreement*).

Recently, some writing teams have incorporated themselves into a single loan-out company. The primary reason for this action is the single tax return and one accountant required at tax time and the one state minimum tax fee that must be paid.

I believe that two tax returns are better than one lawsuit. As mentioned above, it is difficult to separate two people from the bonds of a writing partnership. Now, compound that with the legalities of extracting them from the bonds of their corporation.

WRITER'S COLLABORATION AGREEMENT*

AGREEMENT made at _____, California, by and between _____ and _____, hereinafter sometimes referred to as the "Parties".

The parties are about to write in collaboration an (original story) (treatment) (screenplay) _____ (other), based upon _____, hereinafter referred to as the "Work", and are desirous of establishing all their rights and obligations in and to said Work.

NOW, THEREFORE, in consideration of the execution of this Agreement, and the undertakings of the parties as hereinafter set forth, it is agreed as follows:

1.   The parties shall collaborate in the writing of the Work and upon completion thereof shall be the joint owners of the Work (or shall own the Work in the following percentages:

_____).

2.   Upon completion of the Work it shall be registered with the Writers Guild of America, west, Inc. as the joint Work of the parties. If the Work shall be in form such as to qualify it for copyright, it shall be registered for such copyright in the name of both Parties, and each Party hereby designates the other as his attorney-in-fact to register such Work with the United States Copyright Office.

61

3.   It is contemplated that the Work will be completed by not later than _____, provided, however, that failure to complete the Work by such date shall not be construed as a breach of this Agreement on the part of either party.

4.   It is understood that _____ (both writers) is a/ are/are not "professional writer(s)," as that term is defined in the WGA Basic Agreement.

(It is further understood by the Parties that _____ (and _____), in addition to writing services, shall perform the following additional functions in regard to the Work:

5.   If, prior to the completion of the Work, either Party shall voluntarily withdraw from the collaboration, then the other Party shall have the right to complete the Work alone or in conjunction with another collaborator or collaborators, and in such event the percentage of ownership, as hereinbefore provided in paragraph 1, shall be revised by mutual agreement in writing.

---

*   The Provisions herein are not mandatory, and may be modified for the specific needs of the Parties, subject to minimum requirements of the Writers Guild Basic Agreement.

6. If, prior to the completion of the Work, there shall be a dispute of any kind with respect to the Work, then the parties may terminate this Collaboration Agreement by an instrument in writing, which shall be filed with the Writers Guild of America, west, Inc. [new mediation arbitration procedure in Constitution]

7. Any contract for the sale or other disposition of the Work, where the Work has been completed by the Parties in accordance herewith, shall require that the Work shall be attributed to the authors in the following manner:

8. Neither party shall sell, or otherwise voluntarily dispose of the Work, or his share therein, without the written consent of the other, which consent, however shall not be unreasonably withheld. (It is agreed that _____ to contract on behalf of the Parties without written consent of the other, on the condition that s/he negotiate no less than _____ for the work.)

9. It is acknowledged and agreed that _____ (and _____) shall be the exclusive agents of the Parties for the purpose of sale or other disposition of the Work or any rights therein. Each such agent shall represent the Parties at the following studios only:

X agent   Y agent

The aforementioned agent, or agents, shall have _____ period in which to sell or otherwise dispose of the Work, and if there shall be more than one agent, the aggregate commission for the sale or other disposition of the Work shall be limited to ten percent (10%) and shall be equally divided among the agents hereinbefore designated.

If there shall be two or more agents, they shall be instructed to notify each other when they have begun negotiations for the sale or other disposition of the Work and of the terms thereof, and no agent shall conclude an agreement for the sale or other disposition of the Work unless he shall have first notified the other agents thereof. If there shall be a dispute among the agents as to the sale or other disposition of the Work by any of them, the matter shall immediately be referred to the Parties, who shall determine the matter for them.

10. Any and all expenses of any kind whatsoever which shall be incurred by either or both of the Parties in connection with the writing, registration or sale or other disposition of the Work shall be (shared jointly) (prorated in accordance with the percentages hereinbefore mentioned in paragraph 1).

11. All money or other things of value derived from the sale or other disposition of the Work shall be applied as follows:

a. In payment of commissions, if any.

b. In payment of any expenses or reimbursement of either Party for expenses paid in connection with the Work.

c. To the Parties in the proportion of their ownership.

12. It is understood and agreed that for the purposes of this Agreement the Parties shall share hereunder, unless otherwise herein stated, the proceeds from the sale or any and all other disposition of the Work and the rights and licenses therein and with respect thereto, including but not limited to the following:

a. Motion picture rights
b. Sequel rights
c. Remake rights
d. Television film rights
e. Television live rights
f. Stage rights
g. Radio rights
h. Publication rights
I. Interactive rights
j. Merchandising rights

63

13. Should the Work be sold or otherwise disposed of and, as an incident thereto, the Parties be employed to revise the Work or write a screenplay based thereon, the total compensation provided for in such employment agreement shall be shared by them (jointly) (in the following proportion):

If either Party shall be unavailable for the purposes of collaborating on such revision or screenplay, then the Party who is available shall be permitted to do such revision or screenplay and shall be entitled to the full amount of compensation in connection therewith, provided, however, that in such a case the purchase price shall remain fair and reasonable, and in no event shall the Party not available for the revision or screenplay receive less than _____% of the total selling price.

14. If either Party hereto shall desire to use the Work, or any right therein or with respect thereto, in any venture in which such Party shall have a financial interest, whether direct or indirect, the Party desiring so to do shall notify the other Party of that fact and shall afford such other Party the opportunity to participate in the venture in the proportion of such other Party's interest in the Work. If such other party shall be unwilling to participate in such venture, the Party desiring to proceed therein shall be required to pay such other Party an amount equal to that which such other Party

would have received if the Work or right, as the case may be, intended to be so used had been sold to a disinterested person at the price at which the same shall last have been offered, or if it shall not have been offered, at its fair market value which, in the absence of mutual agreement of the Parties, shall be determined by mediation and/or arbitration in accordance with the regulations of the Writers Guild of America, west, Inc. if permissible pursuant to the WGAw Constitution.

15. This Agreement shall be executed in sufficient number of copies so that one fully executed copy may be, and shall be, delivered to each Party and to the Writers Guild of America, Inc. If any disputes shall arise concerning the interpretation or application of this Agreement, or the rights or liabilities of the Parties arising hereunder, such dispute shall be submitted to the Writers Guild of America, west, Inc. for arbitration in accordance with the arbitration procedures of the Guild, and the determination of the Guild's arbitration committee as to all such matters shall be conclusive and binding upon the Parties.

DATED this _____ day of _____, 19_____.

_____

_____

Chapter 6
PROTECTING YOUR WORK

"TRUST IN ALLAH, BUT TIE UP YOUR CAMEL"

Whatever the peculiar vagaries of the business, one fact is certain—producers won't be able to purchase or produce your work if they don't have access to it. In other words, as a writer, you cannot be unduly afraid of theft but also hope to circulate your work to buyers. No matter what its merits may be, your unread script will remain unsold in the dark recesses of your desk drawer unless you expose it to the light.

That said, there are legitimate concerns about protecting your material from uncompensated appropriation (i.e., having it stolen, ripped-off, snatched in broad daylight—this may sound like an overexaggeration, but it's an emotional issue). To hear the horror stories circulating in restaurants and studios around town, this sort of thing happens all the time. Major producers and directors often exact confidentiality agreements from their employees and will assign code numbers to script submissions, etc.

Certainly, each year, several movies appear which seem to have lifted their plots from the same source material. (Do you remember all the "body exchange" films that came out around the time of *Big*? I can think of six offhand.) But does that mean plagiarism took place? **Conscious stealing** happens less often than we may believe. To most mainstream film executives or producers, stealing an idea is not worth the trouble. Movies cost too much to produce—it makes little sense to cheat on the relatively small amount it would take to secure the appropriate rights. (That's what development budgets are for.) Also, in the long run, it's in the best interest of the studio executives to establish relationships with people who have bright ideas. **Unconscious stealing** is a whole other story. Twenty-five years as an entertainment lawyer, producer and film company executive has taught me this: you absorb a lot of ideas during the course of hundreds of pitch meetings and thousands of script submissions.

65

In a story conference, with plotlines and dialogue tossed back and forth or as writers, producers, director and executives try to beat a deadline or solve a script problem, who really can say where any particular thought originates?

In fact, the concept of "originality" may be more a matter of incorporating old ideas into new form than the solitary creation of an idea that is assumed by copyright. And when a TV series is based upon a film that is based upon a novel, the lines of "originality" blur even further. (Perhaps this explains why the single most litigated issue under the Copyright Act is whether a given work is an infringing derivative work "based upon" another copyrighted work. For while copyright protection does not extend to "underlying ideas" but only to the expression of such ideas, neither does infringement require a word-for-word theft of the original work. Courts have found infringement whenever the new work is "substantially similar" to the copyrighted work.)[1]

One judge in the Midwest is said to have found, as a matter of triable fact, that there are only 29 basic plot ideas in the world, with the most enduring of those realized in the repeatable genre movies that form the staple of Hollywood's diet. Critic Northrop Frye seems to agree: "Poetry can only be made out of other poems; novels out of other novels."

Of course, it is perfectly acceptable for a writer to incorporate *public domain* material (for which copyright protection has expired or was never attached) into his own literary work. In the September, 1998, issue of the *Atlantic Monthly*, Charles C. Mann, writing on the question of copyright and the theft of ideas, made this point:

> Shakespeare derived some of the language in *Julius Caesar* from an English translation of a French translation of Plutarch; he followed a printed history so closely for *Henry V* that scholars believe he had the book open on his desk as he wrote. In this century Eugene O'Neill gleaned *Mourning Becomes Electra* from Aeschylus.

Personally, I subscribe to psychologist Carl Jung's theory of "the collective unconscious." Sometimes ideas are out there, like dreams floating in space, and any number of people laboring over a story might pull them out of the air and adopt them as their own. The novelist P.D. James recently echoed this, saying "a good idea, whether related to plot or theme, is like a benign infection borne on the air, waiting to be caught and used by others if one doesn't get [it] written quickly."

[1] Moore, S. M. *Copyright.* Entertainment Law Newsletter, Los Angeles, 1999.

Still, make no mistake, you have rights with respect to your work product. Even if you have put a new twist on an old plot or you have only presented it orally in a pitch meeting, it is protectable, either by federal copyright or by various state laws which claim that an implied contract exists between you and the potential buyer if your material is submitted, orally or in writing, with the expectation of payment for its use and is, in fact, subsequently used.

All writers are advised to afford themselves the best protection possible against theft of their work. A written agreement is best. If that's not practical at the time (pitch meetings leave writers particularly vulnerable to theft, conscious or unconscious), try to get an oral agreement that your work is being submitted for sale and won't be used without payment. Keep in mind that blind, unsolicited submission of your work is a risky, no-win proposition.

Here are four basic methods of protection:

1. Submit wisely.
Submission through established channels, like agents, entertainment lawyers or literary managers, offers your most basic protection. Regular business relationships are less likely to be put in jeopardy by a rogue attempt to circumnavigate the author's interests.

2. Maintain a paper trail.
Keep records of all correspondence between you and any potential buyer who has been given access to your work. Never submit your material without a cover letter. Save your rejection letters. Take notes of meetings or telephone conversations, being careful to chart date, time, person spoken to and subject matter (these can serve double duty when claiming business expenses on your tax return).

67

3. Copyright your written work.
This is your simplest and best protection. Article 1, Section 8, of the U.S. Constitution gives Congress the power to secure "for limited times" to authors "the exclusive Right to their respective Writings."

What is copyrightable?
Under current law, every "original work of authorship" expressed in a tangible medium is copyrighted at the moment of creation. Mere ideas, concepts, names, titles, facts, etc., are not copyrightable, per se, though other forms of protection may apply. Titles, for example, when registered with the Motion Picture Association of America, are protected from use by other members of the MPAA, though only for a set period of time. Also, a title can become so well-publicized that it acquires a "secondary meaning"—public identification with the title is so strong that to allow it to be cloned would likely cause confusion in the public's mind. (One could not, for example, release a movie about underwater predators and call it

Jaws.) True events are not copyrightable but any original expression of those events, as in a news or magazine article, is protectable.

Who owns the copyright?

The creator of the work is the owner of the copyright, unless that work is created "for hire," in which case the employer (the producer or studio) is considered the author of the work, for copyright purposes. A work "for hire" is any treatment, screenplay or other work (including films) created by an employee for an employer or pursuant to a written contract that expressly provides that it is a "work made for hire." In such case, the creator has no ownership rights to the work created.

The bundle of rights encompassed by the copyright are property rights, protectable from unauthorized use, trespass or encroachment—the same as a piece of land. Similarly, they can be sold, bartered, assigned (all rights), transferred (one or more rights), passed on in a will, or even broken up and auctioned off in parts (but only in writing). For example, a writer may sell the adaptive rights to his work, i.e., the right to make a film or television show based on it, while maintaining the right to publish the work or have it performed on the live stage.

How do I register the copyright?

68

Register your copyright by filling out Copyright Application Form PA, a copy of which and instructions for completing can be downloaded from the U.S. Copyright Office's web site at **http://lcweb.loc.gov/copyright.forms.** The current copyright fee is $20 and a copy of your material must be included in the same envelope as the completed form. Your material is copyrighted as of the date of receipt, but allow about three months for confirmation. An original can be obtained by writing to: Copyright Office, Library of Congress, Washington, D.C. 20599. Recorded information is available 24 hours a day by phoning (800) 688-9889 (toll-free), or call (202) 707-3000 on weekdays to speak to someone in the Copyright Office. You may also access the forms and registration hotline at (202) 707-9100.

Under international copyright law enacted March 1, 1989, pursuant to the Berne Convention, registration of your copyright is optional, but it is strongly recommended. It puts the world on notice of your claim to creation, it establishes

While it is not possible here to cover all the specifics involved with copyright protection, you can contact an attorney who specializes in that area of the law (ask for references from your local bar association). Also, the Writers Guild of America, West, Inc., recently published a thorough pamphlet called *Plagiarism & Copyright Infringement*. It can be obtained for a nominal fee by writing the Guild at: 7000 West Third Street, Los Angeles, CA 90048-4329.

proof of authorship as of a certain date and it is a prerequisite to the extended benefits of any infringement suit you later may be forced to file. On a similar note, it is also no longer necessary to preserve your copyright (or risk having it fall into public domain) through the use of a copyright notice. In fact, for screenplays, a copyright notice is rarely seen. But should you wish to put your readers on notice, place either the word "copyright," an abbreviation for same or "©" on the cover page of your work, followed by your name and the year of copyright.

How long is the work protected?
The Copyright Act of 1976, effective January 1, 1978, and just recently revised by the U.S. Congress, extends copyright protection to individuals for life, plus 70 years (now the same term as for British works); and to a company, in the case of a "work made for hire," for a term of 95 years from the date of publication. For works written prior to 1978, a protected term of 75 years from publication applies. ("Publication," as defined, includes films of the work, although works under the current act need not be published to be granted protection.)

4. Register your work with the Writers Guild.
Both the Writers Guild, West (address above; phone: 323-951-4000) and the Writers Guild, East (555 West 57th St., New York, N.Y. 10019; 212-767-7800) operate a registration program that is widely used by all writers, both Guild and non-Guild. This service is also available over the Internet.

69

Guild registration is recognized throughout the industry as an effective means of corroborating a claim of authorship because it establishes a specific date by which you authored the registered work. It does this by sealing received material (no bindings, covers or brads) in an envelope, recording the date and time and giving you a numbered receipt. The Guild subsequently can be called upon to produce the material in its signed, dated and sealed envelope when necessary.

Guild registration accepts a wide range of material, including scripts, treatments, synopses and outlines for radio, television or film and even for stage plays, novels, short stories, poems and lyrics. However, Guild registration is valid for only a five-year period (renewable), after which it is authorized to destroy the material without notice.

For recorded information on how to register your work, call the Writers Guild, West hotline at (323) 782-4500, or see the Guild's informational pamphlet included at the end of this chapter. Keep in mind that **Guild registration is not a substitute for registration with the U.S. Copyright Office.**

A recent alternative to both Guild and copyright registration is The National Creative Registry. It is priced similarly to the Guild registration but provides a longer registry and certain unique services. You may write to them for information at: 1106 Second Street, Encinitas, CA 92024 or phone them at (619) 942-2660.

Finally, there persists in writers' folklore a practice called a "poor man's copyright," in which the writer sends his material by registered mail to himself or to a few close friends. If push comes to shove, he can produce his script in a sealed, postmarked envelope, thus establishing the date of authorship. This costs almost the same as a copyright or Guild registration and you must be responsible for keeping your envelope safe and preserving its seal, etc. It is not a recommended practice.

CHECKLIST FOR PROTECTING YOUR WORK:

- **Submit wisely**
- **Maintain a paper trail**
- **Copyright**
- **Register with the Guild**

WGA
INTELLECTUAL PROPERTY
REGISTRY

The WGA's Intellectual Property Registry receives over 30,000 pieces of literary material annually and is available to members and non-members. Writers are invited to submit their material to be archived by the Writers Guild to protect their work. For more information on this service, contact the Registry at (323) 782-4540.

PURPOSE AND COVERAGE

The WGA Intellectual Property Registry is available to assist all writers in establishing completion dates for particular pieces of their literary property written for the fields of radio, theatrical and television motion pictures, video cassettes/discs and interactive media.

Registration provides a dated record of the writer's claim to authorship of a particular literary material. If necessary a Registry employee may produce the material as evidence if legal or official guild action is initiated.

The Registry does not make comparisons of registration deposits, nor does it give legal opinions, advice or confer any statutory protections.

71

Registration with the Guild does not protect titles.

PROCEDURE FOR DEPOSIT

Materials may be submitted for registration in person or by mail. The Registry must receive:

1) One (1) unbound, loose-leaf copy of material on standard, 8 1/2" x 11" paper.
2) Cover sheet with title of material and all writers' full legal names.
3) Social security number (or equivalent), return address and telephone number of one writer (the registrant).
4) Registration fee:
   WGAw and WGAE members $10.00
   Non-members $20.00

Payment accepted in cash, check, money order or Visa/MC (expiration date required).

When the material is received, it is sealed in an envelope and the date and time are recorded. A numbered receipt is returned serving as the official documentation of registration and should be kept in a safe place.

Notice of registration shall consist of the following wording: REGISTERED WGAw No.____ and be applied upon the title page.

MEMBER STAMP

At the time of registration, WGAw members may request that a maximum of two (2) copies of the material being registered be stamped with the legend "MEMBER WGAw." The stamp indicates only that one or more of the writers listed as an author on the title page was a WGAw member at the time the material was registered with the title page bearing the stamp. There is no additional fee for use of the stamp.

REGISTRABLE MATERIAL

We only accept written materials.

Registrable material includes scripts, treatments, synopses, outlines and written ideas specifically intended for radio, television and theatrical motion pictures, video cassettes/discs, and interactive media.

The WGA Intellectual Property Registry also accepts stageplays, novels and other books, short stories, poems, commercials, lyrics and drawings.

DURATION AND EXPIRATION

Registration is valid for a term of five (5) years and may be renewed for an additional five (5) years at the current registration rate. Renewals will be accepted up to three months prior to the expiration of the original registration. A grace period will be extended allowing renewals as late as three months following the expiration of the original registration.

At the time of registration, or renewal, you authorize the Registry to destroy the material without further notice to you on the expiration of the first term of registration or any renewal period.

72

REQUESTS FOR REGISTRATION INFORMATION

It is imperative that we DO NOT confirm any registration information over the phone.

Only the writers listed on the registration receipt may request confirmation of the registration, the registration number, date of deposit, or any other information.

The Registry will honor such written requests from writers regarding the registration of their own work(s) only if accompanied by photo identification. All verification or confirmation requests from a writer should contain as much specific information as possible, such as registration number, title of material, effective date, and social security number of writer, and may be submitted by facsimile, mail or in person. The fax number for the Registry is (323) 782-4803.

REQUESTS FOR COPIES OF DEPOSITED MATERIAL

Because the deposited material cannot be returned to the writer without defeating the purpose of registration, registered material may not be withdrawn. It is therefore important to always retain a separate copy of the material being registered.

If a writer finds it necessary to obtain a copy of deposited material, duplicates may be purchased for the price of registration upon written request by one or more of the listed authors, identified by photo identification. In the event an author is deceased, proof of death and consent of the representative of the heirs and/or estate must be presented in order to obtain a copy of the material.

Requests for duplication of deposited material must be submitted by 5:00 PM Thursday of any week. Duplicates will be available Tuesday of the following week.

In no event, except under these provisions, shall any deposited material, copies of deposited material, or information regarding deposited material be provided unless an official guild action, court order, or other legal process has been served.

FREQUENTLY ASKED QUESTIONS
Does Guild registration take the place of copyright registration?
No. Any questions regarding copyright should be directed to the U.S. Copyright Office in Washington D.C. at 1-800-688-9889 or to an attorney specializing in that area of law. Copyright application forms are available to walk-in customers only.

Does registration with the Writers Guild protect titles?
No.

Does registration help a writer become a member?
No. Questions concerning the rules for admission to membership in the guild should be referred to the WGAw Membership department at (323) 782-4532.

73

Does registration help in determining writing credits?
Generally, no. If there is a dispute as to authorship or sequencing of material by date, then registration may be relevant.

Questions concerning the WGA credit determination procedures should be directed to the Credits department at (323) 782-4528.

REGISTRATION HOURS
Monday through Friday, 9:30 AM to 5:30 PM

LOCATION AND MAILING ADDRESS
WGAw Registration
7000 West Third Street
Los Angeles, CA 90048

TELEPHONE NUMBERS
(323) 782-4540	Information
(323) 782-4803	Fax

WEBSITE
www.wga.org

Chapter 7
REPRESENTATION: AGENTS, LAWYERS, MANAGERS AND GUILDS

You've finished the final polish of your script, satisfied there is nothing more that you can do to improve it. There is only one thing left to do, get it in the hands of someone who will actually pay you money for it.

How do you find that person and how do you get him to read your work? Accept this simple caveat and save yourself wasted postage and time waiting for a phone call or letter that will never come: **Most production companies have a firm policy against accepting any material unless it is submitted through an established agency or some other contact with whom they already enjoy a business relationship.**

If you don't have direct contacts you must get in touch with someone who does—someone who can not only get exposure for your script, but for you. This leads to writing assignments, the true lifeline of the free-lance writer.

AGENTS—THE WRITER'S SALES FORCE
Perhaps the single most important concept to grasp in the film business is this—**it's a business of relationships.** Simply put, agents know more movie producers and studio executives than you do. They spend their days cultivating relationships with buyers. And the buyers love agents because agents save them time and money. Agents may not have infallible taste, but they are counted upon to distinguish a professionally formatted and potentially viable screenplay from one that, quite frankly, is just not up to marketable standards. This saves potential buyers piles of money on "coverage" (having your work read, summarized and critiqued). Later, the agent can also act as a buffer zone between producers and clients—a service that becomes more and more indispensable to both as a cherished work winds its way down the rocky path of development.

Agents also confer instant credibility to the new writer: if you have one, **you belong.** (It's a club, after all, and your agent is a member.) In addition, regardless of the individual egos that comprise it, **film is a collaborative art and the business of screenwriting is ultimately about the writer developing into someone with whom others in the business will want to work.** When bonds form, assignments can follow and careers can become established.

Most spec scripts by unknown writers do not sell and agents know this. Your original spec script is your professional calling card, a means of getting you in the door to take the meetings that can lead to assignments.

Agents are also the first line of defense in protecting studios and producers from "nuisance" lawsuits. Find a successful film and you'll find someone who claims, sometimes justifiably, that he sent or phoned in the idea first. *Air Force One,* the nation's top summer box office draw for 1997, was immediately hit with a lawsuit claiming that the original idea was hijacked by the producers from a former helicopter mechanic and his sister. Without commenting on the merits of the case, the film's executive producer stated that "Unfortunately, in our business, this has become an undesirable sign of success."

Most screenplays are written for hire, but it is also true that most writing assignments are doled out to writers with a track record of delivering movies. Agents, then, accept new writers based on **long-term potential.**

The challenge for the agent is getting the new writer exposed in the marketplace. For that to happen, the agent needs a way around the buyer's reluctance to consider new talent. If he can just tantalize the buyer into *reading* the script—even if it is not what the buyer is seeking at the moment—the hope is that the buyer will become engaged by the writing and ask to meet the writer (to see "what

Particularly in television, where the pitch is the lifeblood of series and MOWs (movies of the week), the entree of an agent may be critical in setting up those all important face-to-face meetings with producers and network executives.

else" he's got or to determine if the writer may be right for another project slated for development).

Think of screenwriting as a business with two assets—your inventory of scripts and yourself. An agent is your sales force for both. Writers and their agents should respect and value each other's contribution—that would be the winning attitude.

HOW TO GET AN AGENT

Sometimes it seems as if you need an agent to get an agent. When I asked my own agent to speak to students in my screenwriting class, this was his reply:

"I'd be happy to speak at your class, but on one condition: tell them not to phone me, not to come over to my office, not to send me scripts. Let them do the *work*, find a *prominent* person in the film business, a successful producer, director or writer or a super-successful actor, have *them* read it first and personally recommend it to me and then, and only then, will I read it. There is no shortage of writers or work to represent. It's a highly competitive business and only those who stand out in the eyes of a professional whose opinion I respect are—percentage-wise—worth the investment of time needed to read new writers or evaluate their work."

Not all agents are so blunt (I got lucky), but most conduct business in the same way: through referrals. You, on the other hand, have contacted every person you ever went to school with and simply cannot connect yourself to anyone in a position to personally recommend you and your work. Do not despair; you can get an agent. You'll just have to work at it.

The first thing to be done is to check the current list of Writers Guild signatory agents, the latest version of which is included in the Appendix. (Updated copies may be obtained for $2.50 and a self-addressed, stamped envelope sent to the WGA, west, Inc. or accessed directly on the WGA website: http://www.wga.org). Besides the annual *Writer's Market*, other good sources are *The Hollywood Agents and Managers Directory*, c/o Hollywood Creative Directory 3000 W. Olympic Blvd., Suite 2525, Santa Monica, CA 90404; telephone: 310-315-4815; out-of-state 800-815-0503; fax 310-315-4816; and the annual *Film Producers, Studios, Agents and Casting Directors Guide*, which includes an index of agents and managers, available from Lone Eagle Publishing, 2337 Roscomare Road, Suite Nine, Los Angeles, CA 90077; telephone 310-471-8066 or 800-345-6257; fax 310-471-4969, www.loneeagle.com.

Any of the above sources may list agents outside of Hollywood, but most of these resources are geared to agents in the greater Los Angeles area. The big advantage to Los Angeles or New York representation is **access**. You want an agent who doesn't have to make long-distance calls to keep up his contacts.

If you live far from Los Angeles or the New York metropolitan area, consult your city directory listing for local literary agencies. Contact them, then follow through—determine whether they are Writers Guild signatory agencies and obtain a client list. While many out-of-Hollywood

In Los Angeles, you'll find a high concentration of agents in "Agent's Alley," that small cluster of streets near Sunset Boulevard and Doheny Drive, or along Wilshire, Beverly or Santa Monica Boulevards.

agencies do not offer the writer easy access to studio heads and other powerful clients, there are advantages to a new writer being represented by less mainstream agencies—more personal attention and career advice at a time when you need it most.

Some agencies accept unsolicited submissions; most will flat out hold themselves "closed to new writers." It is true that few agents place a premium on finding or grooming writers. Most agents want writers who will work and generate fees. Yet individual agents at any agency will insist they are always open to good material (translation: a high-concept, star-castable, bidding-war spec script) and are always looking for good writers. So, how do you reach individual agents and interest them in making an exception to "policy" and considering your work?

Blanketing Hollywood with your script is both prohibitively expensive and terribly risky. You'll want an invitation. One way to get an invitation is to promote yourself in a charming, persistent (not annoying) way to the gatekeepers (secretaries, receptionists, assistants) whose mission is to keep solicitors (you) away from the door. Don't appear desperate, but do ask for help in guiding you through the Hollywood maze.

. . . .

78

A friend from the Midwest sent a number of spec scripts through the Hollywood maze and received no response. He left phone messages; no reply. But, he was relentless. One day, when the entire writing staff of a hit TV series was at lunch, he managed to engage the receptionist in conversation. She was from a town near his and a bond was struck. She told him that his script was likely lost in a pile with other unsolicited submissions, but if he would send another, *she* would read it. The receptionist read his script on her lunch break, liked it, and kept putting it on writers' desks until somebody read it. Three months later, he got a call from the executive producer of the show telling him that if he planned on being in LA in the near future, he was invited in to pitch ideas for future episodes. Taking the next flight out, he made an appointment and pitched a bucketful of ideas, all of which were rejected. All the same, the producers liked his attitude and enthusiasm and gave him an assignment to write a show already in active development. Even though they never used *that* episode, they liked *him* and his style enough to offer him a staff position!

. . . .

And there are other options. Find the name of a writer who has written a film similar to yours. Or, if you want an agency that has had recent success with a new writer, check the credits of recent independent films for the name of the writer. The Writers Guild's Agency Department can tell you who represents that writer. Then, contact the agent as a "die-hard" fan; tell him you have a script similar to the one he so brilliantly shepherded toward production and ask if he has interest in representing it. Or, using this method in reverse, try to locate clients the agency represents. This has the added benefit of determining if the agent works mostly in features or television and whether his client list indicates the agency is a formidable one, likely to be well-connected with buyers.

You can also connect with a writer whose work you admire by getting a contact number (other than the agency) from the WGA's Membership Department. Then call the writer and have a chat— it's not as hard as you might imagine. (Most writers don't need to protect their privacy from hoards of crazed fans.) Perhaps you can win the writer over and get him to look at your script. If he is impressed, a personal recommendation to his agent or someone else in the industry could result.

Be as enterprising as your imagination and dedication allow. But if all fails and you despair of ever getting your screenplay through the agency maze, cheer up. There is a way. It may be the weapon of last choice in the writer's arsenal, but it is still remarkably effective.

THE QUERY LETTER

If you don't have a personal contact to an agent already, the query letter is a step toward acquiring one. This is a *brief* but provocative letter introducing yourself as a writer seeking representation. Some regard it as a waste of time and postage, believing your letter doesn't stand a chance of being picked out of a pile of junk mail. First-hand experience has convinced me that the method does indeed work.

Keep your query letter to one page and don't hard sell. It should, naturally, be in proper business letter format and free of typos or grammatical errors. Use only quality paper and the clean, crisp print delivered by a laser printer. Always address your letter to a principal (not a production company) or a specific agent (not an agency)—a phone call should yield you a name.

As a member of the New Members Committee of the Writers Guild, I heard frequent accounts of query letters used to great success. One writer, now scripting for both Ron Howard and Castle Rock, told of how he got his start in the business by sending out over 400 form letters to agents. He received 40 or so requests for scripts, and out of that garnered four solid agency offers. His first screenplay sold within six days of his accepting representation.

79

This one page letter will be the only hint as to the quality of your writing. It should be as clear, concise, compelling, original and intriguing as the premise of your script. It is a matter of personal judgement in what detail you describe your plot, but a succinct summary is favored. As with your screenplay, cut to the heart of your premise, preferably in a single, irresistible paragraph that stamps your work as a sure-fire commercial hit and you as a writer others will want to work with.

Above all, **be creative.** Be quietly persistent. Be a good salesperson, able to get your foot in the door before it is slammed in your face. If you can capture the attention of an overworked assistant, your letter will be placed on the executive's desk—and he will read it.

. . . .

Following is an example of a query letter that caught my attention.

Ronald Suppa Productions, Inc.
Attn: Mr. Ronald Suppa

Dear Mr. Suppa:

I understand you are a former South Philadelphia resident. I grew up in Northeast Philly, but I lived on South Street for five years before coming to California. I spent nine years as a stockbroker, but found what I really enjoy is writing. I recently finished my fifth screenplay and am working on my sixth.

I believe I have a screenplay that may interest you. I'm sure you remember Frank Rizzo; he's hard to forget. I've even read that Sylvester Stallone has said that he'd like to play Rizzo. Personally, I think that Danny Aiello fits him perfectly. My story is about boxers and politicians who get mixed up together weeks before the Philadelphia mayoral election. The character up for re-election is based loosely on Rizzo, known in the story as Ray Rombella. Ray has no reason to take his competition seriously until an old boxer comes forth with information that could bring him down. Ray collides with his past in a dramatic conclusion that involves murder, prize-fight fixing, the old-boy network. . . and a child caught in the middle.

Mr. Suppa, I feel good about this story. It's a world I know very well, having both boxed and been involved in political campaigns, the last being the election Frank most likely would have won had he not died just before the primary.

Please check at the bottom if you would like me to send a copy of my screenplay, along with a release. An SASE is enclosed. Thanks for your time and consideration.

Clearly the writer did his homework. Maybe he read an article that mentioned my connection with Stallone; perhaps he looked up my credits in a Hollywood resource book. The fact is, he made the letter personal.

He then outlined, in general terms, a story that interested my company in the past. He also tied in his work experience, letting me know that his script would offer an insider's view of his subject. This also made the point that he wasn't a novice writer, having taken time from a "real job" to write six screenplays. While this kind of boasting can backfire (if he's been at it awhile, why is there no agent?), I knew, for example, that even Oliver Stone had written a dozen screenplays before garnering his first agent. For me, at least, the point was moot. The general tone of the letter was friendly and respectful—so few letters meet even these rudimentary rules of etiquette.

Finally, the writer made it easy for me. His willingness to supply his own release form marked him as a team player, aware of the exigencies of the industry. And that SASE is a must if you expect a reply to your query letter; some writers enclose a postcard (it calls for less postage and the agent doesn't have to lick the envelope).

I dropped the reply card in the mail. He sent the script the day after receiving my response. It was a workmanlike, professional effort, but we passed. I called the writer and explained our reasons for passing. He didn't get defensive or argumentative; he listened and asked questions to understand exactly what we were looking for. He also told me about another project which he was pursuing. His letter and serious attitude had put him into the game.

81

. . . .

What does every agent and producer look for? Relationships with working writers who have something to sell—a concept so fresh it snaps, crackles and pops off the page. Your query letter may set forth just such a concept—but, do not expect a reply to your letter. A few may respond, most will not. This is the way things are; don't get angry or take it personally. Wait a reasonable period of time—two to three weeks—and follow up your letter with a polite phone call, FAX or e-mail (a strange fact of modern life; people who screen every phone call and letter will read their faxes and e-mail).

If you do phone and successfully get anyone, even a janitor, to stay on the line with you, be nice. Treat everyone as if he were the head of the studio. And, do be sure to thank anyone who does anything to get you closer to your career goals, not only because it's the decent thing to do, but also because the one taking messages and answering the phone today may well *be* the head of production to-morrow (and production heads have notoriously long memories).

Should an agent respond positively to your letter or call, send a copy of your script (never send an original) or your two best samples, if you have more than one. But **do not send a copy of your screenplay until it is asked for.** (And don't bother enclosing a self-addressed stamped envelope; you probably won't get your script back anyway. Just chalk up your copying and postage costs to the price of doing business.) You should also anticipate that an agent or producer may ask for a release form before agreeing to read your work.

THE RELEASE FORM

The release form secures your agreement not to sue if a potential buyer happens to later make a film bearing a resemblance to your submitted script, treatment or pitch. Most producers require them as standard business practice, and most agencies now request them from new (and sometimes not-so-new) writers before considering work for representation.

This practice is not meant to condone or legalize the theft of ideas (although some release forms are so broadly worded as to appear to permit just that, and with near impunity). Rather it is a response to the increasing risk and expense of lawsuits resulting from (often spurious) claims of similarity. Generally, the release form is not used to a writer's detriment but, if you refuse to sign it, your work probably won't be considered.

82

. . . .

"It took a little faith." That's how Microsoft founder Bill Gates viewed his decision to sign the disclosure and release forms presented to him by IBM on that fateful day when the two companies agreed to join forces in the most successful partnership in the history of entrepreneurial enterprise.

Earlier that day, IBM had presented that same set of documents to a competitor of Gates, who called in an army of lawyers and ultimately refused to sign. Today, he's a footnote in computer history while Bill Gates is the richest man in the United States.

. . . .

If you are asked to sign a release form, it is best to do so. You may even wish to supply one on your own volition. In either case, you will be expressing your desire to make it less onerous for those with legal vulnerability to read your material and establish a business relationship with you. For your use, a typical release form follows.

Literary Material Release Form

To: [company]
Re: [title of material submitted hereunder]

Gentlemen:

I am today submitting to you certain literary material, the present title of which is indicated above (hereinafter "the material)," upon the following express understanding and conditions:

1. I agree that I am voluntarily disclosing such material to you at my request. I understand that you shall have no obligation to me in any respect whatsoever with regard to such material unless and until each of us has executed a written agreement which, by its terms and provisions, shall be the only contract between us.

2. I agree that any discussions we may have with respect to such material shall not constitute any agreement, express or implied, as to the purchase and use of any such material which I may disclose to you either orally or in writing.

3. If the material submitted hereunder is not new or novel, or was not originated by me, or if other persons including your employees have heretofore submitted or hereafter submit similar or identical material which you have the right to use, then I agree that you shall not be liable to me for your use of such material, and you shall not be obligated in any respect whatsoever to compensate me for such use by you.

4. I further agree that if you hereafter produce or distribute a motion picture and/or television program or programs based upon the same general theme, idea or situation and/or having the same setting or background and/or taking place in the same geographical area or period of history as the material, then, unless you have substantially copied the expression and development of such idea, theme or situation, including the characters and storyline thereof, as herewith or hereafter submitted to you by me in writing, you shall have no obligation or liability to me of any kind or character by reason of the production or distribution of such motion picture and/or program(s), nor shall you be obligated to compensate me in connection therewith.

I acknowledge that but for my agreement to the above terms and conditions, you would not accede to my request to receive and consider the material which I am submitting to you herewith.

Very truly yours,
[Signature of writer, date, address and phone]

THE AGENCY AGREEMENT

What does an agent look for in a client? First, he needs something to sell: a script that will attract buyers and scream forth your talent and career potential. Without an *available* script (one that is not previously sold), most producers will decline to meet new writers or read their work. It is not the fault of the agent, then, if pitch meetings and assignments never materialize.

An agent also wants a client who will listen, take advice and appreciate that the agency has other clients as well. Of course, should the agent want to represent you, make sure the feeling is mutual. Embarking on an agent-client relationship is like entering into a marriage, so attempt to know your agent as well as possible (either by phone or in person) before you sign.

Agents procure employment and negotiate deals. In California, the state labor and employment code requires all agents to get a license, post a bond and record their agreements with their clients. An agent receives a 10 percent commission on what he sells, whether it is literary material or the writer's services. In no instance should you pay him to read your work, to attempt to sell your work or to represent you. In some cases, a special commission, known as a *packaging fee,* is taken by an agency in lieu of the agent's regular commission. This occurs when certain agencies "package" the major components (such as star, director, writer and producer) of a theatrical film, television movie or series and then sell the package to the studio or other production entity (which pays the packaging fee).

You want an agent who is respected and connected, one who is a strong negotiator and who truly believes in your work. He should take an active interest in promoting you and your writing and be sincerely supportive of your career. He should have integrity, be trustworthy and, when necessary, be capable of delivering a healthy dose of candor.

Should the agency press you to sign an agreement with them, by all means do so (since this formality is more to the agency's advantage than yours, you should not bring it up first). Not every agency will ask. Many agents represent a few clients without a contract (agents call these "pocket clients") so as not to "pad" their lists with non-producing clients and run the risk of making their more valuable clients think they are getting short shrift and switch agencies. Of course, this is a double-edged sword because you are then free to sell your work on your own and not commission the agency on your sale, or you may even work with two agencies at the same time (though should you attempt this, you run an unhealthy risk of "never working in this town again").

If you do decide to sign, resist the temptation to haggle over the agreement. Agents are wary of problem clients and you are protected from a fiasco by the Guild's contract with the ATA (Association of Talent Agents) which allows you to exit an agent if you have not worked within 90 days. For such reasons, negotiating the agency agreement is considered bad form (akin to asking for a prenuptial agreement in the same breath as you propose marriage). Like a pre-nuptial contract, if the marriage works, you'll forget all about it. If it doesn't, a good lawyer can always find a way around it. Which leads to . . .

ENTERTAINMENT LAWYERS: HOLLYWOOD'S BEST-KEPT SECRET

Your screenwriting career does not rest solely on your ability to attract an agent. A good script will always find a home and *after* it does, agents will come knocking. But writers have another powerful ally in this murky world of deals and dealmakers—the entertainment lawyer.

Whether you sell a script or are hired to write one, there will be deal points to negotiate and contracts to sign. An entertainment lawyer can anticipate problems and cover the writer with protective language. Do you need to obtain the rights to a true story, novel, play, biography, magazine article or other source material you wish to adapt for the screen? An entertainment lawyer can draw up agreements that will satisfy both the law and the sometimes more stringent requirements of networks and studios. Even major players in Hollywood—the directors, stars and studio heads you read about over your morning bowl of Wheaties—have agents who may put the deal together, but each also has an entertainment attorney who will close the deal.

Moreover, in an industry where the name of the game is access, I know agents, producers and executives who will put a script sent to them by a reputable film lawyer first on their list of things to read. And film lawyers always get their calls returned, promptly.

Another often overlooked advantage to having an entertainment attorney is having another friendly voice on your side (albeit a paid one). As writer Roger Simon once said, "In a town of liars, you need at least two or three people who will tell you the truth." In the short chain of those on your side, your lawyer should be one you can count on to honestly appraise the wisdom of your career choices.

In addition, an entertainment attorney, like an agent, can put a screenwriter in touch with other clients to create valuable movie packages. A package is the pooling of a group of talents whom a studio might deem desirable to work with, using their combined strength to get a project developed or produced. A lot more attention will be paid

85

to your script if Dustin Hoffman or Sydney Pollack is attached. In providing this service alone, a good entertainment lawyer may be the most valuable gun in Hollywood's arsenal.

. . . .

Attorneys sometimes replace agents altogether. A short while ago, film-maker James Cameron (*Titanic*) gave notice to his long-time agency that henceforth he would be represented solely by his attorneys. The move sent shock-waves through the agency community. If Cameron could walk— and take all of those lucrative commissions with him—what would stop other players from following suit?

Perhaps, it is fear. In a series of now-infamous letters to former superagent Michael Ovitz, writer Joe Eszterhas spelled out his fear of endangering the career he had worked so hard to build after deciding to leave Ovitz for other representation. Eszterhas did leave and survived quite well. But, to be sure, many writers can't switch agencies so easily, as Eszterhas did, or can't pick up a phone and get the head of a major studio to jump to attention, as Cameron can.

. . . .

To be clear, however, entertainment lawyers *won't* get you a deal or get you a job. That's what agents are for—agents are licensed by the state to sell client's work; lawyer's are not (at least not in California). To reach the buyers for your work, you must have an agent or be able to make and exploit your own contacts and do all the legwork yourself. Then, a good film lawyer can review and negotiate a deal for your work as well as (or better than) most agents and they can also help protect you from potentially ruinous lawsuits, such as libel or invasion of privacy.

If you're offered a feature deal, you may need an entertainment lawyer in addition to your agent. The agent will lay out the broad strokes of a deal, most often in a short letter known as a "deal memo." But, agents rarely negotiate "usual and customary" provisions, such as sequel and remake rights, spinoffs, ancillary rights, residual schedules, reversions, warranties and indemnities, nor do they negotiate the fine points of *force majeure, droit morale* and favored nations. And, of course, you'll need an attorney to sort out the mystifying definition of "net profits" (known to run as long as 50 pages in some studio contracts).

As you might expect, entertainment lawyers are not cheap. Most bill anywhere from $250 to $600 per hour. However,

What if your writing partner dies during development—or as a result of it, as John Gregory Dunne almost did? (You can read about this and other travails of the screenwriting life in Dunne's great book, *Monster* [Random House, New York, 1997].) Do you still have a deal? Your lawyer will make sure you do.

some will make a percentage agreement with you; five percent of your deal is the going rate (half what an agent would charge). Should the law firm represent more than one element in a given production (the writer, producer, director or star), it may also earn a package fee which may include a profit share. But again, these fees are similar to and often less than what an agent charges.

Moreover, if you *can* get an appointment with an entertainment lawyer, the initial consultation and the career advice that goes with it is usually free. Many attorneys pride themselves on their ability to develop a client base by representing new talent *pro bono* (for free). Of course, they will eventually exact payment but, usually, this will be a sum that bears a reasonable relation to funds the writer receives from the option or sale of a script (similar to a contingency fee paid to personal injury lawyers).

But, in your shopping for representation, be sure you are seeking the counsel of an *entertainment attorney*. If you know a lawyer who handles divorces and writes wills or is the person to see if you get into an auto accident—he is not an entertainment lawyer. And, you want a lawyer who handles more than contracts. A film lawyer is connected to the film business 24 hours a day, seven days a week. He knows the current salary quotes for a hot actor or director, the sticky points that will break a promising deal, even which two people must never be brought together in the same room, much less the same film. So highly specialized is this area that a half-dozen or so boutique law firms can lay claim to representing 90 percent of the name talent in Hollywood. This can result in one firm or even one lawyer representing both sides in a contract. Recently, this cozy arrangement has been subjected to scrutiny by the courts and has spawned a flurry of "conflict of interest" lawsuits. While it may be true that business has always been done this way, should you find yourself in such a position, separate counsel is recommended.

So how do you obtain such high-powered representation? The best and the brightest are as busy and elusive as top agents. As standard business practice, entertainment lawyers are usually put in touch with new clients through referrals. A phone call to any reasonably established person will often yield you a name and a number. If you possess no such contacts, call the local bar association and request a list of lawyers practicing in entertainment or contract law. Better still, any of the creative guilds (such as, SAG, DGA, WGA, PGA) have attorneys on staff who would be happy to give you a list of attorneys with whom they deal on a frequent basis.

LITERARY MANAGEMENT

What if you have neither an agent nor an entertainment lawyer? Is there still someone out there who knows the ropes and has your best interests, as a writer, at heart?

First, a parable. She was late-fifties, well spoken, a smart dresser, fit, with a demeanor that radiated success. An embossed card presented her as a "Literary Manager." Not an agent, mind you, not a lawyer, not a publicist, but yet another percentage drain on a writer's sweat-income. Her name was reminiscent of wind, or gale or gusts, though my writing partner remembers her as "Air," an homage to her substance (as in empty, as in full of hot . . .)

"Air" contacted us after hearing a development executive glowingly endorse our work. Before I could pocket her business card, she won us over by pronouncing that our admittedly hard-sell political screenplay was a "slam dunk." It was "brilliant, commercial, but also literary!"—all after perusing only a short synopsis we had dutifully carried to our first meeting at the Beverly Hills café of her choice. She made four calls on her cell phone and took two more before flagging down the waiter for a second espresso—she checked her urgent messages, she rescheduled important meetings, she brokered clients. She was such a busy lady, she zoomed out of there, leaving us with the check.

Later that day, she turned up the heat. Her first four faxes asked, in order, for our script via messenger, in-

formed us her "very trusted assistant" was reading our work, suggested no less than ten different pitch meetings she would "immediately" set up, and pleaded with us to allow her to fire our agent for "not properly handling" us or our material. Four hours later, at 2 a.m., a frost set in. A final fax demanded that we contact her first thing in the morning. She now had "serious doubts" about the viability of our work in its present form and felt it needed "major changes" before she could consider representing us further.

The next day, when we contacted her, she dodged specific questions about plot and character and admitted that her concerns were those of her assistant (whom we later learned was a 22-year-old unpaid volunteer who had been in her employ three weeks). Oh, and one last thing: she would be faxing over a document for us to sign which gave her the right to attach herself as a "producer" to any film based on our work, "in lieu of my commission, of course."

Exhausted yet intrigued, we wondered: What could a literary manager do for us and did we really want one? Also, what qualified her to be one? Or, as Sundance asked Butch: "Who are those guys?"

While talent management is not a novel concept, what was once hands-on career guidance for highly-successful actors is now seen as a viable support base for, and income source from, writers as well. The financial carrot is there: an agent is limited by law to 10 percent of a client's gross income and cannot produce or otherwise involve himself directly in a client's film; managers have free reign to take 15 percent or 25 percent or even 50 percent if the client so agrees, and can negotiate freely for credits or employment on a client's film.

And, anyone can declare themselves to be a literary manager—no training, no tests, no experience required. For qualifications, entertainment industry experience and contacts will do. In California, agents are licensed and bonded to procure employment and negotiate deals, while the services of a personal manager (neither regulated nor franchised) are strictly limited to advise and counsel. Many managers, however, cross the line, commonly working (with or without agents) to solicit jobs for their clients. Conversely, former agents seem to take to the management business like a fish to water.

Managers, like agents, are best found via personal recommendations. Or try contacting one listed in *The Hollywood Agents and Managers Directory,* (Hollywood Creative Directory 3000 W. Olympic Blvd., Suite 2525, Santa Monica, CA 90404; telephone: 310-315-4815; out-of-state 800-815-0503; fax 310-315-4816) or the annual *Film Producers, Studios, Agents and Casting Directors Guide* (Lone Eagle Publishing, 2337 Roscomare Road, Suite Nine, Los Angeles, CA 90077; telephone 310-471-8066 or 800-345-6257; fax 310-471-4969).

When a key agent at United Talent Agency left the agency to form a management company, many of his writing clients went with him. More recently, former superagent Michael Ovitz announced the formation of his management company, Artists Management Group; his former client, Robin Williams, promptly exited Creative Artists Agency (with his then agent) to join him. Such developments have left agents wondering out loud whether managers are acting as *de facto* agents. (In California, the argument has reached Sacramento, where legislation is being introduced that would oblige managers to labor under substantially the same rules as agents.)

89

"Why do writers need a literary manager?"
It seems the agency business has over-extended itself. With many new markets to cover and a heavy concentration on packaging clients as a means of circumventing the straight 10 percent commission, agencies are left with little time for grooming new writers or nurturing an existing client's career. The result is a black hole into which an army of untended writers have fallen. And where such a vacuum exists, someone will fill it.

Simply put, writers want work. And *despite the legal constraint in California against managers seeking or obtaining work for their clients,* the *implication* of the management relationship is that the manager will build or enhance the writer's earning capacity.

In practice, a manager can gain employment for his clients and still remain within the law. For example, he can help obtain agency representation or switch the writer to an agent who will more aggressively market the writer and his work. He can prod the agent to action with calls a writer may be loathe to make himself. He can "help" the agent arrange meetings with producers, production company executives and others in order to more widely expose the writer and his work to the film community.

Managers can also help build the rest of the writer's support team, such as publicist, entertainment attorney, business manager or industry-savvy accountant. He may even help a blocked writer find a writing partner to get the creative juices flowing again.

Creatively, he can help identify the current needs of the marketplace and serve as a critical reader of the writer's work before it goes out to potential agents or buyers or he can act as a test audience for a writer's pitch.

> The legal limits on the manager's role sometimes makes for curious justice. As a young lawyer, I represented a Country & Western singer who was suing her manager of ten years after a personal falling out. Her complaint, ironically enough, was that the manager had solicited bookings for her during a rough period when her agents had let her career simmer on the back burner. Though the manager's efforts were, at that time, well-intentioned and encouraged, the judge ordered all of his hard-earned commissions forfeited.

And, managers can make discreet inquiries and receive valuable feedback on what worked or didn't work at those pitch meetings. Perhaps most important for writers who feel isolated at their computers, the manager can serve as a sounding board for the writer's concerns about the day to day activities of the film business and his place in it. A good manager keeps in constant touch with his client, unlike an agent who may speak with his client only upon the delivery of a new script to market.

As if all that was not enough bang for your buck, remember that the manager often toils long and hard and far in advance of any money changing hands. Many managers have few clients and charge as little as 5 percent of the client's gross income (though 10 percent or 15 percent is more the norm) for developing (sometimes engineering from scratch) a client's career.

"So what's the catch?"

The manager-client bond is often the closest of all professional relationships in the entertainment industry and there is much to recommend it. But, any seasoned veteran knows that where money can be made from the exploitation of talent, abuse is possible.

The manager being attached to a client's project—as a producer, for example—is not an uncommon development in the manager-client association. And not, necessarily, an unwelcome one. For the writer, it may mean acquiring an instant producer for a new screenplay as well as a chance to be in business with a trusted ally (hopefully garnering greater respect for his contribution and enjoying an improved status during production). For the manager, having a writer for a client is like getting a free option on good screen material as well as providing a means to profit from the alliance in a way prohibited to agents (who are barred by law from involvement in the production of their client's work).

But, this kind of close relationship can also lead to conflict of interest and fiduciary duty concerns which the writer must vigilantly monitor; i.e. is the manager working primarily for you or for himself? What if a studio wants to bid $1,000,000 for your screenplay, but views you manager-cum-producer as excess baggage—can he hold up *your* deal with demands of his own? Horror stories have been known to happen, especially if a management contract expressly gives permission for your manager to act as the producer of your projects.

"Will I be asked to sign a contract?"

The core of any management relationship is built on trust. Ideally when the arrangement is no longer working, the parties should be able to shake hands and go their separate ways. But ours is not an ideal world; a writer will most likely have to sign a management contract.

Experience dictates that it's better if the terms of the contract are as specific as possible. Unlike an agency contract, which allows the writer to quit the agency if no work is obtained within a 90 day period, a typical management pact is harder to exit gracefully. A writer can find himself contractually bound to a failing relationship or to a vague notion of what services are expected on his behalf.

Forewarned is forearmed; let the following caveats serve as a guideline for your agreement:

1. Be certain that the contract clearly spells out the duties of the manager and the responsibilities of the writer over the term of the contract. These duties can be so specific as to set forth the "meet and greet" contacts the manager will arrange, the number of times a week the manager will contact the writer, and the circumstances under which both parties can be released from the contract.

2. Presumably, you will want a personal manager who is held in high esteem in the industry and it is the personal attention you will receive from this manager that has sparked your interest to begin with. Therefore, you do not want the manager to be free to delegate or assign his duties to third parties without your approval. Similarly,

91

while you may want help in finding an agent or lawyer, you do not want to grant the manager the right to form these associations *without your prior consent.*

3. Finally, be wary of giving your manager power of attorney over any of your affairs, particularly the incurring of debt, the signing of contracts on your behalf or the right to endorse and cash checks payable to you. Also, be careful about granting the right to act as or be credited or paid as a "producer" of your work on the screen.

Sadly, some writers find themselves employing the attorney the manager may have recommended to find a way out of the management contract that same attorney advised them to sign.

THE WRITERS GUILD

Membership

"We're a guild, not a union," Writers Guild of America, west, former President Brad Radnitz liked to tell new members when asked if the WGA can help them gain employment or lessen the competition. In most unions, when the current membership has passed or is otherwise unavailable for an assignment, a prospective employer may look outside the union for workers. Not so in the three top Hollywood creative "guilds"—the Screen Actors Guild, The Directors Guild and The Writers Guild (the latter hereafter sometimes referred to as the Guild)—all of which are open to new members once they have rendered eligible services for a "signatory company." And all of mainstream Hollywood—the studios, networks and many independent film companies—are "signatory" to the WGA's Minimum Basic Agreement (the "MBA"). As the MBA has evolved, even current WGA, west, president, Daniel Petrie, Jr., concedes that it has become "increasingly difficult to understand and interpret." However, there are the two basic edicts:

1. Only a Guild member may write for a signatory company.
The precept is deceiving. The WGA is not a closed shop. A nonmember who sells a script to a signatory company will be offered guild membership. A writer hired to write for a signatory company will have 31 days after employment begins to request membership. In either case, if you pass it up, you won't be offered membership again. But if only Guild members can work for signatory companies, how do some non-Guild members work for the majors? (George Lucas and Quentin Tarantino, two writers who have openly eschewed Guild affiliation, come to mind.) The MBA is not a perfect system; if a company wants to hire a non-union writer, it can create a new non-signatory company for the purpose of making

just that one picture and then hire anyone it wants who is not in the Guild.

2. A Guild member cannot sell to or work for any producer or company that isn't a Guild signatory.
This rule is strictly enforced and it makes it arduous for smaller, non-signatory companies to find talented writers. It's also good news for new writers still honing their skills—just don't check your common sense at the door: trust your instincts, and make sure you are fairly compensated for your work.

There are two separate and distinct branches of the Guild. The WGA, west—largest in terms of membership—serves writers west of the Mississippi; the WGA, east serves those east of the Mississippi. The two branches usually act as one but, in 1998, a dispute over a crucial contract vote emphasized a potentially larger chasm between the two than had previously been envisioned. This dispute was the subject of ongoing conversations between the governing boards of the two branches; however, both are united in a common belief that the Guild serves the writer and it shall not be sacrificed to partisan bickering.

In general terms, admission to the WGA is invited upon the sale or licensing of previously unpublished and unproduced literary or dramatic material or upon the completion of writing services pursuant to a contract of employment ultimately totaling 24 "units of Credit" (a motion picture screenplay or radio play or teleplay 90 minutes or longer earns 24 credits each); said sale, licensing or employment must be with a company or other entity that is signatory to the applicable WGA Collective Bargaining Agreement. (The complete Guild rules of member eligibility are set forth at the end of this chapter.) Should you earn the right to be invited to join, the initial fee is currently $2,500, plus 1.5 percent of your gross income as a writer and quarterly dues of $25.

> A tip: If you and the company you're working with is not Guild-affiliated, you can still ask that the terms of your pact be subject to the MBA, thus affording you the protection, if not the enforcement power, of the Guild. You can also use the Guild *minimums* as a guideline for negotiating your deal. (Minimum wages for script sales and writing services are established by the MBA and are the most visible result of the sometimes protracted and bitter negotiations between the Guild and the signatory companies.)

93

Benefits
There is much to recommend about membership in the WGA, not the least of which are the opportunities you'll have to hang out with other writers (at least during the strikes). Writing is a lonely

experience and it's nice to know that there is always some other writer up at 3 a.m., happy to join you for a cup of coffee or engage in an Internet chat.

The more obvious purpose of the Guild is to serve its members. The agreement negotiated with the signatory companies sets minimum standards of pay and working conditions. While the MBA is no guarantee of job security, it has consistently and considerably improved the conditions under which writing services are performed. In the difficult area of creative rights, for example, the Guild has managed to get employers and purchasers of original material to agree to accord the writer (among other things) certain rewrite rights, the right to be consulted on the director's cut of the film and promotional rights (which insure the writer will not have to crash the premiere of his own film).

Perhaps the most widely heralded benefit is its health fund, which many hold to be the best medical and dental plan in the business. Eligibility is based on earnings tied to the Guild minimum for one half-hour, network primetime story and teleplay. Currently, that means writers must earn around $17,000 within four consecutive calendar quarters for eligibility. Excerpts from the Minimum Compensation Schedule are set forth at the end of Chapter 10.

The Guild also maintains a staff of attorneys to review (but not negotiate) contracts and to protect the writer's creative rights (see Chapter 10) and work, even after the writer has sold it. One of the most crucial of these functions is the policing and collection of **residuals** which may become due as a film based on your work is released to various markets (such as television, cable, video, cd-rom, multimedia games, etc). Guild watchdogs monitor broadcasts and other releases worldwide and bill the producing companies. Signatories that are delinquent in their paying of residuals are placed on the Guild's "Strike" or "Unfair" list.

The prudent writer will not trust his hard earned residuals to this process alone, but will use the internet to check on reports of an airing in other cities and countries. This will help Guild lawyers to bolster (and often to make) their case. (Tip: non-Guild writers might consider asking for an additional flat fee payable upon foreign sales, in lieu of residual payments.)

The WGA library is a script depository without parallel (it is open to the general public) and the Guild publishes a great magazine, *Written By*, which focuses on writers' issues, work and lifestyles, and offers many inside tips. If you write for TV, the Market List, found inside the magazine (complete with contact phone numbers for each series), is a must. Non-members can subscribe.

94

For those of you who ask not what the Guild can do for you, but what you can do for your Guild, there are a wide variety of committees (such as agent and employment access, age and sex discrimination and the women's committee) upon which members may serve.

The Guild also administers a script registration service, a pension plan, a film society that offers first run screenings of most studio releases, a credit union (very useful for a profession marred by erratic income), a free notary service, and when requested, **arbitration for screen credit**. This last function may be the Guild's most frequent source of interaction with its members.

Credit

In today's film climate, it is normal for many writers to work on the same script (whether to fix script problems, accommodate the budget, stars or directors, or simply to placate a nervous studio executive). Therefore, credit on the final film—who is entitled to it and who end up receiving it—is naturally the subject of much debate. The Guild Policy on Credits runs seven pages in the membership manual and while it may not make the best bedtime reading, it confirms that "a writer's credits are essential to building or sustaining his/her career."

For your credits to be determined by Guild policy, you must have your work acquired by, or perform writing services for, a company signatory to the WGA Minimum Basic Agreement and be considered a "professional writer" by Guild definition. Dealing with a non-signatory company places the final credit determination beyond Guild jurisdiction.

When performing work-for-hire, be certain to inquire whether or not there is any assigned source material and whether or not other writers are employed or have been employed on the project. Also, the Guild stresses that writers "keep copies of all materials and accurate records of delivery dates." (To protect yourself, always turn in your assigned material with a cover letter setting forth the material delivered, date and to whom delivered.)

After the movie is completed, the producer must send to the Guild and to all writers who worked on the project (or a prior produced version) a "Notice of Tentative Writing Credits" and a copy of the final shooting script. If any writer disputes the determination or if the writers cannot agree among themselves as to the final credits, the arbitration process takes place. All drafts are then submitted to an arbitration committee (composed of other Guild members) to determine the relative contributions of each writer to the shooting script. Pursuant to Guild rules:

> "Any writer whose work represents a contribution of more than 33 percent of a screenplay shall be entitled to screen-

play credit, except . . . an original screenplay [wherein] any subsequent writer or writing team must contribute at least 50 percent to the final screenplay."

The percentages stated are designed as a guideline. For a second writer to receive credit, the contribution "must consist of dramatic construction, original and different sequences, original characterization and dialogue." Credit may not be shared by more than two writers or, in unusual cases, three writers or two writing teams.

Note: There is a considerable bias in favor of crediting the original writer.

The Guild has published a *Credits Survival Guide* "to provide writers with a plain language guide to the credits determination process and practical tips writers should know to help protect their interests in credits." To obtain a copy, contact the Guild's Credits Department at (323) 782-4528 in Los Angeles or (212) 767-7804 in New York (or check their website at http://www.wga.org or www.wgaeast.org).

All of the hoopla over screen credit is more than a battle of egos—it can translate into a significant amount of money in residuals and much more. An appeals court recently upheld a $7.3 million verdict in favor of a writer who sued Universal Studios, claiming that the studio stole from his original teleplay the idea for the television series Northern Exposure. The ruling was heralded as significant for writers as a recognition by the courts of the impact a screen credit for a hit series can have on a writer's career and future earnings.

> **Credit = credibility and determines fees, power and, ultimately, careers.**

CAREERS

A common question from novice writers is whether a long-term career as a working writer is a reality. Has the Guild been remiss in its duty to act in the interest of all writers in building the *profession* of screenwriting, with its incumbent recognition, job security and perks?

The Guild has insured broad financial gains, to be sure. But has the concentration on the short-term goal of higher pay been at the expense of the dignity, respect and long-term future to which the average working writer aspires? In fact, is there such a thing as an average working writer? Staff writers of episodic television earn big bucks and big residuals—so long as they are able to maintain their jobs. But, less and less freelance work is available.

Some screenwriters (like Joe Eszterhas and Shane Black) garner $1 million or more for a story outline and there is much ballyhoo in the press about the occasional spec script that brings instant wealth to a new writer. But the "middle-class" screenwriter, the writer who earns a decent living wage by consistently selling his work, year in and year out, has almost disappeared.

And though there are affirmative action committees within the Guild, the odds for a writing career dwindle if you are not white, male and under 40. In fact, the Guild recently released a two-year study outlining the decline in employment for older writers: in 1997, 73 percent of Guild writers 30 or younger were employed, compared to 46 percent of those in their forties, 32 percent of those in their fifties, 19 percent of those in their sixties, and a negligible percentage beyond that.

In the interest of *all* writers, it has been suggested that the Guild take a hard line—that it demand owner participation in all media writers create, demand retention of the writer's copyright, refuse to sanction rewrites on the original writer's work, demand creative participation for the writer in the making and marketing of the final film and absolutely demand an end to age, sex and race discrimination.

But in the real world of supply and demand, the studios brush aside such demands. Congress, after all, via the Copyright Act, takes even the title of "author"—the very dignity of authorship,—away from a writer for hire and hands it, along with the copyright to the work itself, to the studio or other employer—those who may never have put pen to paper!

As to the membership itself (the power to strike aside), the Guild has a practical mandate of maintaining employment. Yet, how often has a second writer refused to tinker with the original writer's vision or take full credit for the result? Until writers give value to their work, to their lonely but crucial role as filmmakers and to each other, no reform is possible. Because, after all, even the Guild cannot legislate respect.

97

REQUIREMENTS FOR ADMISSION TO THE **WGA,** WEST, INC.

FILM, TELEVISION, RADIO

An aggregate of twenty-four (24) units of Credit as set forth on the Schedule of Units of Credit, which units are based upon work completed under contract of employment or upon the sale or licensing of previously unpublished and unproduced literary or dramatic material is required. Said employment, sale or licensing must be with a company or other entity that is signatory to the applicable WGA Collective Bargaining Agreement and must be within the jurisdiction of the WGA as provided in its collective bargaining contracts. The twenty-four (24) units must be accumulated with the preceeding three (3) years of application. Upon final qualification for membership, a cashier's check or money order, payable to the Writers Guild of America, west, Inc. in the amount of Two Thousand Five Hundred Dollars ($2,500) is due. Writers residing West of the Mississippi River may apply for membership in the WGA, west, Inc. Writers residing East of the Mississippi River are advised to contact: Writers Guild of America, East, 555 West 57th Street, New York, NY 10019.

SCHEDULE OF UNITS OF CREDIT

Two Units   For each complete week of employment within the Guild's jurisdiction on a week-to-week basis.

Three Units   Story for a radio or television program less than thirty (30) minutes shall be prorated in increments of ten (10) minutes or less.

Four Units   Story for a short subject theatrical motion picture of any length or for a radio program or television program or breakdown for a non-prime time serial thirty (30) minutes through sixty (60) minutes.

Six Units   Teleplay or radio play less than thirty (30) minutes shall be prorated in five (5) minute increments;

Television format for a new serial or series;

"Created By" credit given pursuant to the separation of rights provisions of the WGA Theatrical and Television Basic Agreement in addition to other units accrued for the literary material on which the "Created By" credit is based.

Eight Units   Story for a radio or television program or breakdown for a non-prime time serial more than sixty (60) minutes and less than ninety (90) minutes; Screenplay for a short subject theatrical motion picture or for a radio play or teleplay thirty (30) minutes through sixty (60) minutes.

Twelve Units Story for a radio or television program ninety (90) minutes or longer or story for a feature length theatrical motion picture; or breakdown for a non-prime time serial ninety (90) minutes or longer.

Radio play or teleplay more than sixty (60) minutes and less than (90) minutes.

Twenty-four Units	Screenplay for a feature length theatrical motion picture; radio play or teleplay ninety (90) minutes or longer;
	Bible for any television serial or prime-time mini-series of a least four (4) hours;
	Long-term story projection which is defined for this purpose as a bible, for a specified term, on an existing, five (5) times per week non-prime time serial.
A Rewrite	One-half (1/2) the number of units allotted to the applicable category of work.
A Polish	One-quarter (1/4) the number of units allotted to the applicable category of work.
An Option	One-half (1/2) the number of units allotted to the applicable category of work subject to a maximum entitlement of eight (8) such units per project in any one (1) year. An extension or renewal of the same option shall not be accorded additional units. If an option on previously unexploited literary material is exercised, the sale of this material is accorded the number of units applicable to the work minus the number of units accorded to the option of the same material.

ADDITIONAL RULES FOR THE UNIT SYSTEM

Teams: Each writer who collaborates as part of a bona fide team on the same project shall be accorded the appropriate number of units allotted to the applicable category.

New or Unique Cases: In any case not covered by this Section 4, the Board of Directors shall have the authority to convene a Committee to Review the Unit System, which Committee shall suggest specific units applicable to any such work to the Board. Such unit determinations as may be adopted by the Board shall be submitted for membership approval at the first annual or special membership meeting following the Board's action.

Writer Owned Company: In all cases, to qualify for membership, if the writer's employment, option or purchase agreement is with a company owned in whole or in part by the writer or a member of the writer's family, there must be a bona fide agreement for financing, production and/or distribution with a third party signatory producing company. Failing such an agreement, the script must be produced and the writer must receive writing credit on screen in the form of "Written by, "Teleplay by," "Screenplay by," or (audio credit) "Radio Play by."

Writers In A Managerial Capacity or Writer-Performers: A person who is employed to write or who sells or options literary material to a signatory company while:

a) serving in a managerial capacity with the company; or b) rendering managerial services relating to the project for a network, syndicated television station(s), basic cable or pay television system, a studio, or the like, or (c) employed as a player on the project, shall not utilize this assignment, option or sale to qualify for membership in the Guild unless such script is produced and the individual receives writing credit on screen in the form of "Written by," "Teleplay by," "Screenplay by," or (audio credit) "Radio Play by."

99

Exceptions to the Three-Year Rule: In exceptional cases, the Board of Directors, acting upon a recommendation from the Membership and Finance Committee, shall have the power and authority to grant admission to Current membership based on units earned prior to three (3) years before the membership application was filed.

Comedy-Variety: If three (3) or fewer writers are employed to write literary material for the same comedy-variety program for television, each writer shall be accorded the number of units for teleplay applicable to a program of the same duration (as may be adjusted pursuant to the applicable time period provisions in Appendix A of the MBA). If more than three (3) writers are employed to write literary material for the same comedy-variety program for television, each writer shall be accorded the number of units for teleplay applicable to a program of the same duration but multiplied by a fraction the numerator of which is one and the denominator of which is the number of writers minus two. For example, if there are five (5) writers employed, the multiplier would be one-third (1/3); if there are ten (10) writers, the multiplier would be one-eighth (1/8).

Documentaries and Informational Programming: Telescripts for documentaries and literary material for informational programming shall be accorded the number of units for teleplay applicable to a program of the same duration.

Newswriters: Any person employed as a radio or television news writer, editor, desk assistant or in another job classification cover under the "WGA-CBS National Staff Agreement" (Or successor collective bargaining agreement) may be admitted to Current Membership in the Guild after thirty (30) days of employment in such bargaining unit.

100

INTERACTIVE

A writers and/or designer who has worked for an employing company which has signed the Interactive Program Contract and paid the appropriate Pension and Health contributions may join the WGA as a Current or Associate member. A writer who has earned 24 units of credit—the equivalent to a full length screenplay—is eligible for Current WGA membership.

Units for interactive programs are currently interpreted on a case-by-case basis for projects covered under the Interactive Program Contract. The company you work for must sign this contract and agree to pay 12.5 percent of your gross compensation to the WGA Pension and Health Plan.

To ensure eligibility for Associate or Current membership through the writing of interactive projects you must:

- Work for a company who has signed the Interactive Program Contract and has paid the 12.5 percent Pension and Health contribution.

- You must send your signed contracts, both interactive and personal services contract, along with a completed Membership Application form, a Project Summary Sheet and the project script (and/or the project item itself, if applicable) to the Department of Industry Alliances, Writers Guild of America, west, 7000 West Third Street, Los Angeles, CA 90048.

These materials are reviewed by a subcommittee of WGA members who belong to the Creative Media and Technology Committee (CMAT). This subcommittee assigns the appropriate number of units for the project. If the writer is credited with less than 24 units, then the writer may be eligible for Associate membership. Those writers who become Associate members have three years in which to obtain the 24 units necessary for Current membership. It is the responsibility of Associate members to file additional contracts with the WGA so their eligibility for Current status may be tracked. Should a writer applying for WGA membership submit a project for which 24 units of credit are assigned, he/she must become a Current member. In this case, the writer does not have the option of Associate membership.

For further information, contact the department of Industry Alliances at (323) 782-4511 or (408) 323-1898, or Membership at (323) 782-4532.

Chapter 8
THE MARKETPLACE

PART ONE: THE PLAYERS

A. The Writer: Strategies for Marketing Yourself
In the complex game of selling your work, even the best agents or managers can't (and won't) do it all for you. There are two primary reasons for this. First, many agents and managers have contacts limited to the studios or major independent producers. (Unless you're associated with a very hot spec script or have previously written a hit film, those markets may effectively be closed to you.) Second, the particular sensibilities of your script or your willingness to work cheaply may appeal to less mainstream buyers. (For these markets, you are often on your own.) In both cases, you must do your homework: research the appropriate market for your work, determine what these companies are looking for, how they process and evaluate material and decide how to best present your screenplay and yourself. Here are a few ways to go about it:

> ➤ *Build your team.*
With most buyers, you only get one shot. If you blow it, you're not likely to get another. You will rarely hear: "Do the rewrite and resubmit it; we'll take another look at it then." It is up to you to make sure your writing is the best you have to deliver before you submit it the first time. For this, you need honest, informed, reliable feedback on your writing before you bring it to market.

Two honest allies can save you a lot of negative "coverage" later on. Why two opinions? One will weigh too heavily on you and more than two will likely confuse you. Who should these allies be? You can always give your work to your manager, attorney or agent, if these people are willing to help during the creative stage. But, I recommend against submitting work to your marketing team before it's ready. They may not respond to your draft and turn away from you at this vulnerable point in the writing process.

So contact two good friends, friends who are not adverse to being honest with you. And, when they do comment, listen quietly and take notes (a certain amount of humble pie goes with the territory). Most of all, learn from the experience.

➤ *Make a business plan.*
Approach the selling of your work with the same meticulous care you gave to the writing of it. First of all, become familiar with the business itself. Learn all you can about the people in it—who is hot, who to contact to arrange a meeting, what a particular executive recently bought. Resolve to make others see you as a fellow professional, conversant with the usual and customary way business is done.

The entertainment section of your local newspaper and magazines like *Premiere* or *Entertainment Weekly* keep a finger on the pulse of the industry. Follow who is where and doing what with whom by reading the trades (*Daily Variety* and *The Hollywood Reporter*). Both trades feature a weekly chart on films in production, which tracks the particulars of what films are being produced (thus naming those producers most likely to appreciate the movie you are scripting). Information is power.

Telling your story to your friends is a good first step. Their reaction (or lack of reaction) can be a good barometer of how spellbinding a story you've created. Watch for eyes glazing over as you race over the murky middle, see if they register confusion or ask questions as you try to tip-toe around the weak areas of your work ("oh that, oh well, I have to fix that, just keep listening"). The feedback will help strengthen your script (and improve your pitch) before you present it to those few precious contacts you hold in your back pocket.

Next, understand that not all screenplays sell, even some very good ones—so develop an advance plan for dealing with rejection. Here are two suggestions:

- Start another screenplay before trying to sell the one you have finished. That keeps you in the game for the long haul.

- Make lemons into lemonade—view rejection as an opportunity to become a better writer and to cement a deeper relationship with the person who rejected your work. See if you can get him to explain why the material didn't work for him. Ask him to be candid. Tell him you respect his opinion and want to gain the benefit of his insight. Any dialogue at this point should leave an open door for future work; in a business where rejection too often makes enemies, you will have employed it to make friends.

➤ *Network.*
Don't be afraid to contact those who have established themselves in the business. Many are happy to act as mentors to novice writers

who express a sincere willingness to work. Also, build alliances with your peers; perhaps start your own *writer's table*. Take film classes, attend writing seminars. The USC and the UCLA film schools have become Hollywood legend but strong professional bonds have been built at Yale Drama School, The American Film Institute and other academic institutions as well. For example, executive producer Stephen Bochco didn't look much further than his circle of buddies from Carnegie Tech when he began to staff and cast television shows like *Hill Street Blues*, *LA Law* and *NYPD Blue*.

Screenwriter Robert Towne (*Chinatown*) gives this advice: "Make movies with your friends." (Of course, that's easy when your friends are Jack Nicholson and Warren Beatty.) You may have friends you don't know yet. The party game known as *Six Degrees of Kevin Bacon* (connecting the actor to other actors through common films) is a variation on an old theme; with enough research, you can find someone who will connect you to just about anyone.

> Contacts are not always obvious to you; you have to look for them. If your great aunt has a friend with a son who knows a guy that dates a woman whose cousin works as a secretary for a small LA entertainment law firm—that's a contact!

The goal here is to make and keep connections, at whatever level they are found, with the same relentless drive, creativity and imagination that will serve you well as a writer.

105

➢ *Be your own producer.* Essentially, this means becoming a "packager." Studios can afford to take on the challenge of developing pitches, novels and flawed screenplays into movies; they may be driven by the interest of a star, director, producer or writer with whom they

> Post this advice on your bulletin board: When a group of USC film students asked *Star Wars* creator George Lucas how to go about breaking into the film business, he replied, "Somehow."

wish to be in business or by the underlying compelling nature of the concept. Most independent film companies (with less time, money and development staff) cannot afford that same luxury. They look for a finished screenplay strong enough to attract talent or one with talent (especially a star) already attached. Therefore, the best way to attract independent producers to your work or to raise the money to film your screenplay on your own is to link your work to those who have a track record with both audiences and investors.

Talent is reached through contacts—and approaching talent is not as daunting as a new writer might believe. Stars, too, seek the artistic freedom of more intimate productions, character-driven stories and the chance to work with emerging talent. (Note Harvey Keitel's work in Quentin Tarantino's directorial debut, *Reservoir Dogs*, and the resurgence of John Travolta's stalled career when Tarantino interested him in *Pulp Fiction*.) And, there are always pet projects that well-known creative talent take pride in developing themselves and want to produce outside the constraints of the studio system—many have their own production companies expressly for this purpose. *The Hollywood Creative Directory* is a source of such companies that are in active development and also companies that have development deals already in place with studios or networks. Bankable directors can be contacted through their representatives (names can be obtained through the Director's Guild) and even "A" list actors have their agents or managers listed (with contact information) with the Screen Actor's Guild.

But beware: **attaching talent to your screenplay can be a double-edged sword**. A desirable name can create instant heat on your project but it can also be a deal-breaker for a prospective buyer who may see this talent as more of a burden than a benefit. Attach more than one person and you increase the odds of that happening because some buyers hate baggage. Multiply this warning by 10 for any notion you may have of attaching *yourself* as a producer, director or principal actor. (But, if you have a proven track record in the slot you wish to fill, that's different—or, if your screenplay is so hot you have negotiating leverage, go for it!)

If you've managed to raise the production financing yourself while retaining the authority to cast yourself as director or star, then more power to you. Or, if you would rather burn your screenplay (really, not just bluffing) than sell it without directing or starring in it, etc., then you must follow the dictates of your heart. But, attaching yourself in such a key capacity is bound to do more than just raise eyebrows; it may be a deal breaker. Before you dash a promising career on the rocks of your own ambition, seek the advice of others who have your professional interests at heart, your agent, lawyer or manager or all three.

106

> ➤ *Enter screenwriting contests.*

So many writing contests emerge each year that entire books are devoted to cataloging and updating them. The good news is, a handful of such contests are a legitimate search for talent. Contests sponsored by universities and other well-established educational institutions or by large film companies and studios can offer the novice or unexposed screenwriter access to the movers and shakers of production. Some yield agents and options or cash awards, work stipends or workshops with established professionals. What do the judges look for? Unless the contest targets special genres or select entrants, the answer is usually the "very best of which you are capable."

The bad news is that many contests are not well-established, are difficult to monitor and may even be rip-offs. The fringe of the contest market has become infested with charlatans. Some contests are unconscionable scams that require substantial entry or reading fees but offer winners little or no film contacts, media exposure or real prizes.

In such an unregulated environment, anyone can anoint himself a judge of writing talent. But who are these "judges?" What are their credits and what is their motivation? Gaining access to new talent can be a noble purpose; collecting fees for the chance to "borrow" material from writers is not. How does your entrance fee differ from paying any stranger to read your work? (It is considered unethical for an agent or production company to charge a fee to offset their reader costs, a practice I find particularly abominable.)

A student entered (for a $35 fee) a contest based in New York that certainly sounded legitimate. She won *first prize* (over "close to 10,000" contestants), receiving a nice computerized announcement to that effect but nothing else. Her spec episode was to be "presented" to the producers of the show; she never heard a word. My guess is that the promoter (richer by $350,000 if the entrance figures are accurate) mailed her winning script to the producers who tossed it in the bin along with all other unsolicited manuscripts.

The most important aspect to entering a contest is to determine how winning the contest will benefit the entrant. If the prize is money, is there proof bona fide winners were ever actually paid? If it's industry access or recognition, is there a list of prior winners and their accomplishments which resulted from winning the contest? If it's the promise of a script sale, be especially cautious. (One well-publicized contest requires "potential" finalists to sign a long and onerous legal document effectively transferring, in advance, all rights to their work for an unconscionably low purchase price—which in fact may never be payable and which compels the writer to perform substantial additional writing services over an unspecified period of time at no additional compensation.)

Finally, why submit to contests which hold little industry cache when established contests cost the same to enter? You can choose which to enter from among 42 contests listed in Erik Joseph's guide: *How To Enter Screenplay Contests & Win!* (Lone Eagle Publishing, Los Angeles, 1997), or be among the first to submit to the many new contests opening up yearly, but the following seven are consistent favorites among my students:

(Note: Application deadlines, fees, procedures, awards and contact names and numbers are subject to change. Send a self-addressed, stamped envelope (SASE) for an application, specific guidelines and rules of eligibility.)

Chesterfield Film Company Writer's Film Project: 8205 Santa Monica Blvd., Suite 200, Los Angeles, CA 90046-5912; 323-683-3977. Entry fee: $40. Deadline: June 1. Up to 5 writers receive a $20,000 stipend each for a one-year fellowship program based in Los Angeles.

Nicholl Fellowships in Screenwriting: Academy Foundation, Academy of Motion Picture Arts and Sciences, 8949 Wilshire Blvd., Beverly Hills, CA 90210-1972; 310-247-3000. Entry fee: $30. Deadline: May 1. The nation's most prestigious screenwriting contest, it awards up to 5 $25,000 fellowships and promises publicity and industry contacts.

Sundance Screenwriters Lab: The Sundance Institute, 225 Santa Monica Blvd., 8th Floor, Santa Monica, CA 90401; 310-394-4662. Entry fee: $25. Deadline: June 28 and November 15. Offers a chance to work at Robert Redford's Utah ranch with some of the best writers and other creative talent available and promises publicity and travel expenses.

UCLA Extension Diane Thomas Screenwriting Awards: Writers Program, 10995 LeConte Ave., Los Angeles, CA 90024-2883; 310-825-9415. Entry fee: None. Deadline: January 27. Screenplays must be developed in the Writers Program screenwriting classes; cash awards are presented at an award ceremony attended by top film agents and producers.

Walt Disney Studios Fellowship Program: Fellowship Program Administrator, 500 South Buena Vista Street, Burbank, CA 91521-0880; 818-560-6894. Entry fee: None. Deadline: Between April 1 and April 26. Preference given to women and minorities; WGA members not eligible; 10 to 15 writers are awarded fellowships; out-of-state winners are afforded airfare and some expenses.

Warner Bros. Television Writers Workshop: Warner Bros., 4000 Burbank Blvd., Burbank, CA 91522-0001; 818-954-7906. Entry fee: $25, $450 to participate in the workshop. Deadline: Fall (call for exact date). Professional training, development deals, possible staff positions and assignments are offered.

Writer's Digest **Writing Competition:** 1507 Dana Avenue, Cincinnati, OH 45207; Fax: 513-531-1843. Entry fee: $8. Deadline: May 31. Accepts film and TV scripts; offers cash awards, subscriptions, trips and industry contacts.

Lesser known contests (such as the Wisconsin Screenwriters Forum, 5747 North 82nd Court, Milwaukee, WI 53218—not limited to residents of Wisconsin—and the Austin Heart of Texas Film Festival, 707 Rio Grande #101, Austin, TX 78701) may not yield large prizes or instant publicity, but winning can bring your work to light and bolster your credentials as a writer.

The trades, other film publications and state and local film commissions are sources of information or advertisements for contests. Investigate carefully, use good common sense and make inquiries on the Internet before committing your hopes, entrance fee and postage. And **never**—under any circumstances and notwithstanding flattery or rosy promises—sign anything that could be construed to sell or transfer the rights to your "winning entry" without first consulting a good contract lawyer.

Most large cities and all states have a strong economic interest in promoting local film production. Many sponsor screenplay competitions expressly for the purpose of targeting good scripts which can be shot locally. (See for example, the "Set in Philadelphia" Screenwriting Competition; 3701 Chestnut Street, Philadelphia, PA 19104; 215-895-6593; or, the Lone Star Screenplay Competition; 1920 Abrams Parkway, Suite 419, Dallas, TX 75214; 214-606-3041.) If the setting of your story lends itself to a particular location, write the appropriate state or local film commission for a list of possible contests for which your script may be eligible.

109

> *Employ consultation services.*

Some industry readers, story editors, writing teachers and screenwriters have taken to moonlighting as consultants. Ads are placed offering first-rate, insider analysis of submitted work. Some promise to connect you to agents or buyers or even to produce selected work themselves. Some are competent, well-intended and reasonable. A positive experience with a consultant can net professional feedback and an industry contact. But beware: many so-called consultants may be out of steam, out of work, out of touch, disgruntled, bitter and in need of exorcising their own demons.

Also, examine your own motivations. At this point in your career, do you need help with the mechanics of the writing process or an objective critique of your finished work? Or, perhaps you desire advice on how to market your work, including personal recommendations to agents or production companies. In either case, will you be getting individual attention and advice superior to that you could access yourself (often for less money) through University courses, screenwriting seminars, computer programs and various publications?

The same warning for contests applies here. Check references and track records and ask questions that go to the heart of your expectations before placing your money and dreams on an opinion that may carry little weight with mainstream Hollywood.

It is best to steer clear of mass-marketed consultation services offering "close supervision" of their "highly trained staff." Find out who, exactly, will be doing the reading—the consultant or a paid reader? Will the service include a personal phone consultation or will it be conducted entirely by mail? Will you be paying for a professional reader report—a line by line script analysis and in-depth, truthful *advice* to make you a better writer? Or will you receive an adapted form letter on the general principles of screenwriting?

And note: Whether you submit a concept, outline, treatment or screenplay, whether it is for evaluation by a producer or agent or for entry into a contest, whether it is for grant or scholarship consideration or for professional consultation or analysis—register and/or copyright your work and maintain a good paper trail of all correspondence relating to your submission. The operative phrase here is "buyer beware."

B. The Reader

Executives and independent producers simply don't have the time to read all the screen material that comes to them; they depend on the formidable first defense of any company—the reader.

The reader report, or **coverage** as it is known in the trade, determines whether a screenplay moves up the ladder to the executives who can approve it for development or production. Coverage enables the executive to discuss the work knowledgeably with the writer, agent, producer or other staff members—without actually having spent hours reading the material. (The importance of this function increases in direct proportion to the growing number of script submissions.)

To "cover" the mountain of material that finds its way to the studio gate, studios have "Story Departments" staffed by skilled, full-time readers, adept at plucking the one script out of many that has the attributes the executives they serve are seeking. (These jobs are often unionized—Story Analysts Local 854 serves Los Angeles—with a going rate of about $25 an hour plus benefits.) But outside help must also be employed to read and critique not only spec screenplays but the galleys of soon-to-be-published novels that might be candidates for adaptation to film. To meet this demand, a veritable army of freelance readers has risen up—some only part-time interns with little training, others highly educated and industry-savvy, for whom being a reader is a full-time job (at least temporarily; most readers see their job as a stepping stone to a career as a screenwriter or creative executive).

Coverage typically consists of a brief "log line" of the story (a one sentence description); a one or two-page plot synopsis; and a one page critique of the merits and faults of the story and characters. The report usually concludes with a qualifier such as "Recommend," "Consider," or "Pass," which is based on story, characters, and the company's specific needs. Some companies use a final grading system (known as the "box score") which assigns marks to aspects such as idea, storyline, characterization, dialogue and production values, and sometimes asks the reader to hazard a guess on the budget needed to produce the film.

With more than 40,000 scripts making the rounds each year, getting them read can prove prohibitively expensive, especially for smaller companies. The going rate for freelance readers is about $50 per screenplay (as high as $75 if the reader must pick up and deliver).

Some development executives use the reader report as a quick summary from which they can determine whether a script is worth their personal attention, rather than relying on the reader's critique or recommendations. In fact, most readers will admit that factors beyond their control will go into the ultimate decision of any executive as to what material is pursued to production—such as their employer's connection with or commitments to talent. Very few produced screenplays can attribute their start to a reader's recommendation; it is a testament to the professionalism with which most readers approach their job that this reality does not permanently discourage them.

In fact, the opposite is true— all readers share the desire to find something truly wonderful. The hope is to be the first to discover the hot, new talent—to unearth the jewel hidden in the pile of often poorly executed and formulaic writing. Take the reader on an emotional thrill ride and he will champion your screenplay to executives further up the chain of command. The irony is that—though all are loathe to admit it—like any good gatekeeper, the reader's primary

111

The reader process awaits not only scripts by new writers but also those of established writers with produced credits and agents in tow. In fact, even agents employ readers to limit their reading load. Thus, in effect, the reader becomes the writer's target audience. The writer's task is to put the movie into the reader's head, to create a powerful curiosity in the reader which makes him want to go forward and to avoid turning off a reader by profane, racist or sexist characters or situations.

job is to pass. He must limit the reading load of his boss, not increase it.

C. The Independent Producer

John Gregory Dunne's recent book, *Monster*, reveals the "monster" to be the studio's money which controls Hollywood. But, even the bottom line of corporate giants is a willing slave to the real monster, the public's fickle, growing and insatiable appetite for product. And the majors look chiefly to one main supplier to feed that appetite—the (oft-misunderstood) independent producer.

One reader I know has this motto taped on her bulletin board: "It is easier and cheaper to pass." Do not make it easier still for the reader to say "no"—your script must be technically flawless, have a clear story "hook" in place and be imminently castable (i.e., with lead characters that scream "star turn"). To have a solid reason to contact stars and institute a working relationship is the stuff of a development executive's dreams.

A lot of film has passed through the projector since independent producers such as David O. Selznick and Mervyn LeRoy manipulated and controlled writers, directors and stars in bringing us such screen classics as *Gone With the Wind* and *The Wizard of Oz*. Yet, the way business is done in Hollywood has not changed all that drastically. It's still the indie producer, the savvy insider with a vested interest in finding projects that will make good movies, upon whom studio executives rely.

Who is the independent producer? Someone who puffs long, Cuban cigars and escorts pre-pubescent girls to decadent Hollywood hot tub parties? How about money mavens who count ciphers rather than sheep to fall asleep at night? Those are the popular myths. In reality, the independent producer is often a hustler and a scapegoat and the unsung hero of film history. (How many producers of award-winning films can you name?) He is most often the person who seeks out fresh material and new talent, develops it by supervising the writer through various screenplay drafts, packages it with other creative elements (such as a director or stars), pitches it to the powers on high, garners the necessary funds to film it and nurtures it through its premier to the film festivals and its appearance at your local multi-plex theater.

The producer is the architect of the movie project and the one who carries off the Oscar if the film wins for "Best Picture."

Yet—and here's the important part—it is only on the strength of a well-crafted *screenplay* that the producer can gain admission to those few, powerful executives, directors or stars whose nod of approval can coax millions of dollars to be gambled on a film's production and success in the marketplace. As in a genre love story, the writer chases the indie producer until he catches you!

Today, a growing list of actors and directors have their own production companies (many consist of one-executive and an assistant), often funded by a major studio. Television networks fund such companies for a series creator or star. The mandate is to find material suited to the talents or ambitions of the owner-star. Writers often complain that dealing with such companies almost assures a turn in "development hell," but some "star" companies should be applauded for using their clout to develop and champion many scripts that the studios or networks would be reluctant to adopt, even (at times) providing production financing from their own pocket.

Many independent producers work on a limited budget, offering little option money and asking for free rewrites. The *quid pro quo* is the tenacity with which he will promote your material and the exposure he can offer you in the marketplace. You should also receive a sizable back-end payday (purchase price and profit share) to compensate you for the trust and good faith you've demonstrated in working for less.

When seeking a producer for your script, integrity and current business relationships should be high on your list of desirable qualities. If the producer has an office, try to wrest an invitation to discuss your script there. See if the phone rings, if activity is in the works. Does the producer have a director or star in mind? Can he set a meeting with you that includes that director or star? Since anyone can call himself an independent producer, legitimacy is judged by a provable track record or a contract accompanied by a check. But danger lurks for the writer who does not take early steps to protect himself.

The Problem: The Producer's Home Shopping Network
Sometimes, an unscrupulous producer will ignore the step of paying you to acquire the rights to your work. Instead, he may pitch your story over the phone to his contacts at studios or networks or even to actors with whom he has a relationship—all without a paid option giving him the right to do so. Unless great enthusiasm is expressed on the other end, the producer can simply drop the submission in the wastebasket and no one is the wiser.

Later, the writer, unaware of the producer's illicit activities, may find a legitimate producer willing to buy the material or an agent willing to represent the work, but upon submission to those networks or studios already contacted by the unscrupulous producer,

113

he will receive a curt reply that the material has already been "covered" and rejected. The agent may end his representation of the writer and the honest producer (who paid money in good faith for an option) may sue for return of his funds. Unless the writer attaches a new, marketable element (more than a new title is necessary), the screenplay will be history—and the writer will have a near to impossible task identifying the culprit who did him wrong. In this risky atmosphere, made more perilous by the practice of sending stories over the Internet, ethical producers will find themselves "chilled" from paying options unless they can receive convincing assurance that the material has not "been around."

Even experienced writers have been known to cave in to a producer's request to "let me just have it for a week, to see what I can do with it." A well-connected producer can "cover" the studios and other major markets for a script in a series of phone calls. The writer's script, never having been properly prepared for the marketplace or pitched with the proper degree of thought or energy, is considered "shopped" and may be dead in a weekend.

> **The Writers Guild of America prohibits shopping in its agreement with producers, levying substantial fines on abusers, but the practice continues to be widespread.**

The Solution: Control Your Submission List.

If possible, submit through established channels—agents, attorneys, managers. Do not "shotgun" your material all over town. (Producers you may never be able to trace may take a liking to your work and shop it without contacting you.) Court producers one at a time. Don't give anyone a lot of time to decide about his interest in your work—let him know that you are actively pursuing other contacts.

Then make other contacts. Publications such as *The Hollywood Creative Directory* or *The Film Producers, Studios, Agents and Casting Directors Guide* can provide the names and titles of individuals you may wish to contact. Internet services also list production companies and their current needs—many like to circumnavigate agents and managers and *want* to deal directly with writers.

A query letter will keep you from sending your screenplay to parties who do not accept unsolicited material. A good telephone personality can help you through the first line of defense—the protective assistant—and perhaps receive an offer to submit your work. Follow up any contact with a letter, fax or e-mail confirming the substance of the contact.

However you contact a producer, be cautioned: Clear title (ownership of rights) to your work can be clouded if a producer (or other third party to whom you have submitted your screenplay) later claims that an "oral transfer of rights" was made or a courtesy period of time was extended in which he could consider your script for production. This cloud must be cleared up before any production company can obtain the "E & O" (Errors and Omissions) insurance policy necessary to begin production. So take good notes and keep meticulous records; make it a business practice to follow up all meetings with letters which clearly document any understandings reached.

D. The Studio Executive

"How do all these bad movies get made?" we ask. The "suits," as studio executives are nicknamed around town, do not always deserve the blame. After all, they face a revolving door (most executive jobs last only a few years) and during their short tenure they are under great pressure to find a blockbuster that will guide them up the ladder of success before they are knocked off. Since movies have long gestation periods (two years or more from development to release), job pressure begins on day one: the executive must establish and nurture relationships with people who can help find or develop unique stories that will attract the same few major stars or directors being besieged daily by the competition.

115

Preying on these fears and needs is a cadre of agents, lawyers and managers who profess to have the hot script to put the executive's career into orbit. If you go to enough Hollywood movies, you know there just aren't that many hot scripts around. But the executive cannot shut his door on these people; one of whom may actually have that blockbuster. So bad decisions are made, good scripts are mangled, outrageous budgets are greenlighted and super-star salaries rise—and the executive is the scapegoat when that potential blockbuster is a big-budget failure. (Of course, it is also true that the executive can get *too much credit* when one film out of twenty they greenlight *does* find an audience).

But what is the writer to do when faced with story conferences called because the executive felt lonely, when two years of work is jettisoned for an idea hatched at a 2 a.m. House of Blues concert? Remember you labor in a collaborative art; *maybe the work will get better.* Or not. And don't despair: Any executive with

> To many studio executives, in the immortal words of critic Pauline Kael, "A good script is a script to which Robert Redford will commit himself. A bad script is a script which Redford has turned down. A script that 'needs work' is a script about which Redford has yet to make up his mind."

a history in the business knows, in his gut, that it is the power of the word—the script—that spawns any blockbuster and not the actor or the director or the mega-budgeted special-effects. It is the responsibility of every writer to never let him forget that—especially in the beginning, when he needs you most. That's your chance to **make him respect you.** Have your agent extract more money for that dialogue polish, or perhaps some future perk that involves you in casting and location scouts. If the studio is to get first crack at future scripts, make them honor both the letter and the spirit of those rewrite commitments. Do all this and you may not feel (at least for a time) the inevitable need to direct in order to preserve the integrity of your artistic vision.

Should you manage a face-to-face with any development or production executive, it may help to remember that the meeting is not, in the final analysis, about you or your script— it's about how making a deal with you will help further that person's *own* career ambitions. As writer David Mamet said: "Your business is writing movies, theirs is to get ahead in the movie biz."

PART TWO: THE MARKETS

A. The Major Studios

In early 1997, William Goldman wrote in *Premiere* magazine that he had just witnessed the worst year in Hollywood history. Not *movie* history, he was quick to remind, not in a year that was loaded with memorable films. It was just that, in his opinion, none of them—save one—was made by the mainstream studio system, a system that Goldman sees as having finally crushed art beneath the boot of commerce, a system where, in Goldman's words, "the studios are making movies for mouth-breathers in foreign lands, testosterone-filled young men who get off on the violence."

The much-heralded summer of 1997 fared no better with reviewers. Writing that "*Con Air, Batman & Robin* and *Speed 2* deserve to be tortured and killed," highly-regarded *Newsday* film critic Jack Mathews added, "If [Hollywood is] going to spend $80 million to $140 million on a picture, why not include a compelling story as well as a tricky premise? Why not characters as well as stars? Would a few subplots and a little relevance—just the least food for thought is all we ask—really cost them at the gate?"

Therein lies the problem. The gate. The box-office. The big bucks. And, in 1998, James Cameron's *Titanic*, which cost close to $300 million to make, proved that a very expensive film could be a sound investment after all. In the wake of its *billion* dollar-plus worldwide gross and near-sweep of the Academy Awards (it was not, however, even nominated for a writing award), the major Hollywood studios (Warner Bros., Twentieth Century Fox, Disney, Sony Pictures, Paramount, MGM/UA, and Dreamworks) can be counted on to continue to greenlight "event" movies, some of which will become movie classics, but many others of which—saddled with dumb plots and dumber dialogue—will be lost to film history.

A big hit in the world marketplace means big stars, bigger budgets and high concepts. Hollywood has taken notice of the resurgence of the independent film but, at the cost of making films today, downside risk (potential financial disaster) must be limited. Their best protection is to deliver to the audience what has been successful in the past. In a sense, then, the audience has itself to blame for getting the same old stuff: mindless action, recycled plots and aging stars.

Should you desire to write for mainstream Hollywood, the guideposts are the same as they have for years: write a high-concept or character-driven genre film that sports a strong starring role (preferably for a male). The financial rewards for success are considerable. But if this doesn't sit well with your passions or your soul, consider the following alternatives:

B. The Independents
117

For personal stories with morally ambiguous points of view, for stories that challenge established filmmaking formats—the daring, often controversial stories that many screenwriters must tell—you may wish to court smaller production companies with the freedom to produce product for select, target audiences. (The nurturing of and marketing to such audiences has become an art unto itself.) In the eyes of the critics, audiences and even the venerable voting members of the Academy of Motion Picture arts and Sciences, these small, independent pictures have finally matured to A-list status.

The dominance of *Titanic* at the various 1998 film awards and *Saving Private Ryan* in 1999 does not obliterate the lessons of recent history. Alongside *Titanic* stood the independently financed *The Full Monty* and *Good Will Hunting,* and in competition with *Saving Private Ryan* were independent films such as *Shakespeare in Love, Life is Beautiful* and *Elizabeth*. In 1997, only the star-turn of Tom Cruise in *Jerry Maguire* broke the spell of an independent sweep of the nominations that included *The English Patient* (winner), *Fargo, Secrets & Lies* and *Shine*. In 1996, two little engines that could—*Il Postino* and *Babe*—were Best Picture nominees and, in 1995 (for films released in 1994), all five nominees for Best Original Screenplay—Miramax Films' *Bullets over Broadway, Heavenly Creatures, Pulp Fiction* and *Red,* and Gramercy Pictures' *Four Weddings and a*

Funeral—were offbeat, diverse, and independently produced. In all, Miramax Films, received 22 nominations that year, more than any major film studio.

And where have these celebrated ideas and talents, so anathema to the mega-budgets, formula heroes and calcified story structures of the majors, been nurtured?—through the festival circuit.

Film festivals have become an increasingly important component to the nurturing and discovery of new talent. Producing your own work or having it produced by film students (or even former video store clerks) may not pay much, but if your film is then accepted into one of the premiere festivals, it can bring you exposure, honor and perhaps even turn you into a hot commodity.

At festivals such as Sundance, Toronto, Telluride, Cannes, New York, MIFED, The Los Angeles Independent Film Festival and the American Film Market, independent film producers, studio executives and distribution companies (large and small) fan out in search of the daring, the unconventional and the unsigned. Even the unproduced, first-time writer can attend and rub elbows with those creative talents, producers and executives that would be near-to-impossible to get on the phone back in Hollywood.

For a comprehensive list of festivals, deadlines, awards and tips from those who run them and those who have been there, Chris Gore's *The Ultimate Film Festival Survival Guide* (Lone Eagle Publishing, Los Angeles, 1999) will serve as an excellent resource.

C. The Alternative Markets

Writers need not labor only in the more glamorous fields of the entertainment business—feature films and network series television. There are, in fact, significant advantages to writing for what have been labeled "alternative" markets.

For years, alternative markets such as animation, cable and first-run syndication, to name a few, suffered a "poor cousin" reputation. Often low-paying and unmonitored by the Writers Guild, many mainstream agents shied away from actively representing writers in these markets. But the Writers Guild has recently legitimized many such markets by creating and monitoring specific guidelines for employment. An increasing number of writers are now availing themselves of the higher pay, creative freedom and job security these markets may offer.

Should you aspire to write for a particular market, identify a current show in that market and try to obtain and then study writing samples of that show to familiarize yourself with the style and format. Then submit writing samples appropriate to that market. Be forewarned: writing required for these markets is often very specific. A sample for one market may not be effective as a sample for any other market. Helpful material for breaking into any specific show/market may be available in your local library or through the Internet—or from a contact within such show/market, the best way to plug yourself into any new area of employment.

Caveats in place, here are some fields that may capture your interest:

➤ *Animation*

The Lion King, Aladdin, Hercules, A Bug's Life, The Prince of Egypt, Antz, Mulan—the film list grows by leaps and bounds each passing season. In TV, shows like *The Simpsons, Rugrats,* or *Hey, Arnold* are scoring rating victories over network shows with highly-paid live talent. Once a "Disney thing," virtually every studio now has a long-term commitment to develop and produce animated features and television. Equally significant for writers is the animation industry's recent recognition of the importance of writers to develop that programming. Previously, characters were conceived by the cartoonist and plots were often devised by what was possible in the medium or simply fun to draw. Today—sometimes before a drawing is rendered—writers are working in consort with the animators in applying the principles of the three act film structure, defining character arcs and developing full storylines.

In a recent, two-day course on structure and characterization for Disney Television's animation team, it was encouraging to witness animators' desire to learn how to better work with writers on story and character development from the early concept stages. The Writers Guild has taken notice: animation writers are now being accepted as Associate Members and the Guild has begun the process of bringing animation writers fully under the Guild's jurisdiction.

➤ *Children's Programming*

Shows like *Sesame Street, Barney, The Puzzle Place, Teletubbies* and *Mr. Rogers' Neighborhood* have become staples on morning television. Entire family-oriented cable networks like The Discovery Channel, The Animal Channel or The Disney Channel also provide a platform for children's programming. There are also children's afternoon specials which focus on issues of interest to teens and pre-teens and a burgeoning market in children's and young adult direct-to-video films. (The Olsen twins, those loveable girls who began on the television series *Full House,* have turned their unique personalities into a $50 to $100 million enterprise, releasing everything from shorts and direct-to-video movies to more ambitious feature films.)

119

➤ Cable Television

Cable television is another market in need of programming to supply the explosion of new channels and operating systems. Made-for-Cable films and episodic series (e.g., *Sex in the City, The Sopranos*) are proliferating. Suppliers like Home Box Office, Showtime, The Movie Channel, The Disney Channel, Turner Broadcasting, etc. usually require agency submissions, however a contact or good query letter and writing sample may make breaking in a lot easier. The pay is generally only slightly less than that of the networks.

➤ Non-Dramatic Programming

This wide category includes documentary (e.g., *Biography*), musical/comedy/variety (e.g., *Late Show with David Letterman, The Tonight Show with Jay Leno*), quiz and audience participation shows (e.g., *Jeopardy, Wheel of Fortune*), award shows (e.g., *The Academy Awards, The Grammy Awards*) and even news programming (e.g., *Nightline, 48 Hours*). Never forget that it is writers who research and fill the categories for *Jeopardy*, draft David Letterman's "Top Ten List" and compose those short, seemingly informal exchanges the presenters at an award show squint to read off a monitor.

➤ Syndication

120

There are many first-run syndication shows, including talk shows (e.g., *Oprah, Larry King Live, The Jerry Springer Show*), game shows— soon to get their own cable channel (e.g., *The Dating Game, Hollywood Squares*), magazine shows (e.g., *Entertainment Tonight, Extra*), and reality programming (e.g., *Unsolved Mysteries, LAPD: life on the beat.*) Add to that the almost daily bombardment of the "news as entertainment" shows (e.g., *First Edition, Hard Copy*) and the real action in syndication—first-run one-hour dramatic series programming.

Aided by an expanding number of foreign broadcast companies and a burgeoning market for supplying cable and satellite delivery systems, there are currently more than two dozen first-run, one-hour syndicated dramatic shows on the air. Following closely behind the hugely-successful *Star Trek* franchise (which has yielded billions of dollars to Paramount) and *Baywatch* (a network-canceled show currently in its third billion of worldwide revenue for Pearson All American Television), Universal Television has written new chapters in worldwide marketing and merchandising profit due to the sale of its two first-run syndicated hits, *Xena, The Warrior Princess* and *Hercules: The Legendary Journeys*. Not to be outdone, virtually every other major studio or cable supplier are flexing their programming muscles in the same market.

Lured by greater creative control, less management interference and 22-episode commitments, writers such as Lee Goldberg and

William Rabkin bounce between story editing duties on syndicated smashes like *Baywatch* to showrunning network staples like CBS' *Diagnosis Murder.* Even well-established feature producers like Oliver Stone (with *Witchblade*), Francis Ford Coppola (with the sci-fi series *First Wave*) and Jerry Bruckheimer (*Soldier of Fortune*) have entered the arena with multi-episode commitments—and lots of new jobs for writers.

The writing staff of a syndicated show is usually leaner and more restricted by budget and time, but usually receive greater responsibility for the creative direction of the show, from writing a greater number of episodes to being consulted during production and postproduction. This kind of experience pays off in producer positions on their next network post. On the downside, less staff and more episodes translates to long work hours (six or seven days to churn out one episode), less pay (about two-thirds of the network fee), and fewer residuals (about one-third of the network rate). Still, in his article for the February, 1998 Writers Guild publication, *Written By,* Steve Brennan admits that, for the moment at least, "the reality of producing 22 episodes in one season in syndication puts the writer in the driver's seat."

➤ *Interactive Multimedia*
Studios, animation and special effects companies are escalating the production of electronic programming, including feature films (e.g., *The Pagemaster*), direct-to-video films (including cassettes, CDs and laser discs), video games, interactive programming, multimedia and CD-Roms. Even new writers can gain direct access to the leading producers of these media without an agent—usually all that's required is a solid concept, sometimes augmented by a flow chart and/or a treatment that is three to ten pages in length. But caution: essentially unregulated and in a state of evolution, abuses are frequent. Writers are doing three times the work for one-third the pay and often denied credit arbitrarily. You should query the WGA staff for guidelines in accepting employment in this market.

➤ *The Foreign Markets*
The foreign market for feature films (for both theatrical and video consumption) gobbles up all the majors can deliver and hungers for more. This hunger for American product has created a universal respect for the way American movies are made, i.e. with writers. Foreign productions were historically the product of an auteur system in which scripts were improvised by actors under the guidance of a director usually working from a fleshed out treatment at best. Today, writing conferences are popping up all over Europe and Asia and the invited stars are American writers. Just following American principles of structure and character development can almost automatically

121

raise your screenplay to a competitive level in such markets. And submission there is more a matter of contacts than credits.

➤ *Daytime Serials*
Employment opportunities abound in the area of daytime soaps due to high staff turnover (long hours, low pay). And, new writers can submit writing samples outside the soap arena (almost any dramatic piece will suffice) since the plot lines of soaps are planned a year in advance and are folly to predict.

➤ *PBS*
Produced by local stations or independently by producers or documentary filmmakers, PBS airs shows (such as *American Playhouse*) which attract CPB (Corporation for Public Broadcasting) and corporate funding, and grants from such foundations as the National Endowment for The Arts. After having queried programmers on their interest in your proposed project, contact appropriate funding sources. Many writers consider the low fees and small production budgets a fair trade for creative freedom and the chance to contribute to quality programming.

➤ *Documentaries, Industrial, Educational and Training Films*
122 The non-broadcast audio-visual industry may employ more writers than the film and television industries combined. Research the industry of your interest and contact local production facilities for lists of producers working in that area. Local film commissions may also have a detailed list of such companies. Some schools and corporations have video or in-house educational managers you can contact. Access is surprisingly easy (a premium is placed on enthusiasm and almost any writing sample will do) although the pay is usually low.

➤ *Public Access Television*
Every citizen (writers included) has the right to take advantage of the public access station in his particular city to create his own

---

ALTERNATIVE MARKETS AT A GLANCE:

- **Animation**
- **Children's Programming**
- **Cable Television**
- **Non-Dramatic Programming**
- **Syndication**
- **Interactive Multi-media**
- **The Foreign Markets**
- **Daytime Serials (soaps)**
- **PBS**
- **Documentaries, Industrials, Educational and Training Films**
- **Public Access Television**
- **Radio**

programming. For your 15 minutes of TV fame, check your phone directory for the cable companies in your area and inquire about their public access programming. Many provide training, equipment and even technical support.

➢ *Radio*

Radio has enjoyed a proud history of drama, comedy, horror and suspense programming long before television was invented. Contact your local radio stations for employment guidelines and opportunities. For minimum terms and conditions of the Writers Guild Radio Agreement, contact the Guild Contracts Department.

123

Chapter 9
ADAPTATIONS AND TRUE STORIES

Half of the screenplays nominated for Writers Guild of America Awards or Academy Awards are for works *based upon material previously produced or published*. And television has an infatuation with dramas based on real people and true stories culled from the headlines. For the writer who desires to tap into this rich well-spring of ready-to-wear character and story, certain rudimentary guidelines can save valuable time and costly legal fees.

ADAPTATIONS OF PREVIOUSLY PRODUCED
OR PUBLISHED WORK

Good story material may be found to be as near as your own bookshelves or the dusty back room of a neighborhood used book store. Of course, to adapt a novel, play or other written or produced material for the screen, you must first secure the underlying rights, usually referred to as the *motion picture, television and allied rights* in and to the material to be adapted. These rights are severable from the bundle of rights encompassed by the copyright and are normally retained by the author when publication or live theater rights are sold. Acquiring these rights may require you to put on your producer's hat. Don't be intimidated; as some executives say, a producer is only "someone who knows a writer."

For **books**, a simple phone call or letter to *the subsidiary rights or ancillary rights division* of the publisher, or a letter to the author addressed in care of the publisher, should establish if the film rights are available. If they are, determine who owns or controls the copyright and has the power to grant such rights to third parties such as yourself. If the book or play you seek is not a recent publication (e.g., a book 40 or 50 years old might catch your fancy), you may find that the publisher is out of business or is under new management and the information you desire may not be available or readily forthcoming. In this case, you will have to go directly to the author.

Your local library should stock author directories that may be helpful, including the *Writers Directory*, which lists writers from around the world who have at least one work published in English, and *Contemporary Authors,* which at 165 volumes and listing over 100,000 authors may be the most complete source of author information available; for information about either book, contact Gale Research, toll-free at 800-877-4253. You can also communicate with The National Writers Union (212-254-0279) or The Authors Guild (212-563-5904); either will access their membership files to help you locate an author.

For **best sellers,** past or present, it is best to invest in a copyright check by an attorney versed in copyright law. Two firms that are well known for their expertise in title searches on literary properties are Thompson & Thompson and Brylofsky & Cleary, both based in Washington, D.C. and accessible through their own web sites. The U.S. Copyright Office charges only $20 an hour to search its indexes for information on copyright ownership and/or assignments, or you can do a search yourself through an established checking service like the Library of Congress (202-707-3000) or other companies offering the service (for a small fee) on the Internet. If film rights do appear to be available, you will want to know if such rights have been previously transferred and to whom (namely, producers—have they already been shopped in Hollywood with no success). Keep in mind that since copyright owners are not required to register their work, even the best research may prove inconclusive.

Obtaining rights to a bestseller can be expensive (tens of thousands of dollars), so you will likely want an agent or lawyer to help you craft a deal that is fair to all concerned. For a lesser-known work, the author or his representative may be inclined to grant a writer a favorable arrangement since your interest may help sell the film rights to a dormant novel. With both parties going on good faith, the option fee can be as little as one dollar (or, it can even be free), and a one page deal memo is often the only documentation needed to get the ball rolling.

The Writers Guild has carved out a **"no option" exception** to their minimum payment schedule for a work targeted for television, where a few phone calls may serve to cover the universe of potential buyers. In such cases, option money need not be paid to the writer for the period during which the potential purchaser of the rights actively seeks financing for the project. This practice is referred to as an *if-come* deal. In such a deal, a purchase price, while agreed upon beforehand, is only paid upon setting the project up at a network or other television venue.

To adapt a **stage play,** contact the author or his agent and proceed as above.

To embark on a **sequel or remake** of a previously produced motion picture, begin your rights inquiry with the distributor. In most cases, your quest will end there as well. (Studios are not keen on unsolicited attempts to exploit their libraries.) But don't be dissuaded if you truly believe in the project; you may spark a renewed interest in a previously forgotten or ignored gem. While the studio is under no legal obligation to connect you to the project they own, the executives may work with you if you provide a *truly novel and substantial twist* in story or approach—in which case, an *implied contract* will arise to protect you against the studio exploiting your ideas without compensation. (An implied contract is a legal fiction; consult your lawyer if you suspect it may apply in your case.)

Finally, if the rights you seek are not available, you can still contact the current owner and offer to share your vision and enthusiasm for the material; you just might land a contract to perform writing services on the project.

. . . .

You can *write* a screen adaptation of any published or produced work without acquiring the rights. But, you can't *sell* your screenplay based on that work without them (unless you sell it to someone who already owns or plans to acquire those rights). Any other buyer will require a clear and complete chain of title from the "based upon" material through to the final draft screenplay. Still, you can always use your adaptation as a *writing sample* to showcase your talent at adapting plot, characters and dialogue to the screen. However, such a work may offer little hint of your talent for creating story and character from scratch.

127

. . . .

THE LIMITS OF COPYRIGHT: PUBLIC DOMAIN

Copyright is not granted in perpetuity. When it expires, the work falls into the public domain. This means it is up for grabs by anyone—for free. (Witness the recent host of films based on the works of Jane Austen. The writers who brought her novels to the screen were paid—not Austen's heirs.)

You don't have to go back to Jane Austen's time to find public domain material. *For work created before January 1, 1978,* the copyright survives for 28 years after the registration date or the date the work was first offered in the marketplace. The copyright is renewable for a term of 47 years (effective with the Copyright Act of 1976), for a total protectable term of 75 years. However, due to neglect or oversight, many copyrights are not renewed.

For works registered with the copyright office or first offered in the marketplace after 1978, the copyright term is for the life of the author plus 75 years. For joint authorship of a work (the creation of which is deemed not to be separable) the 75 years runs from the demise of the last surviving partner. In the case of a work "for hire," the protected term is 95 years from publication. When these terms expire, the work falls into the public domain and is free for the taking without permission or payment.

ADAPTING TRUE STORIES

In writing classes across America, students are urged to delve into their personal experience to find material about which they can write with knowledge and passion. Do you hate your boss? Write a thinly veiled character in his likeness and let the world know what you think of him. Did your girlfriend leave you for another woman? And poor you left with only those juicy secrets shared into the night. . . it beats seven years of therapy, doesn't it? But what if they recognize themselves in your work and decide to sue you? Doesn't the First Amendment protect freedom of speech and aren't you, as an artist, allowed a little artistic license with the facts? What about libel? You're only writing the truth and isn't the truth considered an absolute defense to a libel action? Or, what if you believe you have found the perfect subject for an MOW from yesterday's head-line news: the cheerleader mom who plots to blot out her daughter's competition or the beauty contestant found strangled in the base-ment of her parent's home. What rights must you obtain to depict those people in a movie and why?

128

   Fine Print Caveat: what follows, for reasons of brevity and ease of comprehension, is an overview of the subject. It does not at-tempt to cover all the intricacies, exceptions and technical minu-tia of the applicable legalities and their exceptions. For a legal opin-ion on your specific circumstances, you should consult with an entertainment attorney.

The Law of Libel

The law of libel protects against false written statements, commu-nicated to another, which damage the reputation of the defamed person or entity, or subjects him/it to hatred, contempt or ridicule. (The law of slander applies to the spoken word.) The deceased are excepted; you cannot libel the dead because defamation is a per-sonal right which does not descend to the estate. Defamation of the deceased, could, however, lead to liability to members of his family, partners in his business or others directly damaged by your libelous statements.

   There is also an exception for so-called "**public figures.**" In order that the press may freely publish opinions and criticism about in-dividuals in the public eye (politicians, celebrities or other subjects of media attention), the published statement must *not only* be false to be actionable, but the writer or publisher of the statement must have either known it to be false or have held a negligent and reck-less disregard for whether or not it was false.

Even if everything you've written about an individual can be proven to be true, you may still have legal problems. The rights of privacy and publicity may carve out exceptions to your ability to protect yourself with even the veil of truth.

The Right of Privacy

While libel seeks to protect a person's reputation, the right of privacy seeks to protect an individual's damaged feelings.

Even if they are true, if facts are revealed which are "highly offensive" to a person of "ordinary sensibilities" and are of a nature to which the public has "no legitimate concern," they are *not* protected by the "truth" defense to a libel action.

And, there is yet another weapon given to the aggrieved and sensitive victim of the poison pen: the law of **false light**— a close cousin to libel law, false light has all the characteristics of the law respecting invasion of privacy. A false light lawsuit must prove not only that materially false facts objectionable to a reasonable person have been published (a term of art extending to any medium), but also that the way those facts have been presented has placed the complaining individual in a false light in the public eye, hurting his feelings or interfering with his ability to exist peacefully in the community. A public figure must also satisfy the "knowingly false or reckless disregard for the truth" criteria outlined above to successfully sue under this admittedly murky legal theory.

It may be true that your girlfriend engages in kinky sexual activity, but the law does not condone your revealing the sordid details to the world. Of course, if your true love is sadly departed, that's another matter; like libel, an individual's right of privacy ends with death.

129

The Right of Publicity

Recognized in about half of the country, including the entertainment capitals of California, New York and Florida, the right of publicity protects against the unauthorized use of a person's name, face, voice or image for commercial benefit. You may not, for example, appropriate the likeness of Kevin Costner to help sell your video spoof on golf without his prior approval or consent. Moreover, this is a right that can survive the individual—it is capable of being passed down to heirs and estates. (You can't put that likeness of W.C. Fields on a cereal box without paying a royalty to the attorney paid to administer the Fields estate's right of publicity.)

As you may guess from the above examples, these are not often screenplay problems, as the First Amendment protects the use of names and likenesses in that arena. But if your work is destined for multimedia exposure, such as on billboards or games used for "purposes of trade or advertising" you may have legalities to consider.

OBTAINING RELEASES OR ACQUIRING
THE RIGHTS TO LIFE STORIES

Unless the real-life person you intend to portray is a public figure or deceased and you don't have a prevaricating or malicious bone in your body, the rights of privacy and of publicity and laws against defamation make it advisable to obtain, in writing, the rights to his life story and a release of liability for your portrayal of that life.

If you can't manage to obtain a free release (for a limited period and with payment of a stated sum due should you sell the project), you may have to buy it. This usually involves an option and a purchase price attached to an exclusive term (say, one year). During that term, you have the right to seek the development and production of a film based on that true story. If you fail to exercise the option, all rights revert back to the individual from whom they were obtained.

What you are buying is his complete cooperation, and that of his family and heirs, in depicting the events of his life, including your access to private conversations and writings (such as letters and diaries). And no matter how he pleads for it, **never give him script approval**.

Any such agreement should also include the following:

1. A representation that the person understands he is giving the right and permission to depict the events of his life in a movie or television film and that the purchaser of those rights (or his assignee) has the right to embellish, fictionalize, dramatize and adapt the facts of that life story in any manner in which he chooses, at his sole discretion.

2. A representation and warranty that he agrees never to bring suit in any court of law in any venue based on defamation and invasion of rights of privacy or publicity.

3. That the rights granted are fully assignable to any other person or entity.

A bit of paperwork, sure—but better than the potential legal liability from a film based on the life of an uncompensated, living, breathing, sensitive and angry individual. Besides, a studio or network may demand nothing less. It is common practice for producers of biographies, fact-based fiction, true stories pulled from the headlines, etc., to require the writer to *annotate as to source* each line of dialogue, each twist and turn of the plot, every detail of setting or characterization that is not totally invented.

Annotation requires the writer to substantiate the source of every non-fictionalized word, whether by taped interviews or courtroom transcripts or from double and triple substantiation by witnesses and testimony to actual events or conversations. In some cases, the writer may create a scene necessary for plot or character development and annotate it by showing that, from what he can prove was said or done, the character in this circumstance *could have, would have* or *should have* displayed the character traits exhibited.

CONCLUSION

As the above may serve to illustrate, there can be no clear rules in an area of the law that seeks to assign monetary damages for bruised egos and tarnished reputations. Perhaps free speech and literal truth give license to say that Miss Milky Way has put on so many pounds that her title refers to a candy bar rather than an asteroid belt. But remember—anyone can bring a lawsuit and people that are hurt badly enough by someone generally do. In the end, being right or ruled non-liable may be little consolation to you for the lost time and legal fees incurred defending yourself.

Where real people are concerned, your best protection is in your art. **Fictionalize.** Use your relatives, friends and enemies as springboards, not as substitutes, for your imagination. Change men to women, jocks to nerds, doctors to lawyers. If someone has to stretch to identify himself, he'll have a hard time getting a lawyer, much less a court, to find merit in his case. And you'll likely sleep a lot better.

131

Chapter 10
SELLING YOUR SCREENPLAY OR TELEPLAY: THE DEALS

PART ONE: FEATURE FILMS

In February 1999, Sony-owned Columbia Pictures made an announcement: henceforth, it would grant a select group of top screenwriters a share of the gross revenue of the movies they scripted. "Without writers, we'd have nothing," Columbia President Amy Pascal was quoted as saying. "They're the foundation of the movie business." Industry reaction was swift: "First, they broke the $20 million mark for actors and now this—and for writers; please, not for writers!" Of course, nobody said that out loud; rather, the competition rushed to point out that writers *deserved* to share in the success of their blockbusters, along with the many stars, directors, producers and studios that have been gross profit participants for years. It was just that, well, these are rough times in tinseltown; there's not all that much profit to go around, is there?

Joe Eszterhas wrote *Basic Instinct* on a manual typewriter in three weeks and sold it to Carolco for $3.5 million. Later, he was handed $4 million in cash by a Las Vegas investor and an equal amount by a major studio for verbal pitches of high-concept ideas (both films were bombs: *Showgirls* and *An Alan Smithee Film: Burn Hollywood Burn*). Is this business great, or what?

133

To be sure, Hollywood is feeling the worldwide recession just like everyone else. Development deals are down 80 percent at some studios. Production companies may still promise the world for a "high concept" screenplay but, in reality, the producers only pay off when—and if—they can get a studio to pick up the tab. And although the trades still report million dollar spec sales on the front page, the actual purchase price is usually pared down considerably before the deal closes (though it's in no one's interest to relay *that* bit of news to the public.) To be sure, good material will always command a price. As proven by the last Writers' strike, the industry would grind to a halt without it. If your screenplay is hot enough to attract a bidding war among eager buyers, the sky is the limit. If not, even if they love your script, a new writer can usually expect not much more than Writers Guild minimum, plus 10 percent (to cover the cost of your agent).[1]

One high-ranking studio executive threatened that Columbia's deal with the writing elite "is going to force us to take more chances on newer, less expensive writers." From his mouth to God's ear.

Not that that's chump change. Effective May, 1999, the minimum payment for an original screenplay, *including* treatment (for a film budgeted at $2,500,000 or more) is $82,444. Of course, after splitting that with your writing partner and after paying the agent, attorney, Guild, IRS and all relevant taxes, your windfall may not be enough to retire on. You also may not get it all at once; outright purchases are becoming as extinct as the T-Rex.

This makes it all the more important for you to understand—and to have that understanding clearly set forth in a writing signed by all parties—what amount of money you are to receive should an option taken on your work not be exercised, should your writing services be terminated or should the movie you've written never be made. **The first written agreement among buyer and writer (or employer and writer) that delineates these and other crucial bargaining points is usually set forth in a brief "deal memo."**

A. The Deal Memo
The deal memo is a written confirmation of the fundamental terms of any purchase or employment agreement. While giving the appearance of an informal letter (often only one or two pages long), the deal memo is a binding agreement between the parties and governs all later writings on the subject. In practice, it is sometimes the only document the parties will ever actually sign. It should, therefore, be as complete as possible and fully executed, with all essential deal points in place and purchase monies or commencement monies paid before any submission of original material is permitted or writing services are begun.

If the deal memo is for the purchase of literary material, it should clearly set forth the rights being granted, the purchase price, any bonus or contingent payments that apply, provisions for screen credit and other creative rights, including any turnaround provisions or rewrite obligations to the original writer on the part of the buyer.

---

[1] Portions of the Schedule of Minimums of the Writers Guild of America 1998 Theatrical and Television Basic Agreement for both features and television are printed at the end of this chapter.

If the deal memo sets forth an employment agreement, it should clearly state the services to be performed, the payment due for those services, exactly what you are required to deliver in order to get paid, to whom, where and when such delivery is to be made and a complete payment schedule. The writer should also be made aware of any other writers on the project—whether previous, simultaneous or subsequent to the writer's contribution—and the ownership status of any source material supplied to the writer.

Most deal memos contemplate further, more detailed written agreements by the parties. Following are the two basic contractual formats all screenwriters should become familiar with: the *option/purchase agreement* (whereby the rights to your literary work is acquired by a third party), and the two most common *writer employment agreements*—the development deal and the step deal. (Note especially the various forms of compensation payable under either contractual arrangement and the provisions affording writers greater creative control over their work product.)

B. Option/Purchase Agreements

A Literary Purchase (or Assignment of All Rights) agreement can be lengthy, but it is fairly self-explanatory. Pared down to its essentials, the writer sells the motion picture, television and allied rights (or other negotiated rights) to his screenplay and receives money in exchange. If the writer is a member of the WGA or dealing with a company signatory to the Minimum Basic Agreement, applicable minimum terms and purchase prices are set. However, most producers (and even studios) are reluctant to lay out the full price for material only to find out later that their enthusiasm has waned or is not shared by others (such as bankable stars). They'll "option" it instead.

➤ The Option Agreement

In an option agreement, the writer receives a fraction of the agreed-upon purchase price in exchange for granting the producer the exclusive right—over a given period of time (the option period)—to rewrite, package and/or make the financial arrangements for the production of the material. At the end of the option period, the option owner can:

- Exercise the option by paying the balance of the purchase price—thereby gaining ownership of the material, in which case the writer has no more control over it (subject to contractual exceptions); or

- Pay an additional fee to extend the option (if the deal allows for that); or

135

- Allow the option to lapse, in which case all rights to the material revert back to the writer, who keeps the option fee.

An option agreement must be in a writing executed by all parties and is customarily attached to a fully negotiated and detailed Literary Purchase Agreement which becomes effective when the option is exercised. Without an already agreed-upon price and definite terms for the purchase of the movie rights, the option is, on its face, too vague to be enforceable.

For years, this was business as usual in Hollywood; option fees kept a writer going between sales or assignments. Today, despite a booming economy and yearly theatrical box office grosses totaling $65 billion and climbing, studio chiefs worry about runaway costs and are looking for ways to tighten the belt; one casualty has been the slow death of the option fee. Today, producers want a *free* option—maybe even a free rewrite in the bargain. And it isn't that they are necessarily cheap; the real cause lies with the changing nature of the business itself.

Many screenplays are developed but few are produced. Since the average cost of production hovers around $53.5 million, executives in charge of giving the green light to films tend to get picky—they like to window shop but they rarely buy. When the deep pockets cut back on their development slate, it is the independent producers who feel the pinch. Option fees and script development costs—if unreimbursed—can quickly drain the resources of the most well-heeled production company. Even established producers will offer only a small sum against a **set-up fee** payable when a studio or other financier signs onto the project.

Unsolicited submissions to opportunistic producers willing to "shop" a project they do not own—a clear contravention of Writers Guild policy—has been a key factor in the serious decline in option payments to writers, particularly new writers without representation. To protect yourself from this practice, see the methods outlined in the section on the Independent Producer in Chapter 8.

➢ *Standard Terms*

If an option agreement is proposed to you, terms might involve an **option payment** of perhaps 10 percent of the purchase price (as a rule of thumb), although options have been had for as little as a dollar or for as much as several hundred thousand dollars. The payment covers an **option period**—typically one year with the right to renew for a second year at a similar payment. The first option payment is often expressly *applicable* against the purchase price, while any subsequent option payment should be made *not applicable* to the purchase price. (There would otherwise be no incentive for the option owner to exercise and pay the full purchase price; he could just keep his money in the bank and pay the writer off in small yearly amounts until a film based on the work is made.)

Following is the compensation package of a recent option of a spec screenplay written by a first time writer as set forth in a deal memo executed by a well-known producer. The array of payments possible in negotiating for the rights to an original screenplay are well represented:

> $5,000 for a one-year option from the date of execution against a $75,000 purchase price, with an option to renew for another year for an additional $5,000, non-applicable against the purchase price, plus a contingent payment of 2.5 percent of 100 percent of the net profits of any film based on the work, the definition of net profits to be no less favorable than any other net profit participant in the film, plus a bonus of $50,000 payable upon the commencement of principle photography of any film based on the work in which the writer receives sole screenplay credit or $25,000 payable upon the commencement of principle photography of any film based on the work in which the writer receives screenplay credit shared with not more than one other person, plus an additional $50,000 bonus, payable upon the commencement of principle photography, if the final budgeted cost of the film exceeds $10 million, plus $100,000 deferred, payable out of first profits, *pari passu* with any other deferred profit participant.

137

Naturally, if the option is never exercised, the writer keeps the initial $5,000 and the rest of the paperwork is moot.

On the following pages is an option agreement, in letter form, which was recently negotiated by a literary agency for a respected writer/client. In this instance, the writer desired a working relationship with the producing company and was willing to forego an initial option payment in exchange for other concessions; terms included or excluded may, therefore, be peculiar to this particular bargain. For space considerations, exhibits are not reprinted here, but all were consistent with "boiler-plate" language typically found in such option/purchase agreements.

· ·

OPTION AGREEMENT

Date _____

Dear _____ :

In consideration of the mutual covenants and undertakings set forth herein and for ten dollars and other good and valuable consideration, receipt of which you hereby acknowledge, we mutually agree as follows:

1. You grant to the undersigned (hereinafter "Producer") the exclusive and irrevocable right and option (hereinafter the "Option") to purchase, exclusively and forever, the motion picture, television and allied rights (all as are more particularly set forth in Exhibit "A" [Assignment Of All Rights] attached hereto and made a part hereof) in and to the unpublished, original screenplay written by you currently entitled "X" (hereinafter the "Work"). In the event Producer shall exercise such Option in accordance with the terms hereof, Exhibit "A" shall become a binding and valid agreement between us.

2. Producer may exercise said Option at any time during a period of one year commencing on the above date, and may extend the period during which said Option may be exercised for an additional one year term only by payment to you of the sum of Fifteen Thousand Dollars ($15,000) on or before the expiration of the initial one year option period, time being of the essence to both any extension and exercise of the Option. You agree that Producer may during the option period, as the same may be extended, at the sole risk and expense of Producer and without prejudice to your rights if the Option should not, for any reason, not be exercised, undertake or cause others to undertake production and pre-production activities, including but not limited to changing, altering, rewriting or in any other manner adapting the Work, in connection with all or any of the rights granted by you hereunder.

3. Producer shall exercise the Option granted to it hereunder only by giving you written notice of its election so to do and by paying to you as full consideration for all rights granted or conveyed by you to Producer the following:

(a) As fixed compensation, the sum of One Hundred and Fifty Thousand Dollars ($150,000), less the option payment, if made, set forth above, such sum to accrue and be payable to you, one-half concurrently with the exercise of such option and one-half upon commencement of principle photography of the first feature motion picture or movie-for-television based upon the Work (hereinafter the "Film");

(b) As deferred compensation, the additional sum of Seventy Five Thousand Dollars ($75,000) payable only out of and against first profits, if any, from the production and exploitation of the Film, and payable pari passu with any and all other deferments out of first profits of the Film, it being understood that first profits shall be computed and deducted prior to the computation of any other participation in profits; provided, however, that any participation in box office or distributor's gross proceeds shall not be deemed a participation in profits for the purposes hereof;

(c) As contingent compensation, an amount equal to ten percent (10%) of one hundred percent (100%) of the "Net Profits" of the Film, which amount Producer may reduce, at its option, to seven and one-half percent (7-1/2%) of one hundred percent (100%) of said Net Profits by making payment to you of the Seventy Five Thousand Dollar ($75,000) deferment as set forth in sub-paragraph (b) above as a cash payment upon commencement of principal photography of the Film. "Net Profits" shall be defined, computed, accounted for and paid without deduction of any participation in profits except for first profits and on terms no less favorable to you than those accorded Producer or any other participant in profits in any agreement relating to the financing and distribution of the Film; provided, however, that any participation in box office or distributor's gross proceeds shall not be deemed a participation in profits for the purposes hereof;

139

4. You agree to render your services in good faith to Producer at its written request, and at two times (2X) the appropriate Writers Guild Minimum therefore, for one rewrite and/or one polish of the Work in accordance with the instructions of any director contracted to direct the Film.

5. You agree that all representations, covenants, warranties and indemnities set forth in Exhibit "B" attached hereto shall be deemed incorporated herein and made a part hereof as if the same were set forth in full herein.

6. In the event Producer exercises the option set forth above, the following additional terms shall be contained in the formal documentation by which Producer shall acquire the rights in and to the Work as set forth above:

(a) Retained rights. You will retain live television, radio, stage and publication rights, subject to standard exceptions and holdbacks which shall be accorded to Producer, its heirs or assigns, including the following specific terms:

(i) Publication rights subject to a 7,500 word exception;

(ii) Radio rights subject to a holdback of five (5) years from the exercise date of the Option or three (3) years from the release of the Film, whichever should first occur, and subject to a fifteen minute exception;

(iii) Live television rights and dramatic stage rights subject to the standard five (5) and seven (7) year holdbacks.

(b) Remake and Sequel Rights. You grant to Producer the right to produce remakes and sequels of any Film and Producer agrees to pay to you an amount equal to thirty-three and one-third percent (33-1/3%) and fifty percent (50%), respectively, of the purchase price, including deferments, but not including contingent compensation as set forth above, upon each separate exercise of the applicable rights.

(c) Television Series Rights. You grant to Producer television series rights, provided that these rights may not be exercised unless the Film has been made and released first. Should Producer exercise such series rights, a per segment royalty shall be paid to you as follows: Fifteen Hundred Dollars ($1,500) for each segment thirty minutes or less in length, Two Thousand Dollars ($2,000) for each segment more than thirty minutes but not more than sixty minutes, and Two Thousand Five Hundred Dollars ($2,500) for each segment over sixty minutes in length. Additionally, One Hundred Percent (100%) of any such royalties shall be paid and spread equally over the first five (5) reruns of any such segment. Additionally, you will receive ten percent (10%) of one hundred percent (100%) of the net profits from any television series and for any spin-offs one-half (1/2) of the royalties and rerun payments plus five percent (5%) of one hundred percent (100%) of the net profits from any such spin-off. Also, you retain rights of first negotiation and first refusal to write any pilot for any such television series, such rights to be exercisable by you in writing within fourteen (14) days following written notice to you by Producer or its assignee of any such contemplated pilot.

(d) Credit. You shall receive credit in accordance with The Writers Guild Basic Agreement, as the same may from time to time be amended or modified (herein the "WGA Agreement"), on all positive prints of the Film and on all paid advertising issued by or under the control of Producer, subject to normal exceptions and exclusions; provided that in any event you shall receive exclusive story credit on the Film. On any television series or spin-off, you, alone or with no more than one other author, shall be accorded separate card credit as Creator or Creator of the characters on which the series is based.

(e) Health, Pension and Welfare. Producer shall, in a timely manner, pay the Employer's share of all health, pension and welfare benefits to which you may be entitled hereunder in accordance with the WGA Agreement.

7. If Producer shall resell the Work to a third party, you shall participate in any profits derived from such sale as follows: The sum paid to you for the Work shall be deducted from any such sales price and you shall receive ten percent (10%) of the remainder. In addition, any such third party shall be made to assume all obligations to you hereunder and no such sale shall relieve Producer of its obligations to you hereunder unless such sale is to one of the so-called majors in the field of motion picture distribution, in which case Producer shall be relieved of its obligations to you hereunder.

It is contemplated that we shall enter into more formal agreements reflecting the terms set forth above as well as all other usual terms and conditions not inconsistent herewith as are customarily contained in agreements of this nature. In the interim, this letter shall constitute a binding agreement between the parties and may only be modified by a subsequent writing between the parties.

If the forgoing reflects our understanding and agreement, please sign in the space provided below.

. . . .

In the event the option is exercised, the result is the same as if the work is sold outright: the writer loses all control over it, subject to contractual exceptions. This means that the new owner of the material can change it, sell it, film it or discard it. And, the writer may never see or hear from the producer again.

Fortunately for the writer, there is one very common exception:

➤ *The Turnaround Provision.*
There are a variety of reasons why many scripts are developed and so few made. Quality isn't the only factor. The "heat" may be off a story genre or an actor for whom the project was developed; executives or producers who championed the project may have changed studios or agendas or just lost interest in "trying to make the story work." In any case, many such projects are placed in a state of limbo the studios call "turnaround" (and many writers call an early grave).

A typical turnaround clause in the sale of literary material allows the writer only a set period of time—at some future date and under certain conditions—to "buy back" his abandoned work. Though not every contract allows this second chance, a good lawyer will usually negotiate this reversion provision for his client. The writer may then try to set up the script with some other buyer, subject to reimbursing the original buyer for an agreed-upon price. (Usually, the reimbursement is for the purchase price paid to the writer plus, if a film is made, all other expenses and fees attributable to the project, including rewrites, overhead, interest, etc.)

As this can sometimes be prohibitively expensive, the Writers Guild has built into its agreement with producers a little-known provision that allows a writer of original material a two year window of opportunity in which to buy back a script at the *original purchase price* from the current owner who, after a five year period, does not have the work in active development. And the writer does not have to dig into his own pocket for the cash; the re-purchase monies can be from any buyer the writer has solicited.

C. Employment Contracts

In one type of employment agreement (known as a **flat deal**), a writer is hired to write for a specified period of time; usually a weekly paycheck for a week's work. The Writers Guild has set minimum amounts payable for this labor and non-members can use the figures as a guide for their negotiations.

In the more common type of employment agreement, the writer must deliver a certain work (outline, treatment, screenplay, rewrite or polish) within a specified period of time. Typical delivery periods might be six weeks for a treatment or beat outline, 12 weeks for a first draft, six weeks for a rewrite and three weeks for a polish. While this employment agreement is often known as a "development deal," there are actually two distinct types of arrangements:

142

➤ *The Development Deal*

As the name implies, this is an agreement by a producer to pay a writer to develop an outline, treatment or script from material or concepts initiated by the writer or some third party, or to adapt a novel, true story or some other work already owned by the studio/producer. The writer is guaranteed payment whether or not the producer is satisfied with the work and whether or not the work makes it to production. If the employer is dissatisfied, his only recourse is to not hire the writer again.

It is also common for a development deal to be made part of an outright purchase agreement for original material. In fact, should you sell your story, treatment, screenplay or other work for screen or television, it is prudent to also include in the same agreement an assignment to further develop or rewrite such material. This will keep you in the process for as long as possible, ideally enabling you to champion your original vision and see it fully realized.

. . . .

For WGA members, an automatic first rewrite must be offered to the writer of original material. In addition, subject to certain exceptions, such writer must also be offered the opportunity to perform an additional set of revisions if a new director or principal actor is later assigned to the project. And, this employment

mandated by the Guild has a further added benefit: It not only allows the writer to qualify for pension, health and welfare benefits (all such benefits being tied to employment), but pursuant to a recent ground-breaking change secured under the latest Guild contract, for the first time ever contributions to the writer's Pension Plan and Health Fund will also adhere to the underlying purchase of "literary material" (as defined by the WGA MBA)—provided the purchase is from a writer also employed to perform at least one rewrite or polish of such material. For this reason, if for none other, *every WGA writer is strongly advised not to waive his/her right to perform such additional writing services.*

. . . .

Should you be assigned to rewrite your script, be forewarned: Should the option on your screenplay expire and the rights revert to you or should the buyer of your screenplay fail to produce it and you are able to reacquire it, you will get your screenplay back—but not the rewrite. The producer (or studio) will keep your work-for-hire. Thus, some of your best work and brightest ideas on your own screenplay may be lost to you. A solution is to put a provision into your contract that ties your rewrite to your original work as part of any reversion of rights agreement. Of course, you or a subsequent buyer of the screenplay may need to reimburse any monies paid for the rewrite (or some other mutually agreed-upon sum).

143

Regrettably, some development deals do not carry the prospect of being paid at all. Producers may concoct all sorts of arrangements to lock up rights to a screenplay or the writer's most inventive creations, while the writer is made to execute endless rewrites (often for a nominal fee or no fee at all!). Hence, the creation of the phrase "stuck in Development Hell!"

Beware of producers who promise you big things down the line under the proviso that you do a "little" work on your screenplay (or someone else's)—"just polish it up a bit for me—c'mon, it's as easy as filling in the dots." Of course, you're flattered someone wants your work and you want to please him. To be fair, most first dealings with indie producers may involve no money at all changing hands—the producer may ask you for a free option period or want you to fix "that problem in the second act." Particularly if you're a newcomer desperate to break in, you may not want to thumb your nose at someone who shows sincere interest in your work.

Sometimes passion is a worthwhile trade-off for money. But what else do you get in the bargain? Does the producer have a star or director they plan to attach to your project? If you believe that the producer has connections that can increase your script's chances of gaining attention in the marketplace and if you believe that the producer will actively promote you and your work, maybe you'll choose to do a rewrite if necessary—as long as it's on your material.

But, **never write for free when it involves rewrite services on someone else's work or on ideas supplied by a producer** (who can then claim he owns the underlying material and thus leave you with nothing). That is, **no** rewriting, **for anyone**, except yourself. As Samuel Johnson said, "No man but a blockhead ever wrote, except for money." Tell the producer to have his secretary "fill in the dots" if it's so easy.

➤ *The Step Deal*

This is a development deal in which the writer is paid for the work in stages (story, treatment, first draft, etc.), with the producer having specified *reading periods* (typically ranging from one week to one month) in-between each step to consider the work; this also gives the producer the concurrent right to exit the deal at any stage. It is the writer's responsibility to clarify the exact writing services to be performed, how many "steps" are guaranteed and the monies to be paid for each step.

A professional writer is a paid writer. "If we work for hire, we are hacks. If we work for nothing, we are chumps," noted one contemporary pundit. All too often, the value placed on your work is the price paid for it.

The step deal is usually a flat deal; the monies payable to the writer for each step are guaranteed for work actually performed through that step. (The Guild's sample Writer's Theatrical Short-Form Contract appears at the end of this chapter; a version for use in loan-outs is also available.) For example, the writer may be hired to write and deliver an original story (perhaps based on a pitch he previously made) for a fee of $10,000. In the next step, the writer is employed to write a treatment or long outline based on his story for an additional fee of $20,000. Perhaps an additional fee of $30,000 will be payable for a first draft screenplay, with a balance of $30,000 upon delivery of a final draft. There may even be a polish step—a sort of mini-rewrite in which dialogue is improved or scenes paired down to meet budget restrictions—for an additional $10,000. That's $100,000 altogether for the final polished script—a fair sum.

But the writer must be vigilant: In a typical step deal, the writer is only entitled to be paid for work performed for a particular step in the writing process. The WGA has minimums ("scale") that must be met for every step and encourages writers to make "overscale" deals whenever possible. However, this is no protection for the writer who provides, in the initial story step, the core of the plot, character and structure, only to find himself cut off from other writing services (and money) and replaced by another writer in the later stages. The writer must always keep in mind how much money will be due him if the employer chooses not to renew the writer's services beyond a step in the deal—this is the only money the writer can count on.

You may wish to build in safeguards against being cut too early from a project, especially one born from your concept or your particular take on a producer's concept. For example, while the producer can choose not to use you beyond the treatment stage, your contract can require him to pay you through the first draft stage (or perhaps pay some percentage of what would be owed you). This is known as a "pay or play" deal and it gives employers a strong incentive to keep you on the project.

Also, as you move through the development steps, you can anticipate that you will receive "notes," those helpful suggestions from executives and producers (and just about anyone else). Notes can be valuable or they can be the death of a project (if given by an insecure and fickle employer). You may wish to suggest that all persons give their notes at the same time. Also, if you are asked to change the plot or characters substantially from your pitch or initial story conference, get the executive to initial the requested changes before embarking on the next step. Later, if he claims that the script you delivered wasn't the script he bought, show him the initialed changes. Absent such precautions, you may find yourself the scapegoat in a development process that has slipped out of control.

145

D. Compensation: Fixed, Bonus, Deferred, Royalty and Contingent

➢ *Fixed Compensation*
Every writer has heard the refrain: "Get what you can up front." Up to now, that's what we have been discussing: the *fixed compensation* that a writer receives for the sale of his work. These are the monies payable as option fees, purchase fees and whatever other monies are contractually due and payable even if a movie of the subject screenplay is never made. For example, all Writers Guild minimum payments must be met by a purchaser or employer whenever a screenplay is sold or writing services performed. All work-for-hire is payable upon the delivery of the material contracted for and may not be withheld for any reason.

A contract for the sale of film rights may also provide for *bonuses, deferments, royalties and/or contingent payments;* however these are usually (but not always) tied to the actual production of a film based at least in part upon the writer's material.

➢ *Bonuses*
There are as many bonus possibilities in a contract as the writer's agent or attorney can envision. For example, if a novel is purchased

as the basis for a movie, the author could receive a bonus for each week the book appears on the *New York Times* Best Seller list. For a musical, sales of the soundtrack may trigger writer bonuses. Production bonuses are often offered to a writer who receives sole screenplay credit on the final film; a smaller bonus could apply if the final screen credit is shared by not more than one other writer or writing team or perhaps a sum smaller still if the credit is shared with not more than two other writers or teams, and so on.

➢ *Deferments*

A typical deferment is a sum payable out of the first net monies available to profit participants in the film. When all possible fixed sums have been demanded from the buyer, why not ask for a substantial deferment? Since it is payable only out of the profits of the film (which means the film must be hugely successful), the producer doesn't expect to pay it anyway and he may well grant a deferment to close the deal. If you have a deferment in your contract and the film should become a blockbuster (in terms of revenue in relation to cost), you'll have an easier time getting a settlement of the sums due you than you would in a straight lawsuit over net profits.

➢ *Royalties*

146   Residual payments, sometimes called royalty payments, are due when a film the writer has authored (at least in part) is broadcast in another medium, such as home video or foreign television. Collection of such payments is monitored and administered by the Writers Guild. If you are not a member of the Guild, provision for this payment will be hard to include—it is rare for any contract with a nonsignatory employer to provide for the payment of residuals and it is rarer still for a non-Guild writer to actually collect these residuals.

However, all writers contracts should provide for royalty payments or fixed bonuses should any film based in whole or in part upon the writer's work be used as the basis for a TV series (a "spinoff"), a *sequel* motion picture (following the characters through a new story) or a *remake* motion picture (essentially, the same characters in the same story). These payments are due whether or not the writer is involved in the actual writing of the spinoff, sequel or remake (if the writer is involved, a new payment for new work is negotiated). The royalty fee for spinoffs and sequels is typically 50 percent of the original purchase price, including bonuses; the norm for remakes is 33-1/3 percent.

➢ *Contingent Compensation*

Contingent compensation can be based on:

1. gross receipts;
2. adjusted gross receipts (including gross after breakeven);
3. net profits.

True gross participation (that is, a percentage share of the actual monies collected at the box office) is rare, even for superstar male action heroes. When those in the film business speak of someone getting a gross participation, they are usually referring instead to the payment of an agreed percentage of the gross monies that a distributor receives from the exhibition and exploitation of a film—this is known as "first dollar gross;" no distribution fees are chargeable and either no costs or only selected hard costs of distributing the film are taken "off the top." In practical terms, this category is reserved for very powerful stars whose salary is too large for the production budget or for whom this method of payment is deemed a more accurate determination of their worth. Jack Nicholson, for example, got very wealthy from his gross participation in *Batman*.

Deals based on adjusted gross receipts provide for gross profits less specified distribution expenses (and perhaps a lower distribution fee than would be customarily chargeable). Once the sole prerogative of super-star directors and actors (or some of Hollywood's most successful producers; e.g. Scott Rudin or Brian Grazer), only a few writers (typically writer-producers or writer-directors; e.g. Michael Crichton or Woody Allen) have managed to negotiate gross participation—until Sony-Columbia's recent announcement stunned the movie industry. Pursuant to Columbia's deal, certain screenwriters will receive 2 percent (1 percent for those receiving shared screen credit) of the studio's distribution receipts after it has recouped all of its production and marketing costs. So, for example, if a film has a negative cost (the cost of production) of $50 million and marketing expenses of another $50 million, and the studio's income from all sources of exploitation (including theatrical, television and video) amounts to $200 million, the writer will get 2 percent of $100 million, or $2 million.

147

. . . .

Initially, Columbia extended its deal to a select "power list" of more than 30 top screenwriters (known informally as "The Thursday Night Gang," for the night they met for the purpose of devising a plan to net writers a greater profit share in their movies)—getting in exchange a one-script commitment from each over the next four years. Other writers can "qualify" for the deal if they've received $750,000 for any one writing assignment or $1 million for the sale of a spec script or have been nominated for an Oscar or Writers Guild of America award. According to attorney Alan Wertheimer, who helped negotiate the details of the Columbia deal, approximately 300 writers currently qualify.

. . . .

A popular adjusted gross calculation defines the point of profit sharing as occurring after "**breakeven**" has been reached. Breakeven can range from recovery of the distributor's out-of-pocket costs, including the cost of production, to any other cost the distributor can fathom. In a gross-after-breakeven deal, costs accumulate but cease to be chargeable to the profit participant after the point of breakeven. This differs from "net profits," wherein fees and expenses, including interest, continue to accrue even after the film has attained a profit position.

For most writers, a net profit participation is the contingent payment they can expect—(the back end, or "points" as they are known in the business.) The actual definition of "net profits"—the legal calculation of what receipts from the exploitation of the film are considered "income" and what charges to the film may be deductible as fees and "expenses"—has been known to run to 50 pages in a writer's contract. Yet, as notoriously difficult as net profits are to achieve, they are routinely granted. Therefore, certain negotiating points should be kept in mind.

It is standard practice to calculate net profits *after* first deducting any gross participation. Thus the very payment of adjusted gross profits to a profit participant can single-handedly ensure that "net" profits are never reached. So it was that Eddie Murphy's gross profit participation in *Coming to America* kept that mega-million dollar boxoffice smash technically and legally in the red.

1. Even a new writer, if he demands it, will probably be accorded a percentage of net profits. Percentages from 1 percent to 5 percent are customary, the amount depending on such factors as whether the script is written for hire or is an original spec screenplay sale, etc.

2. Net profits should always be calculated as a percentage of 100 percent of net profits from the picture (e.g. 5 percent of 100 percent), as opposed to owning a share of just "net profits." In the latter case, net may be read as "producer's net," and if the producer receives 50 percent of net (the financier/distributor getting the other half) and then shares that portion with various other net profit participants, such as stars or director, the writer may end up with a part of only 25 percent or less of the actual "net profits" on the film. (In a worst-case scenarios, the percentage may be that of a production company later discovered to be a shell corporation which is not entitled to **any** profits on the picture.)

3. It is sound business practice to tie the writer's definition of net profits and rights of accounting to those of the producer's. There is even a notion of "favored nations" whereby the writer shall be entitled to no less of a favorable definition of net profits than any other participant (director, star) in net profits on the film.

Unfortunately, whatever the writer's definition of net profits, and despite the ever-expanding profit base from the worldwide marketing and exploitation of a film, it will take a hugely successful picture for a net participant to ever see an actual distribution of monies.

The notion of any film actually achieving "profit" continues to be an ethereal concept. Screenwriter William Goldman in his book, *Hype & Glory*, tells of a famous producer who likened film profit to the horizon: "It always recedes as you get closer."

A typical net profit scenario might unfold something like this:

Begin with a $30 million film (well below average cost for a studio picture)—that's the cost of physically making the picture (called the **negative cost**). Now, say there are no gross profit participants on the film and it grosses $300 million at the box office. You're rich, right? Wrong.

Only about half that money—$150 million—is returned to the distributor of the film (e.g., Paramount) as **"rentals."** The other $150 million is the **exhibitor's share** for running the print in the theater (the popcorn sales are like a tip). Then, the distributor takes a **distribution fee** for renting the film to the exhibitor. This fee is based on gross receipts of the film (including video, merchandising and soundtrack income, for example), and is calculated as a percentage of that income, usually averaging 35 percent, but as high as 40 percent for foreign exploitation and for licensing the film to television. (A full distribution fee is often charged even where a subdistributor is employed that charges a fee for its services, even if the subdistributor is the distributor's own affiliate—resulting in double fees being charged to the film!) Even under a conservative calculation, with only a single fee of 35 percent charged, we are left with $97.5 million.

Then comes **distribution expenses** (in studio legalese "all costs relating to the distribution of the film, including without limitation . . ."). These costs will be detailed to include every cost the distributor has incurred, including multiple prints of the film, trucking the prints to theaters, trade shows, festivals, long-distance phone calls made when promoting the film overseas, residual payments to talent, checking costs, collection fees, taxes, etc. The most important of these expenses is **advertising** (trailers, television, print, computer network services). While some

149

distributors try to contain expenses to about one-third the cost of production, aggressive marketing campaigns and promotional tie-ins can easily see the marketing costs exceed the cost of the film itself. And these expenses are not fixed. The more markets to which the film is sold (television, foreign, video, etc.), the more money the film earns, the more costs increase (causing a "**rolling breakeven**"). Hence, there is never a point when the film is *clearly* in profit. (After *Forrest Gump* had grossed more than $300 million at the box office, Paramount Pictures had it on the books at $62 million *in the red* and losing more every day! This was due primarily to the gross participants who siphoned off the income before it could be applied to profit.)

For the sake of argument, let's say that the distributor spent $30 million for prints and advertising and all other expenses. That leaves $67.5 million. Except now we have to deduct that $30 million negative cost. That should still leave $37.5 million to divvy up, right? Wrong again.

The studio adds **overhead** to the actual cost of making the picture (somebody has to pay for secretaries, parking spaces and paper clips). A typical overhead charge can run from 15 percent to 25 percent of the negative cost. Taking the latter figure, that's another $7.5 million. (Expensive paper clips.) There are also "penalty" situations (to keep the production team more budget-conscious) in which—for purposes of calculating profits—the actual cost of production may be doubled when the budget is exceeded by more than 5 or 10 percent. (Since the writer is typically not present during production or post, it seems unfair to charge this against his participation—but that's the one place, of course, where the writer can count on equal treatment.)

Now we have to factor in the **interest**—at a given percentage *over* the bank's prime lending rate (higher than the distributor's actual cost of funds) for all the production costs committed to the film. (You never realized they were just *lending* the money, did you?) As a final kicker, interest is often calculated from the time, years before, when the studio first decided that this might be a good project to undertake. If you know anything about compound interest, you know it could easily exceed the $30 million left. But, just in case it doesn't, the studios might include a clause that charges *interest on overhead,* and then *overhead on interest!* (It takes a good lawyer to crawl out from under that one.)

. . . .

E. Creative Rights

In early 1933, a group of screenwriters met at a social club "for the purpose of discussing the betterment of conditions under which writers work in Hollywood." They sought higher wages, better working conditions, fair credit, and—crucial to all of them—industry recognition and a modicum of dignity for their art, otherwise known as "creative rights." The fruits of that meeting led to the founding of the Screen Writers Guild, known today as the Writers Guild of America. Many personal sacrifices and tortuous strikes later, great strides indeed have been made on behalf of writers. But, writers are still a long way from being viewed as a partner among equals. Studios still hold the copyright to the work of writers, directors still receive the possessory credit "A Film By," original work is rewritten, lines, scenes and whole plots changed at the whim of executives who may never have wielded a pen and, if the writer is invited to the set, it is still considered a privilege.

The battle stubbornly continues for those elusive creative rights. The novice writer who works for or sells his work to a non-signatory company must depend on the negotiating skills of his attorney or agent to remain involved through the rewrite stage—or even to get a seat at the premiere.

The WGA has made progress, however, and the fruits of its labor have been summarized in a checklist (available through the Guild) for use by its members as a reference guide to some of the rights to which they may be entitled under the WGA Minimum Basic Agreement (the "MBA"). While the provisions of the MBA may not always be enforced and while they certainly offer no protection to anyone working for a non-signatory company, that checklist may be used by *all* writers as a bellwether when making deals for their material or their services.

151

The following are possible deal points for writers seeking greater control over their work. They are suggested in part from those gains made by the MBA; they are not intended, however, as a creative rights bible nor should Guild members rely upon them as a substitute for reviewing the actual protection afforded by the MBA.

1. For the sale or option of an original screenplay or teleplay, the writer should be granted the first reasonable opportunity to rewrite the material. In addition, if a new element (e.g., director or star) is added within three years of the rewrite and a new writer has not been assigned, the original writer should get an opportunity to make another set of revisions.

2. If a writer sells or is employed to write an original screenplay or teleplay and the purchaser or employer contemplates replacing that writer, a reasonable opportunity should be provided for all parties to meet and discuss the continuing services of the writer.

3. The writer should have an opportunity to view the director's cut of the film in a time sufficient to allow for any approved suggestions by the writer to be incorporated into the film.

4. Credit, if due, should be included in all publicity and advertising of the film wherever the director of the film receives such credit, in a size and placement no less prominent than that of the director.

5. A credited writer should be included in all aspects of publicity and promotion of the film, including press kits, previews, premieres, film festivals and press junkets.

PART TWO: TELEVISION

As noted, movies for television are often begun with a pitch and are developed through many drafts in order to meet the requirements of the network. As the programmer's needs are much more immediate than in feature films, work schedules are shorter and the pay accordingly less. To the extent possible, payment is made upon delivery or when the network pays its license fee to the employer, the Executive Producer (aka the supplier-producer). However, in no instance should payment be made *contingent* upon delivery to or acceptance by a network, or upon payment being made by the network.

Under such intense writing pressure and close supervision, it is less likely than in features that a writer will be replaced. If replacement is contemplated, pursuant to Guild rules, the creative executive or producer must give the writer an opportunity to meet and discuss his views and attempt to work things out so the writer may continue on the project.

The Schedule of Minimums of the Writers Guild of America 1998 Theatrical and Television Basic Agreement is a fair barometer of compensation levels for most television writing. It is set forth at the end of this chapter, along with the Guild's Standard Form Freelance Television Writer's Employment Contract. Additionally, bonuses discussed above for feature writers can also apply to television writers credited with sole or shared credit. And, there is almost always a special bonus payable should a proposed Movie of the Week be released as a feature film (often, a sum equal to the total amount the writer was paid for the TV movie).

By way of example, here is a typical writer's deal for a story, first draft, two sets of revisions and polish for a television movie:

> $60,000 upon final delivery of the polished teleplay, *plus* a 20 percent production bonus for sole teleplay credit, or a 10 percent bonus for shared teleplay credit, *plus* a 100 percent theatrical release bonus should the film be exhibited first as a feature film domestically or internationally, or 50 percent should the film play as a feature following its initial television exhibition, *plus* a 2 percent net profit participation from all markets.

If a TV movie that was originally intended to stand alone is used as the pilot episode for a series (called a "back door pilot") another set of bonuses is incorporated for the writer as the **creator** of the characters and situation which is now the prototype for the series. (This is similar to the per episode royalties and series production bonus to which the creator of any series—the writer who receives the coveted "Created By" credit—would be entitled.)

To be credited as the creator of a television series usually translates to a hefty net profit (or adjusted gross) participation. But these writers may face the same futile scenario as feature writers when it comes to actually seeing payment. *Hundreds of millions of dollars* in profit can be realized by a successful series (i.e., one that enters its fourth year of original programming) if it is sold to syndication (local programming for each U.S. city or territory and other off-network venues—*each* of which pays a price per episode rivaling the original cost to produce the show). However, significant per-episode deficits (the difference between what it costs to produce the show and the license fee the network pays for the right to air the show) and years of mounting interest often make such dizzying profits a fantasy.

For this reason, most series creators or other writers with the power to demand it usually ask for a **guaranteed advance** against any profit participation to which they may be entitled. Meaning, whenever the production of the show hits a certain point (e.g., the fourth year, the fifth year), a bonus is payable regardless of where the actual series stands in the profit picture.

153

If you've simply written an episode of a series (and thus lack the negotiating clout that attaches to an A-List writer, creator or producer of the show), you can expect WGA minimum and an episode rerun bonus equal to the minimum payment, but no profit participation. These deals are so standard that they are almost always ne-

Television writers are also among the hardest working people in Hollywood. The daily grind of turning out a weekly show—from the "table readings" where as many as 20 or more writers, producers, cast and network staff "fine tune" your first draft to the frequent all-night rewrite sessions—may be one reason why many television writers are secretly banging out spec screenplays on the side.

gotiated on a short form directly with the writer's agent. If a multiple episode assignment is negotiated (a guaranteed number of episodes), a **staff position** may follow.

The possibility of becoming a **"hyphenate"** is a quest of all television series writers. The term refers to the combination of jobs and titles (with commensurate fees) earned by many series staff writers—such as writer-story editor, writer-supervising producer, writer-producer, etc. The goal in television is to eventually make it to **executive producer** of the series. This is where real money from television writing is made.

Remember, in series television, the producing jobs are all held by WRITERS! Besides salaries (which can run from a low of $5,000 per episode for a "consultant" to as high as $50,000 per episode for a series producer or executive producer) the writer-producer is responsible for the look, feel and growth of the show that grants him a creative participation unknown by his counterpart in feature films. Also, guaranteed production bonuses and profit participation on a hit series can ultimately put a writer on an earnings par with such well-known series executive producers as Aaron Spelling (one of the few who is not a writer), David E. Kelley and Jerry Seinfeld & Larry David, to name a few.

WRITERS THEATRICAL SHORT-FORM CONTRACT

Date : _____

1. NAME OF PROJECT:_____ ("Project")

2. NAME/ADDRESS OF COMPANY:_____ ("Company")
   _____
   _____

3. NAME OF WRITER:_____("Writer")
   Social security number _____

4. WRITER'S REPRESENTATIVE:_____

5. CONDITIONS PRECEDENT: [ ] W-4   [ ] I-9   [ ] OTHER, if any

6. COMPENSATION:
   A. GUARANTEED COMPENSATION (see 11, below): $ _____
   B. CONTINGENT COMPENSATION (see 11, below): $ _____
   C. PROFIT PARTICIPATION: IF SOLE WRITING CREDIT, _____% OF
      (NET/GROSS) PROCEEDS; REDUCIBLE FOR SHARED CREDIT
      TO _____% (see 27, below)

7. SPECIFIC MATERIAL UPON WHICH SERVICES ARE TO BE BASED, IF ANY
   (a copy will be sent to Writer under separate cover):

8. OTHER WRITERS EMPLOYED ON SAME PROJECT OR FROM WHOM
   MATERIAL HAS BEEN OPTIONED/ACQUIRED, and dates of material, IF ANY:

155

9. COMPANY REPRESENTATIVE AUTHORIZED TO REQUEST REVISIONS:

10. COMPANY REPRESENTATIVE TO WHOM/PLACE WHERE MATERIAL
    IS TO BE DELIVERED:

11. SERVICES TO BE PERFORMED, INCLUDING NUMBER OF STEPS
    (e.g., story and first draft, two rewrites and a polish):

    A. For step 1:   [ ] GUARANTEED   [ ] OPTIONAL
         Writing period: _____ weeks
         reading period: _____ weeks
         payment due: $_____
         (50% due on commencement, 50% on delivery)

    B. for step 2 (if applicable):   [ ]GUARANTEED   [ ] OPTIONAL
         Writing period: _____ weeks
         reading period: _____ weeks
         payment due: $_____
         (50% due on commencement, 50% on delivery)

    C. for step 3 (if applicable):   [ ] GUARANTEED   [ ] OPTIONAL
         Writing period: _____ weeks
         reading period: _____ weeks
         payment due: $_____
         (50% due on commencement, 50% on delivery)

D. for step 4 (if applicable):   [ ] GUARANTEED   [ ] OPTIONAL
Writing period: _____ weeks
reading period: _____ weeks
payment due: $_____
(50% due on commencement, 50% on delivery)

E. for step 5 (if applicable):   [ ]GUARANTEED   [ ] OPTIONAL
Writing period: _____ weeks
reading period: _____ weeks
payment due: $_____
(50% due on commencement, 50% on delivery)

F. ADDITIONAL STEPS (if applicable):
_____
_____

12. COMPANY SHALL PAY THE ABOVE GUARANTEED AMOUNTS DUE IF
READING PERIODS PASS AND COMPANY DOES NOT REQUEST SERVICES;
HOWEVER, if there has been no intervening writer(s), SERVICES SHALL BE
DUE, SUBJECT TO WRITER'S PROFESSIONAL AVAILABILITY, FOR A PERIOD
NOT TO EXCEED _____ MONTHS.

13. BONUS:
A. For sole writing credit: $_____
B. For shared writing credit: $_____
Shared credit bonus will be paid on commencement of principal photography
if no other writer has been engaged; balance to be paid on determination of
writing credit.
C. For "green light" or engagement of an "element": $_____
If Writer is writer of record or is most recent writer on the Project at the time
the Project is given a "green light" by a studio or an element is attached on a
pay-or-play basis, Writer shall be given a bonus of _____ Dollars
($_____) which may __ may not __ be applied against the bonus in A. or
B., above.

14. CREDITS AND SEPARATED RIGHTS: Per WGA MBA.

15. EXISTING CREDIT OBLIGATIONS REGARDING ASSIGNED MATERIAL, IF ANY
(subject to WGA MBA):

16. VIEWING CUT: Per WGA MBA: Writer shall be invited to view a cut of the film in
time sufficient such that any editing suggestions, if accepted, could be reasonably
and effectively implemented. Writer shall also be invited to [___] other screenings.

17. PREMIERES: If writer receives writing credit, Company shall __ shall not __
provide Writer and one (1) guest with an invitation to the initial celebrity premiere,
if held, with travel and accommodations at a level not less than the director or
producer of the project.

18. VIDEOCASSETTE: Per WGA MBA.

19. TRANSPORTATION AND EXPENSES: If Company requires Writer to perform
services hereunder at a location more than _____ miles from Writer's principal
place of residence, which is _____, Writer shall be given first
class (if available) transportation to and from such location and a weekly sum of
$_____ ($_____ per week in a high cost urban area).

156

20. SEQUELS/REMAKES: If separated rights,
   - Theatrical sequels = 50% initial compensation and bonus; remakes = 33%.
   - Series Payments: $ _____ per 1/2 hour episode; $ ____ per 1 hour episode; $ _____ per MOW (in network primetime or on pay television, otherwise $ _____ per MOW); $ _____ per sequel produced directly for the videocassette/videodisc market; $ _____ per product produced for the interactive market based on the Project; _____ [other, e.g., theme park attractions based on the Project].
   - Spin-offs: Generic—1/2 of above payments
     Planted—1/4 of above payments
   - If Writer is accorded sole "Written by" or "Screenplay by" credit, Writer shall have the right of first negotiation on all audio-visual exploitation, including, but not limited to remakes and sequels and MOWs, mini-series and TV pilots (or first episode if no pilot) for a period of seven (7) years following release.

21. NOTICES: All notices shall be sent as follows:
    TO WRITER: TO COMPANY:

22. MINIMUM BASIC AGREEMENT: The parties acknowledge that this contract is subject to all of the terms and provisions of the Basic Agreement and to the extent that the terms and provisions of said Basic Agreement are more advantageous to Writer than the terms hereof, the terms of said Basic Agreement shall supersede and replace the less advantageous terms of this agreement. Writer is an employee as defined by said Basic Agreement and Company has the right to control and direct the services to be performed.

23. GUILD MEMBERSHIP: To the extent that it may be lawful for the Company to require the Writer to do so, Writer agrees to become and/or remain a member of Writers Guild of America in good standing as required by the provisions of said Basic Agreement. If Writer fails or refuses to become or remain a member of said Guild in good standing, as required in the preceding sentence, the Company shall have the right at any time thereafter to terminate this agreement with the Writer.

157

24. RESULTS AND PROCEEDS: Work-Made-For-Hire: Writer acknowledges that all results, product and proceeds of Writer's services (including all original ideas in connection therewith) are being specially ordered by Producer for use as part of a Motion Picture and shall be considered a "work made for hire" for Producer as specially commissioned for use as a part of a motion picture in accordance with Sections 101 and 201 of Title 17 of the U.S. Copyright Act. Therefore, Producer shall be the author and copyright owner thereof for all purposes throughout the universe without limitation of any kind or nature. In consideration of the monies paid to Lender hereunder, Producer shall solely and exclusively own throughout the universe in perpetuity all rights of every kind and nature whether now or hereafter known or created in and in connection with such results, product and proceeds, in whatever stage of completion as may exist from time to time, including: (i) the copyright and all rights of copyright; (ii) all neighboring rights, trademarks and any and all other ownership and exploitation rights now or hereafter recognized in any Territory, including all rental, lending, fixation, reproduction, broadcasting (including satellite transmission), distribution and all other rights of communication by any and all means, media, devices, processes and technology; (iii) the rights to adapt, rearrange, and make changes in, deletions from and additions to such results, product and proceeds, and to use all or any part thereof in new versions, adaptations, and other Motion Pictures including Remakes and Sequels; (iv) the right to use the title of the Work in connection therewith or otherwise and to change such title; and (v) all rights generally known as the "moral rights of authors."

25. WARRANTY AND INDEMNIFICATION:

A. Subject to Article 28 of the WGA Basic Agreement, Writer hereby represents and warrants as follows:

1. Writer is free to enter into this Agreement and no rights of any third parties are or will be violated by Writer entering into or performing this Agreement. Writer is not subject to any conflicting obligation or any disability, and Writer has not made and shall not hereafter make any agreement with any third party, which could interfere with the rights granted to Company hereunder or the full performance of Writer's obligation and services hereunder.

2. All of the Work (and the Property, if any) shall be wholly original with Writer and none of the same has been or shall be copied from or based upon any other work unless assigned in this contract. The reproduction, exhibition, or any use thereof or any of the rights herein granted shall not defame any person or entity nor violate any copyright or right of privacy or publicity, or any other right of any person or entity. The warranty in this subparagraph shall not apply to any material as furnished to Writer by Company (unless such furnished material was written or created by Writer or originally furnished to Company by Writer) or material inserted in the Work by Company, but shall apply to all material which Writer may add thereto.

3. Writer is sole owner of the Property together with the title thereof and all rights granted (or purported to be granted) to Company hereunder, and no rights in the Property have been granted to others or impaired by Writer, except as specified, if at all, in this Agreement. No part of the property has been registered for copyright, published, or otherwise exploited or agreed to be published or otherwise exploited with the knowledge or consent of Writer, or is in the public domain. Writer does not know of any pending or threatened claim or litigation in connection with the Property or the rights herein granted.

4. Writer shall indemnify and hold harmless Company (and its affiliated companies, successors, assigns, and the directors, officers, employees, agents, and representatives of the foregoing) from any damage, loss, liability, cost, penalty, guild fee or award, or expense of any kind (including attorney's fees (hereinafter "Liability") arising out of, resulting from, based upon or incurred because of a breach by Writer of any agreement, representation, or warranty made by Writer hereunder. The party receiving notice of such claim, demand or action shall promptly notify the other party thereof. The pendency of such claim, demand, or action shall not release Company of its obligation to pay Writer sums due hereunder.

B. Company agrees to indemnify Writer and hold Writer harmless from and against any and all damages and expenses (other than with respect to any settlement entered into without Company's written consent) arising out of any third party claim against Writer resulting from Company's development, production, distribution and/or exploitation of the Project.

26. NO INJUNCTIVE RELIEF: The sole right of Writer as to any breach or alleged breach hereunder by Company shall be the recovery of money damages, if any, and the rights herein granted by Writer shall not terminate by reason of such breach. In no event may Writer terminate this Agreement or obtain injunctive relief or other equitable relief with respect to any breach of Company's obligations hereunder.

27. PROFIT PARTICIPATION: Terms to be negotiated in good faith. If the parties fail to reach agreement within [   ] months after execution hereof, either party, upon 30 days notice to the other, may submit the matter to what is known as a "baseball arbitration," in which each party presents one profit proposal and the arbitrator is required to adopt one of the two proposals. The arbitrator shall be selected and the arbitration conducted pursuant to the Voluntary Labor Arbitration Rules of the AAA.

28. AGREEMENT OF THE PARTIES: This document [including Attachment 1, if any] shall constitute the agreement between the parties until modified or amended by a subsequent writing.

By: _____   By: _____
           [Name of writer]   Title

cc: WGA Contracts Department

ATTACHMENT 1

ADDITIONAL PROVISIONS, IF ANY: 159

_____

_____

_____

_____

_____

STANDARD FORM FREELANCE TELEVISION WRITER'S
EMPLOYMENT CONTRACT

Agreement entered into at _____, this _____ day of _____, 19_____ between _____, hereinafter called "Company" and _____, hereinafter called "Writer."

WITNESSETH:

1. Company hereby employs the Writer to render services in the writing, composition, preparation and revision of the literary material described in Paragraph 2 hereof, hereinafter for convenience referred to as "work." The Writer accepts such employment and agrees to render his services hereunder and devote his best talents, efforts and abilities in accordance with the instructions, control and directions of the Company.

2. DESCRIPTION OF WORK

    (a) IDENTIFICATION
    Series Title: _____
    Program Title:_____
    Based On (If Applicable)_____

    (b) FORM
    ( ) Story   ( ) Option for Teleplay
    ( ) Teleplay   ( ) Pilot
    ( ) Rewrite   ( ) Polish
    ( ) Sketch   ( ) Narration
    ( ) Non-Commercial Openings and Closings ( ) Format
    ( ) Plot Outline - Narrative Synopsis of Story ( ) Bible

    (c) TYPE OF PROGRAM
    ( ) Episodic Series ( ) Unit Series   ( ) Single Unit
    ( ) Strip/5 per week ( ) Comedy/Variety ( ) Documentary
    ( ) Dramatic   ( ) Other Non-Dramatic Program
    ( ) Quiz & Audience Participation   ( ) News

    (d) PROGRAM LENGTH: _____ minutes

    (e) METHODS OF PRODUCTION & DISTRIBUTION
    ( ) Film   ( ) Videotape ( ) Live   ( ) Video Cassette
    ( ) Network   ( ) Syndication ( ) Pay TV ( ) Basic Cable

3. (a) The Writer represents that (s)he is a member in good standing of the Writers Guild of America, (West or East), Inc., and warrants that (s)he will maintain his/her membership in the Writers Guild of America, (West or East), Inc., in good standing during the term of this employment.

(b) The Company warrants it is a party to the WGA 1995 Theatrical and Television Basic Agreement (which agreement is herein designated MBA).

(c) Should any of the terms hereof be less advantageous to the Writer than the minimums provided in said MBA, then the terms of the MBA shall supersede such terms hereof; and in the event this Agreement shall fail to provide for the Writer the benefits which are provided by the MBA, then such benefits for the Writer provided by the terms of the MBA are deemed incorporated herein. Without limiting the generality of the foregoing, it is agreed that screen credits for authorship shall be determined pursuant to the provisions of Schedule A of the MBA in accordance with its terms at the time of such determination.

4. DELIVERY

Pursuant to Article 13.B.9. of the 1995 MBA the following information must be completed:

(a) Name(s) and function of the person(s) to whom delivery of all work is to be made by Writer:_____

(b) Place where delivery of all work is to be made by Writer:_____

(c) Name of person who is authorized on behalf of Company to request Writer to perform rewrites of the work:_____

161

Company shall give Writer written notice of any changes in the name(s) of the person(s) to whom delivery is to be made and/or the name(s) of the person(s) authorized to request rewrites.

If the Writer has agreed to complete and deliver the work, and/or any changes and revisions, within a certain period or periods of time, then such agreement will be expressed in this paragraph as follows:

5. COMPENSATION

As full compensation for all services to be rendered hereunder, the rights granted to the Company with respect to the work, and the undertakings and agreements assumed by the Writers, and upon condition that the Writer shall fully perform such undertakings and agreements, Company will pay the Writer the following amounts:

(a) Compensation for services $_____
(b) Advance for television reruns $_____
     (If Applicable)
(c) Advance for theatrical use $_____
     (If Applicable)

No amounts may be inserted in (b) or (c) above unless the amount set forth in (a) above is at least twice the applicable minimum compensation set forth in the MBA for the type of services to be rendered hereunder.

If the assignment is for story and teleplay, story with option for teleplay or teleplay, the following amount of the compensation set forth in (a) above will be paid in accordance with the provisions of the MBA:

    (i) $_____ following delivery of story.

    (ii) $_____ following delivery of first draft teleplay.

    (iii) $_____ following delivery of final draft teleplay.

6. WARRANTY

With respect to Writer's warranties and indemnification agreement, the Company and the Writer agree that upon the presentation of any claim or the institution of any action involving a breach of warranty, the party receiving notice thereof will promptly notify the other party in regard thereto. Company agrees that the pendency of any such claim or action shall not relieve the Company of its obligation to pay the Writer any monies until it has sustained a loss or suffered an adverse judgment or decree by reason of such claim or action.

IN WITNESS WHEREOF, the parties hereto have duly executed this agreement on the day and year first above written.

_____   _____
      (Writer)   (Company)

Address _____   By_____
_____   Title_____
_____   Address _____
_____   _____

WGA 1998 THEATRICAL AND TELEVISION BASIC AGREEMENT
THEATRICAL COMPENSATION+

		First Period Effective 5/2/98 - 5/1/99	
		LOW	HIGH
A.	Original Screenplay, Including Treatment	$43,952	$82,444
	Installments:		
	Delivery of Original Treatment	19,917	32,980
	Delivery of First Draft Screenplay	17,310	32,980
	Delivery of Final Draft Screenplay	6,725	16,484
B.	Non-Original Screenplay, Including Treatment	38,466	71,531
	Installments:		
	Delivery of Treatment	14,423	21,988
	Delivery of First Draft Screenplay	17,310	32,980
	Delivery of Final Draft Screenplay	6,733	16,563
C.	Original Screenplay, Excluding Treatment **or** Sale of Original Screenplay	29,536	60,455
	Installments for Employment:		
	Delivery of First Draft Screenplay	22,810	43,972
	Delivery of Final Draft Screenplay	6,726	16,483
D.	Non-Original Screenplay, Excluding Treatment **or** Sale of Non-Original Screenplay	24,036	49,464
	Installments for Employment:		
	Delivery of First Draft Screenplay	17,310	32,980
	Delivery of Final Draft Screenplay	6,726	16,484
E.	Additional Compensation for Story included in Screenplay	5,500	10,992
F.	Story or Treatment	14,423	21,988
G.	Original Story or Treatment	19,917	32,980
H.	First Draft Screenplay, with or without Option for Final Draft Screenplay (non-original)		
	First Draft Screenplay	17,310	32,980
	Final Draft Screenplay	11,536	21,988
I.	Rewrite of Screenplay	14,423	21,988
J.	Polish of Screenplay	7,215	10,992

163

+The MBA provides for a discount with respect to employment on a flat deal basis of a writer who has not been previously employed under a Guild MBA in television, theatrical films or dramatic radio, subject to an adjustment to full minimum if a photoplay is produced and the writer receives any writing credit. For details, contact the Guild Contracts Department.

1

WGA 1998 THEATRICAL AND TELEVISION BASIC AGREEMENT
__THEATRICAL COMPENSATION+__

		Second Period Effective 5/2/99 - 5/1/00	
		LOW	HIGH
A.	Original Screenplay, Including Treatment	$45,490	$85,330
	Installments: Delivery of Original Treatment	20,614	34,134
	Delivery of First Draft Screenplay	17,916	34,134
	Delivery of Final Draft Screenplay	6,960	17,062
B.	Non-Original Screenplay, Including Treatment	39,812	74,035
	Installments: Delivery of Treatment	14,928	22,758
	Delivery of First Draft Screenplay	17,916	34,134
	Delivery of Final Draft Screenplay	6,968	17,143
C.	Original Screenplay, Excluding Treatment or Sale of Original Screenplay	30,570	62,571
	Installments for Employment: Delivery of First Draft Screenplay	23,608	45,511
	Delivery of Final Draft Screenplay	6,962	17,060
D.	Non-Original Screenplay, Excluding Treatment or Sale of Non-Original Screenplay	24,877	51,195
	Installments for Employment: Delivery of First Draft Screenplay	17,916	34,134
	Delivery of Final Draft Screenplay	6,961	17,061
E.	Additional Compensation for Story included in Screenplay	5,692	11,377
F.	Story or Treatment	14,928	22,758
G.	Original Story or Treatment	20,614	34,134
H.	First Draft Screenplay, with or without Option for Final Draft Screenplay (non-original)		
	First Draft Screenplay	17,916	34,134
	Final Draft Screenplay	11,940	22,758
I.	Rewrite of Screenplay	14,928	22,758
J.	Polish of Screenplay	7,468	11,377

164

+Explanation of discounts on page 1.

WGA 1998 THEATRICAL AND TELEVISION BASIC AGREEMENT
THEATRICAL COMPENSATION+

		Third Period Effective 5/2/00 - 5/1/01	
		LOW	HIGH
A.	Original Screenplay, Including Treatment	$47,082	$88,317
	Installments: Delivery of Original Treatment	21,335	35,329
	Delivery of First Draft Screenplay	18,543	35,329
	Delivery of Final Draft Screenplay	7,204	17,659
B.	Non-Original Screenplay, Including Treatment	41,205	76,626
	Installments: Delivery of Treatment	15,450	23,555
	Delivery of First Draft Screenplay	18,543	35,329
	Delivery of Final Draft Screenplay	7,212	17,742
C.	Original Screenplay, Excluding Treatment or Sale of Original Screenplay	31,640	64,761
	Installments for Employment: Delivery of First Draft Screenplay	24,434	47,104
	Delivery of Final Draft Screenplay	7,206	17,657
D.	Non-Original Screenplay, Excluding Treatment or Sale of Non-Original Screenplay	25,748	52,987
	Installments for Employment: Delivery of First Draft Screenplay	18,543	35,329
	Delivery of Final Draft Screenplay	7,205	17,658
E.	Additional Compensation for Story included in Screenplay	5,891	11,775
F.	Story or Treatment	15,450	23,555
G.	Original Story or Treatment	21,335	35,329
H.	First Draft Screenplay, with or without Option for Final Draft Screenplay (non-original)		
	First Draft Screenplay	18,543	35,329
	Final Draft Screenplay	12,358	23,555
I.	Rewrite of Screenplay	15,450	23,555
J.	Polish of Screenplay	7,729	11,775

165

+Explanation of discounts on page 1.

3

WGA 1998 THEATRICAL AND TELEVISION BASIC AGREEMENT
THEATRICAL COMPENSATION

THEATRICAL BUDGET THRESHOLDS

LOW BUDGET - Photoplay costing less than $2,500,000
HIGH BUDGET - Photoplay costing $2,500,000 or more

ISSUANCE OF DEAL MEMO

The MBA requires timely delivery, generally 10 to 12 days, of a deal memo to the writer or the writer's representative after agreement on the major deal points. Contact the Guild Contracts Department for details.

PAYMENT SCHEDULE

Upon commencement of writing services, the writer is to receive **the greater of**:
(a) 10% of the agreed compensation for delivery of first material;
or (b) $3,321 (effective 5/2/98 - 5/1/99);
$3,437 (effective 5/2/99 - 5/1/00);
$3,557 (effective 5/2/00 - 5/1/01).

In addition, Company will make its best efforts to pay writer within 48 hours of delivery but in no event more than (7) days after delivery.

Payment shall not be contingent upon the acceptance or approval by the Company of the literary material so delivered, or upon any other contingency such as obtaining financing.

PURCHASES FROM A PROFESSIONAL WRITER

The Flat Deal minimums shall apply to purchases of literary material from a "professional writer" as that term is specifically defined in the Basic Agreement.

OPTIONED MATERIAL (THEATRICAL)

166

Company may option literary material from a "professional writer" for a period of up to 18 months upon payment of 10% of minimum. Each renewal period of up to 18 months requires an additional 10% of minimum.

WEEK-TO-WEEK AND TERM EMPLOYMENT

Compensation Per Week++	Effective 5/2/98 - 5/1/99	Effective 5/2/99 - 5/1/00	Effective 5/2/00 - 5/1/01
Week-to-week	$3,577	$3,702	$3,832
14 out of 14 weeks	3,321	3,437	3,557
20 out of 26 weeks	3,068	3,175	3,286
40 out of 52 weeks	2,820	2,919	3,021

++The MBA provides for a discount for a limited period of time with respect to employment on a week-to-week or term basis of a writer who has not been previously employed under a Guild MBA in television, theatrical films or dramatic radio. For details, contact the Guild Contracts Department.

WGA 1998 THEATRICAL AND TELEVISION BASIC AGREEMENT
THEATRICAL COMPENSATION

<u>NARRATION</u>   (written by a writer other than writer of Screenplay or Story & Screenplay)

Minimums for narration are based on status of film assembly and nature of previously written material as follows:

Nature of Material Written prior to employment of narration writer	Film Assembled in Story Sequence	Film Footage Not Assembled in Story Sequence
None	Applicable Screenplay excluding Treatment Minimum	Applicable Screenplay including Treatment Minimum
Story Only	Applicable Screenplay excluding Treatment Minimum	Applicable Screenplay excluding Treatment Minimum
Story and Screenplay	Per Rate Schedule A	Per Rate Schedule A

Rate Schedule A	Effective 5/2/98 - 5/1/99	Effective 5/2/99 - 5/1/00	Effective 5/2/00 - 5/1/01
Two minutes or less	$ 673	$ 697	$ 721
Over two minutes thru five minutes	2,378	2,461	2,547
Over five minutes of narration	Applicable Polish Minimum		

167

THEATRICAL AND TELEVISION

<u>PENSION PLAN AND HEALTH FUND</u>

All employment under the WGA 1998 Theatrical and Television Basic Agreement is subject to employer contributions of:

6% to the PRODUCER-WRITERS GUILD OF AMERICA PENSION PLAN.

6 1/2% to the WRITERS GUILD-INDUSTRY HEALTH FUND.

Effective 5/2/99 and 5/2/00, Health Fund contributions may be increased or decreased by up to 1/2%. In this event, minimums for that period will be reduced or increased by the same percentage. Contact the Guild in the second and third periods to ensure that the minimums and contribution rates have not changed.

Employer reporting forms and information regarding benefits are available from the Pension Plan and Health Fund offices:

Producer-Writers Guild of America Pension Plan
Writers Guild-Industry Health Fund
1015 N. Hollywood Way
Burbank, California 91505
Telephone: 818/846-1015

WGA 1998 THEATRICAL AND TELEVISION BASIC AGREEMENT
<u>**TELEVISION COMPENSATION**</u>

<u>NETWORK PRIME TIME</u> (ABC, CBS, NBC and FBC)

<u>Applicable minimums</u>	Effective 5/2/98 - 5/1/99	Effective 5/2/99 - 5/1/00	Effective 5/2/00 - 5/1/01

Length of Program: 15 minutes or less

STORY+	$ 3,106	$ 3,199	$ 3,295
TELEPLAY	7,542	7,768	$ 8,001

Installments:
+First Draft: 90% of minimum or 60% of Agreed Compensation,
                          whichever is greater
Final Draft: Balance of Agreed Compensation

STORY & TELEPLAY	9,331	9,611	9,899

Installments:
+Story: 30% of Agreed Compensation
First Draft Teleplay: The difference between the Story Installment
                         and 90% of minimum, or 40% of Agreed
                         Compensation, whichever is greater
Final Draft Teleplay: Balance of Agreed Compensation

. . . .

Length of Program: 30 minutes or less (but more than 15 minutes)

STORY+	$ 5,692	$ 5,863	$ 6,039
TELEPLAY	12,248	12,615	12,993

Installments:
+First Draft: 90% of minimum or 60% of Agreed Compensation,
                          whichever is greater
Final Draft: Balance of Agreed Compensation

STORY & TELEPLAY	17,076	17,588	18,116

Installments:
+Story: 30% of Agreed Compensation
First Draft Teleplay: The difference between the Story Installment
                         and 90% of minimum, or 40% of Agreed
                         Compensation, whichever is greater
Final Draft Teleplay: Balance of Agreed Compensation

168

+On pilots only, the writer is to be paid 10% of the first installment (as an advance against such first installment) upon commencement of services.
The applicable minimum for a pilot is 150% of the applicable minimum set forth above.

WGA 1998 THEATRICAL AND TELEVISION BASIC AGREEMENT
<u>**TELEVISION COMPENSATION**</u>

<u>NETWORK PRIME TIME</u> (ABC, CBS, NBC and FBC)

	Effective 5/2/98 -	Effective 5/2/99 -	Effective 5/2/00 -
<u>Applicable minimums</u>	<u>5/1/99</u>	<u>5/1/00</u>	<u>5/1/01</u>

Length of Program: 60 minutes or less (but more than 45 minutes)

STORY+	$10,019	$10,320	$10,630
TELEPLAY	16,522	17,018	17,529

Installments:
+First Draft: 90% of minimum or 60% of Agreed Compensation, whichever is greater
Final Draft: Balance of Agreed Compensation

STORY & TELEPLAY	25,116	25,869	26,645

Installments:
+Story: 30% of Agreed Compensation
First Draft Teleplay: The difference between the Story Installment and 90% of minimum, or 40% of Agreed Compensation, whichever is greater
Final Draft Teleplay: Balance of Agreed Compensation

. . . .

Length of Program: 90 minutes or less (but more than 60 minutes)

STORY+	$13,387	$13,789	$14,203
TELEPLAY	23,805	24,519	25,255

Installments:
+First Draft: 90% of minimum or 60% of Agreed Compensation, whichever is greater
Final Draft: Balance of Agreed Compensation

169

STORY & TELEPLAY	35,336	36,396	37,488

Installments:
+Story: 30% of Agreed Compensation
First Draft Teleplay: The difference between the Story Installment and 90% of minimum, or 40% of Agreed Compensation, whichever is greater
Final Draft Teleplay: Balance of Agreed Compensation

+On pilots and one-time programs 90 minutes or longer, the writer is to be paid 10% of the first installment (as an advance against such first installment) upon commencement of services.
 The applicable minimum for a pilot is 150% of the applicable minimum set forth above.

WGA 1998 THEATRICAL AND TELEVISION BASIC AGREEMENT
TELEVISION COMPENSATION

NETWORK PRIME TIME (ABC, CBS, NBC and FBC)

	Effective 5/2/98 -	Effective 5/2/99 -	Effective 5/2/00 -
Applicable minimums	5/1/99	5/1/00	5/1/01

Length of Program: 120 minutes or less (but more than 90 minutes)
NON-EPISODIC

STORY+	$19,513	$20,098	$20,701
TELEPLAY	33,332	34,332	35,362

Installments:
+First Draft: 90% of minimum or 60% of Agreed Compensation,
whichever is greater
Final Draft: Balance of Agreed Compensation

STORY & TELEPLAY	50,817	52,342	53,912

Installments:
+Story: 30% of Agreed Compensation
First Draft Teleplay: The difference between the Story Installment
and 90% of minimum, or 40% of Agreed
Compensation, whichever is greater
Final Draft Teleplay: Balance of Agreed Compensation

. . . .

Length of Program: 120 minutes or less (but more than 90 minutes)
EPISODIC

STORY+	$17,880	$18,416	$18,968
TELEPLAY	30,546	31,462	32,406

Installments:
+First Draft: 90% of minimum or 60% of Agreed Compensation,
whichever is greater
Final Draft: Balance of Agreed Compensation

STORY & TELEPLAY	46,491	47,886	49,323

Installments:
+Story: 30% of Agreed Compensation
First Draft Teleplay: The difference between the Story Installment
and 90% of minimum, or 40% of Agreed
Compensation, whichever is greater
Final Draft Teleplay: Balance of Agreed Compensation

+On pilots and one-time programs 90 minutes or longer, the writer is to be paid 10% of the first installment (as an advance against such first installment) upon commencement of services.
The applicable minimum for a pilot is 150% of the applicable minimum set forth above.

WGA 1998 THEATRICAL AND TELEVISION BASIC AGREEMENT
TELEVISION COMPENSATION

PAYMENT SCHEDULE

Company will make its best efforts to pay writer within 48 hours of delivery but in no event more than (7) days after delivery.

Payment shall not be contingent upon the acceptance or approval by the Company of the literary material so delivered, or upon any other contingency such as obtaining financing.

In certain instances on long-form television movies, the network (or other licensee) has agreed to reimburse the Company for a "producer's draft," even when such draft is not delivered to the network (or other licensee). Please call the Contracts Department for further information.

MADE-FOR-PAY TELEVISION OR VIDEO CASSETTE/VIDEO DISC

The minimum initial compensation for a writer shall be the same as the applicable minimum initial compensation for a "free" television program. Where the program is of a type generally produced for network prime time, the network prime time rates are to be utilized.

MADE-FOR-BASIC CABLE

For high budget dramatic programs, the provisions of the MBA apply. For all other types of programs, the terms of the MBA may be used to employ writers. Producers wishing to negotiate modified provisions may contact the Guild Contracts Department.

INTERACTIVE/MULTI-MEDIA PROGRAMMING (DISC, CARTRIDGE, CD-ROM, TELEVISION, THEATRICAL, ETC.)

The Guild is currently offering a modified contract for Interactive/Multi-Media writing. Contact the Industry Alliances Department at WGAW or the Signatories Department at WGAE for information on applicable provisions.

171

INFORMATIONAL PROGRAMMING

For informational programming the Guild offers a special contract. Contact the Industry Alliances Department at WGAW or the Signatories Department at WGAE for details.

ANIMATION

The Guild negotiates terms and conditions for animated projects. Contact the Industry Alliances Department at WGAW or the Signatories Department at WGAE for details.

Chapter 11
WHAT HAPPENS AFTER YOU SELL IT?

**"The main thing about screenwriting is learning
how to fight without making enemies."**
—Frank Pierson, screenwriter (*Dog Day Afternoon*)

The time comes when you have been compensated for your work
and released from further writing services. Like any good parent, it
is with more than a little dread that you watch the child you bore,
raised and protected through its difficult gestation finally being
turned out into the world. But assume, this once at least, all the
hard work and sleepless nights and families growing up without
you has paid off: your agent phones—your screenplay has been
"greenlighted" for production by the head of the studio!

What can you expect now? What will happen to your script from
this point on? Will you be involved with further writing or other
aspects of the production? What is the process?

The first order of business in pre-production is to have your script
"broken down" for production, a task often delegated to the production manager or the first assistant director. That means retyped
with scenes numbered and all sound, special effects and prop cues
highlighted. This will help the producer to estimate the cost of
filming your screenplay. A director, if not already attached, must
be found and a preliminary budget agreed upon. Then, comes the
attempt to attract stars to the lead roles. A casting company will be
assigned the job of filling principal roles by matching desired talent to budget and availability.

Simultaneously, the key production team is assembled: the director will need a director of photography, a production designer and
an editor and the producer will want a production manager (if one
has not already been brought on board) to fine tune the budget
and hire the rest of the crew. Locations must be scouted, permits
obtained, insurance binders executed. Similarities between fictitious
names and actual persons or entities will be researched; if deemed

necessary, names maybe changed. Rights to existing music and art work must be cleared as well.

Then there will be more rewrites. Perhaps these will be done by the original writer, perhaps not. By this time, the director and the stars all have their own movie in mind, their own careers to nurture, their own favorite writers. There will also be increasing pressure to lower the budget; certain writers are known for being "budget conscious" in paring down scenes and camera moves and in losing characters and dialogue—all designed to save time in production. (Time is money; principal photography can cost a half million dollars a day or better.) From here on, the screenplay will not necessarily get any better, just different.

Since production personnel are already hard at work implementing the needs of the script in its current draft, all changes will be put on colored pages, a different color for each new, dated set of revisions.

As the start of production approaches, there will be round table readings of the script by the cast, after which a "polish" of the script may be required. This may be the last time a writer's hand is permitted to touch the material to be filmed. If the logistics and planning of pre-production go well and the budget has not skyrocketed out of control, the magical first day of principal photography will, miraculously it may seem, arrive.

174

And that's the day you must learn to let go. The production, not the script, is the new priority. The focus will be on the director and the stars; any journalist sent to cover the production will write of it as the director's film or the star's next big hit and the producer has long since thought of it as "my movie." As for the writer's vision, make no mistake: Directors are sturdy individualists known to adapt the very structure of the film to suit the way the wind may be blowing on any given day. And stars, often being the motivating force behind the movie being made at all, are known to freely change their dialogue and "tinker" with everyone else's right on through the final day of shooting. Except in unusual circumstances, in the heart and mind of almost anyone connected to the film, the writer may as well have ceased to exist.

Sure you will want to be involved, your advice sought in picking the director, cast, locations; you'd like to be consulted on those critical choices to be made in the editing room. If there is any rewriting to be done, you would like to do it. But in truth, more often than not, your work is done; thanks and goodbye.

Will you at least be invited to the set? That depends on the director. If you are, a chair will be provided for you, discreetly out of the way. Do not bring your camera or expect to get chummy with the actors. If one does stroll over to discuss his part, it's best to smile and nod your support, but mum is the word. Directors are known to get frosty fast and withdraw their invitation in the face of any possible second-guessing at this point. And if your services should be called upon for dialogue changes or last minute edits, do not expect additional payment; the budget is set. The producer may furnish your accommodations and meals, and if generous, a modest per diem for the days you actually reworked the script, but no more.

In the evenings, you may be invited to dailies (when the day's work is shown for a select audience), but it's best not to comment unless your comment is solicited, and, even so, be very tactful. During post-production, it is again up to the whim of the director (for television, it's the producer) whether or not you will be invited to the editing room to help smooth out any story wrinkles. If you are a Guild member, there will usually be a screening set up for you, but whether your comments are taken to heart will depend upon the good will you have stored up. Do not expect to be asked for your marketing advice.

Finally, your bio is likely to be included in press kit materials (though rarely will a writer be included in press junkets) and you'll be invited to attend premieres (though rarely previews). Hopefully, your contribution will be mentioned in reviews of the film.

And that's all, folks—unless, of course, you've won a huge marketing gamble with your script and successfully attached yourself as a director, producer or lead actor. Woody Allen and John Sayles see their vision realized all the way through to release on any film they write. Award-winning screenwriters Matt Damon and Ben Affleck could paint you a rosy picture of their experience as writer/ actors on *Good Will Hunting*; so can writer/director/actors Billy Bob Thornton on *Sling Blade* or Roberto Benigni on *Life is Beautiful*. And certainly, Sylvester Stallone can serve as the poster child for launching a full spectrum mega-career by writing the one screenplay which, arguably more than any other in the history of Hollywood, has brought the most success to its author—*Rocky*.

Those success stories (and others) notwithstanding, most screenwriters can better relate to the lament of Academy Award winning screenwriter Peter Stone (who traded his screen career for the less lucrative but more professionally satisfying world of the stage): "Minutes after the script leaves my computer, it's best I be put to sleep."

175

Chapter 12
A WRITER'S NOTEBOOK

There is more to the business of screenwriting than writing. It's a *war* out there and writers go into the trenches daily with no better weapons than a sharpened pencil or a mouse. We need a survival manual—our own uniquely tailored *Art of War*—that has nothing to do with what to write or how to write or why we write or even what to do after we write. There are manuals enough to fill a lawyer's bookcase on all that. No, we need a political guide, something with the expediency, craftiness and duplicity of Machiavelli's *The Prince*. So I've raided my store of "life's lessons" (and borrowed from my well-worn copy of *The Wisdom of Baltasar Gracian*) to share with you these "notes to myself" and six basic "laws" for surviving as a writer in Hollywood.

ON THE WRITER'S LIFE:
• Write every day, if to be a writer is your aim. A salesman without inventory is a hollow boaster.

• Avoid those who do not understand the value of what you do (even if what you do all day is stare at a blank page).

• Find a mentor. Inspiration, technique, success, strategy and contacts rub off.

• Consider a writing partner. Two people have ten times the strength of one. Partners give the illusion of a club; each conferring grace upon the other, they are harder to attack.

• When you're having a bad day, turn off the computer, reschedule the lunch, go work out or read a book; retreat and regroup. There is always tomorrow.

• Do something positive each day to advance your career goals, your character or your knowledge. Boring person = boring writer.

- Set higher, more far-reaching goals—and then set deadlines to achieve them.

- Store goodwill like a squirrel stores chestnuts for the winter; people really do make movies with their friends.

- Enjoy the creative process. It's that long second act and not the big finish that makes a life.

ON THE WORK:
- Reason, ruminate, plot and outline—but eventually, write; the world spins while you stand still in your bathrobe.

- Write for yourself. Not for money; there are easier and faster ways to earn money. Not for fame; those who achieve fame are condemned to spend the rest of their life in fear of losing it.

- Expose your work to the marketplace; but submit your work carefully. A merchant must exhibit his wares to attract buyers, but never brings forth his best cloth first.

- Remember: only completed scripts sell. A 30-page screenplay is a dust-collector.

- Never rush to market. Submit too soon after the first blush of completion and a script's imperfections will forever taint it. Even nature does not bring forth her children until they are ready to be seen.

- Hold your tongue. In a story conference, when receiving those script "notes," wait until you fully comprehend the problems in your script before offering solutions.

- Dwell on the work that has brought you pride, rather than on the crumbled pages. Writer's block and depression are the triumph of the few losses over the many victories.

- Creative work invites rejection, so be good to yourself. Find things that bring you joy and indulge in them from time to time; treat yourself generously if you expect others to.

- Write more. A famous race car driver once shrugged off his long record of victories with a simple explanation: "I win more because I race more."

ON THE BUSINESS:

• Become an optimist. There is pleasure and pain to be had in almost any situation—it is all a matter of perspective.

• A thin line separates friendly rivals and bitter enemies. Be careful about sharing your best ideas or work-in-progress.

• Some people will forever misunderstand your clear meaning, twist the plot of your best writing, misinterpret every character's actions—just don't have this person for an agent.

• Never celebrate your "horror stories"—especially to a prospective buyer or employer. Nobody follows a man who can't swim into the water.

• Keep your weaknesses and your losses to yourself so they don't mark you as a loser even after you overcome them.

• Maintain the long vision; do not be easily discouraged by the script that hasn't sold.

• Be slow to believe (or to doubt) all those rumors of your talent. Persistence, opportunity and hard work may have had something to do with it.

179

• Accept responsibility for your failures. Learn from them and move on. Don't make excuses or waste energy trying to explain them.

• Speak well of those who speak ill of you; it will make you appear invulnerable to their enmity. To put others down only reduces your own esteem.

• Accept that, in any profession there are monsters. Work with, around, through them, but never let them know they are the enemy; why let them plot even harder against you?

• Be careful in sharing your secret hate list. Your confessor today can be lunching with your enemy tomorrow.

• Avoid speaking of your successes (lest you diminish them) or your failures (lest you magnify them). If others praise you, it will be heard tenfold; if they scorn you, it will be discounted.

• Avoid placing your happiness on the outcome of events you cannot control. Don't allow the accidents of fortune to determine yours.

- If you play, play to win. Stop repeating losing patterns. Not every script will sell, but consistency in failure is no virtue.

- All fails the desperate and the unlucky; find or make little successes and hold on to them until you change an unlucky pattern (and never let them see you sweat).

- Good friends are your best asset. Work hard at keeping them or ten times harder making new ones.

- Your words are powerful; be careful. A letter sent can never be recalled; joy and anger fade, but the written word burns on the page.

- Follow the dictates of *your* vision, not those of a development executives. As Baltasar wrote three centuries ago: "talent outshines position."

- Run your own race. Stay focused on your goals, not the speed of others in the race. In Hollywood, as in life, there can be more than one winner.

180

- You can't please everyone or win every argument. Listen, take notes, but never argue with an arguer. A well-timed retreat can leave your nemesis flailing at the wind.

- A handshake is not a contract. (Not in this business.)

- Success is the best revenge. Enjoy your work, your spouse, your friends, and you make the whole world envious.

- Do not envy the success of others; it suffocates your own spirit, dwarfs you and gains nothing.

- Never celebrate a victory or bemoan a defeat until after the battle is over. Take advantage of the ebbs in your work to gather strength and allies for the next surge.

- Never forget the value of good public relations—to have your achievements known is to achieve them twice.

SIX LAWS OF THE SCREENWRITER'S CAREER

1. The Law of Rejection—Don't let rejection dissolve your resolve.

Don't let the big desk intimidate you. Behind it sits some cherub-faced Senior Executive Vice President in Charge of Worldwide Production, 27, fresh from Harvard Business School and genuinely frightened for his job (his predecessor was traded for two development execs and a future draft choice). Fear rules here. Remember: it takes only one person to say "yes."

2. The Law of Change—There is no job security in Hollywood.

Executives change jobs like a con changes aliases; every 18 months on average they show up somewhere else under a new title. So should your screenplay; then, it can be considered all over again. And, new doors open up every day so keep knocking on them.

3. The Law of Changes—We all have to make them.

If your screenplay is rejected by many for the same reasons, consider rewriting it. Until a screenplay is produced, it is always a work-in-progress.

4. The Law of Birth—Keep those babies coming.

As soon as you finish one screenplay, start another—you'll still be fresh and brimming with ideas and undeterred by rejection.

181

5. The Law of Burying the Dead—Gulp and move on.

There comes a point when you've done all you can. It's only one screenplay. Sometimes you must learn to let it go. They can't all be winners.

6. The Law of Survival—Don't quit your day job.

But never forget why you started writing—because you *had* to!

. . . A FINAL NOTE

"Go to London," they said to me.
"In the great city you will make songs
from the sore hard light of your breast."
And I strove with myself for many years
      thinking of those streets,
      men with sharp power in their gaze,
      and illuminated glittering taxis
      lighting the windows of my mind.
But tonight sitting by the fire
and the hills between me and the sky
listening to the empty silence
and seeing the deer come to my call
      I am thinking of another man
      who spoke the words that are true:
      "Look directly down through wood and wood.
      Look in your own heart and write."
                    —*Iain Crichton Smith*

SUGGESTED READING

A select cross section of books can sometimes provide as deep an education in a given subject as an exhaustive bibliography. These seven have made my short list:

Goldman, William. *Adventures in the Screen Trade*. New York: Warner Books, 1983.

Aristotle's Poetics. Translation and commentary by Stephen Halliwell. Chapel Hill: University of North Carolina Press, 1986.

Egri, Lajos. *The Art of Dramatic Writing*. New Jersey: Simon & Schuster, 1972.

Bach, Steven. *Final Cut*. New York: William Morrow and Company, 1985.

Campbell, Joseph. *The Hero with a Thousand Faces*. Second Edition. New Jersey: Princeton University Press, 1982.

Dunne, John Gregory. *Monster*. New York: Random House, 1997.

Booth, Wayne C. *The Rhetoric of Fiction*. Second Edition. Chicago: University of Chicago Press, 1983.

APPENDIX

GUILD-SIGNATORY AGENTS & AGENCIES

On the following pages is a comprehensive list of the WGA's signatory agents and agencies. Check the WGA's web site (www.wga.org) for the most current information.

The WGA cannot offer assistance in finding or recommending an agent. However, this list can serve as a detailed starting point for your own research.

Each literary agency may have its own policy regarding the conditions under which it will accept submissions. The Guild suggests that you first write or telephone the agency, rather than directly send in your script "cold." Explain any credentials you feel are appropriate and briefly describe the nature of the material you want to submit. The agency will likely then advise you whether it is interested in receiving the material with a view toward representing it.

As a courtesy to writers, most agencies will generally return material sent to them if a self-addressed stamped envelope accompanies the submission. However, agencies are under no obligation to return any literary material to a writer seeking representation, nor can the WGA assist in seeking the return of material.

Signatory agencies have agreed not to charge fees other than a commission to WGA members. If you find that any of these agencies do attempt to charge fees, please contact the Guild.

If you believe an agency is a signatory and you do not see it listed here, contact the Guild's Agency Department at (323) 782-4502.

LEGEND

[*] This agency has indicated that it will consider newwriters

[**] This agency has indicated that it will consider writers ONLY as a result of references from persons known to it

[P] A packaging agency is one that represents several people associated with a film or television project, rather than just one client. They receivea commission from the producer for the group of clients they representedrather than the usual 10 percent from the individual clients.

[S] Society of Authors Representatives signed thru WGAE only

[L] Letter of inquiry only.

If there are no symbols next to the agency, this agency will not accept unsolicited material.

ARIZONA

[**] **Creative Authors Agency**
12212 Paradise Village Pkwy
South #403-C
Phoenix, AZ 85032
(602) 953-0164

Momentum Marketing
1112 East Laguna Dr
Tempe, AZ 85282-5516
(602) 777-0957

CALIFORNIA

[*] **A Total Acting Experience**
20501 Ventura Blvd #399
Woodland Hills, CA 91364-2350

[**] **Above The Line Agency**
9200 Sunset Blvd #401
West Hollywood, CA 90069
(310) 859-6115

[**] **Acme Talent & Literary Agency**
6310 San Vicente Blvd #520
Los Angeles, CA 90048
(323) 954-2263

[**,P] **Agency For The
Performing Arts**
9200 Sunset Blvd #900
Los Angeles, CA 90069
(310) 888-4200

[**,P] **Agency, The**
1800 Avenue Of The Stars #400
Los Angeles, CA 90067
(310) 551-3000

Allen Talent Agency
3832 Wilshire Blvd 2nd Floor
Los Angeles, CA 90010-3221
(213) 896-9372

[L,P] **Alpern Group, The**
15645 Royal Oak Road
Encino, CA 91436
(818) 528-1111

[L] **Amsel, Eisenstadt & Frazier**
5757 Wilshire Blvd #510
Los Angeles, CA 90036
(323) 939-1188

[L] **Angel City Talent**
1680 Vine St #716
Los Angeles, CA 90028
(323) 463-1680

[**] **Arthur, Irvin Associates, Ltd.**
9363 Wilshire Blvd #212
Beverly Hills, CA 90210
(310) 278-5934

[L] **Artist Network**
8448 Melrose Pl
Los Angeles, CA 90069
(323) 651-4244

[P] **Artists Agency, The**
10000 Santa Monica Blvd #305
Los Angeles, CA 90067
(310) 277-7779

Artists Group, Ltd., The
10100 Santa Monica Blvd #2490
Los Angeles, CA 90067
(310) 552-1100

186

[**]   **Becsey, Wisdom, Kalajian**
9200 Sunset Blvd #820
Los Angeles, CA 90069
(310) 550-0535

Bennett Agency, The
150 South Barrington Ave #1
Los Angeles, CA 90049
(310) 471-2251

[**]   **Black, Bonnie Talent Agency**
4660 Cahuenga Blvd #306
Toluca Lake, CA 91602
(818) 753-5424

[**]   **Bliss Frederick And Associates**
292 S. La Cienega Blvd #202
Beverly Hills, CA 90211
(310) 657-4188

[L]   **Bloom, J. Michael & Assoc.**
9255 Sunset Blvd, 7th Floor
Los Angeles, CA 90069
(310) 275-6800

[**]   **Bohrman Agency, The**
8899 Beverly Blvd. #811
Los Angeles, CA 90048
(310) 550-5444

**Borinstein, Oreck,
Bogart Agency**
8271 Melrose Ave #110
Los Angeles, CA 90046
(323) 658-7500

[**]   **Brandon, Paul & Associates**
1033 North Carol Dr #T-6
Los Angeles, CA 90069
(310) 273-6173

[**,P]   **Brandt Company, The**
15250 Ventura Blvd #720
Sherman Oaks, CA 91403
(818) 783-7747

[P]   **Broder/Kurland/Webb/Uffner**
9242 Beverly Blvd #200
Beverly Hills, CA 90210
(310) 281-3400

[**,P]   **Brown, Bruce Agency**
1033 Gayley Ave #207
Los Angeles, CA 90024
(310) 208-1835

[**,L,P] **Buchwald, Don & Associates**
6500 Wilshire Blvd #2200
Los Angeles, CA 90048
(310) 655-7400

Career Artists International
11030 Ventura Blvd #3
Studio City, CA 91604
(818) 980-1315

[**]   **Carroll, William Agency**
139 North San Fernando Rd #A
Burbank, CA 91502
(818) 845-3791

[L]   **Catalyst Literary &
Talent Agency**
(818) 597-8335

[**]   **Cavaleri & Associates**
405 South Riverside Dr #200
Burbank, CA 91506
(818) 955-9300

[**]   **Chasin Agency, Inc., The**
8899 Beverly Blvd. #716
Los Angeles, CA 90048
(323) 278-7505

[L]   **CNA & Associates, Inc.**
1925 Century Park East #750
Los Angeles, CA 90067
(310) 556-4343

[*]   **Coast To Coast Talent Group**
3350 Barham Blvd
Los Angeles, CA 90068
(323) 845-9200

[**]   **Coppage Company, The**
3500 West Olive #1420
Burbank, CA 91505
(818) 953-4163

[**]   **Coralie Jr. Theatrical Agency**
4789 Vineland Ave #100
North Hollywood, CA 91602
(818) 766-9501

[L]   **Dade/Schultz Associates**
6442 Coldwater Cyn #206
Valley Glen Ca 91606
(818) 760-3100

187

[**,L] Douroux & Co.
445 South Beverly Dr #310
Beverly Hills, CA 90212
(310) 552-0900

[L] Durkin Artists Agency
127 Broadway #210
Santa Monica, CA 90401
(310) 458-5377

[**,P] Dytman & Associates
9200 Sunset Blvd #809
Los Angeles, CA 90069
(310) 274-8844

[L] Ellechante Talent Agency
274 Spazier Avenue
Burbank, CA 91502
(818) 557-3025

[**,L,P] Endeavor Agency, The
9701 Wilshire Blvd, 10th Floor
Beverly Hills, CA 90212
(310) 248-2000

Epstein-Wyckoff-Corsa-Ross
& Associates
280 South Beverly Dr #400
Beverly Hills, CA 90212
(310) 278-7222

[*] ES Agency, The
55 New Montgomery #511
San Francisco, CA 94105
(415) 543-6575

Favored Artists Agency
122 South Robertson Blvd #202
Los Angeles, CA 90048
(310) 247-1040

[P] Field-Cech Agency, Inc., The
12725 Ventura Blvd #D
Studio City, CA 91604
(818) 980-2001

Film Artists Associates
13563-1/2 Ventura Blvd
2nd Floor
Sherman Oaks, CA 91423
(818) 386-9669

[L] Film-Theater Actors Exchange
582 Market St #306
San Francisco, CA 94104
(415) 433-3920

Flate, David Talent Agency
9300 Wilshire Blvd. #300
Beverly Hills, CA 90212
(310) 828-6289

[L] Freed, Barry Company, Inc., The
2040 Avenue Of The Stars #400
Los Angeles, CA 90067
(310) 277-1260

[**,L,P] Fries, Alice Agency, Ltd.
1927 Vista Del Mar Ave
Los Angeles, CA 90068
(323) 464-1404

Gage Group, Inc., The
9255 Sunset Blvd #515
Los Angeles, CA 90069
(310) 859-8777

[**] Garrick, Dale International
8831 Sunset Blvd
Los Angeles, CA 90069
(310) 657-2661

Geddes Agency
8430 Santa Monica Blvd #200
West Hollywood, CA 90069
(323) 848-2700

[**] Gelff, Laya Agency
16133 Ventura Blvd #700
Encino, CA 91436
(818) 996-3100

[**] Gerard, Paul Talent Agency
11712 Moorpark St #112
Studio City, CA 91604
(818) 769-7015

[P] Gersh Agency, Inc., The
232 North Canon Dr #201
Beverly Hills, CA 90210
(310) 274-6611

[**,L] Gordon, Michelle & Associates
260 South Beverly Dr #308
Beverly Hills, CA 90212
(310) 246-9930

[**] Greene, Harold R. Agency
13900 Marquesas Way
Building C #83
Marina Del Rey, CA 90292
(310) 823-5393

188

[L] **Gusay, Charlotte Literary**
Agent/Artists Representative
10532 Blythe Ave.
Los Angeles, CA 90064
(310) 559-0831

Grossman, Larry & Associates
211 South Beverly Dr #206
Beverly Hills, CA 90212
(310) 550-8127

[**] **Henderson/Hogan Agency, Inc.**
247 South Beverly Dr
Beverly Hills, CA 90212
(310) 274-7815

[*] **Herman, Richard**
Talent Agency
124 Lasky Dr, 2nd Floor
Beverly Hills, CA 90212
(310) 550-8913

[**] **Homan, Maybank, Lieb**
9229 Sunset Blvd. #700
Los Angeles, CA 90069
(310) 274-4600

[**] **HWA Talent Representatives**
3500 West Olive Ave. #1400
Burbank, CA 91505
(818) 972-4310

[P] **Innovative Artists**
1999 Avenue Of The Stars #2850
Los Angeles, CA 90067
(310) 553-5200

[P] **International Creative Mgmt.**
8942 Wilshire Blvd
Beverly Hills, CA 90211
(310) 550-4000

Kallen, Leslie B. Agency
15303 Ventura Blvd #900
Sherman Oaks, CA 91403
(818) 906-2785

[**,P] **Kaplan-Stahler-Gumer**
Agency, The
8383 Wilshire Blvd #923
Beverly Hills, CA 90211
(323) 653-4483

[**] **Karg, Michael & Associates**
12220 1/2 Venice Blvd.
Los Angeles, CA 90066
(310) 205-0435

Kjar, Tyler Agency, The
10643 Riverside Dr
Toluca Lake, CA 91602
(818) 760-0321

[**,L] **Klane, Jon Agency**
120 El Camino Dr #112
Beverly Hills, CA 90212
(310) 278-0178

[**,P] **Kohner, Paul Inc.**
9300 Wilshire Blvd #555
Beverly Hills, CA 90212
(310) 550-1060

[L] **L.A. Premiere Artists Agency**
8899 Beverly Blvd #510
Los Angeles, CA 90048
(310) 271-1414

[**,P] **Lake, Candace Agency, Inc., The**
9200 Sunset Blvd #820
Los Angeles, CA 90069
(310) 247-2115

[**,L] **Larchmont Literary Agency**
444 North Larchmont Blvd. #200
Los Angeles, CA 90004
(323) 856-3070

[**] **Lenhoff & Lenhoff**
9200 Sunset Blvd #1201
Los Angeles, CA 90069
(310) 550-3900

Lenny, Jack Associates
9454 Wilshire Blvd #600
Beverly Hills, CA 90212
(310) 271-2174

[**] **Lichtman, Terry Co., Agency**
12216 Moorpark Street
Studio City, CA 91604
(818) 655-9898

Luker, Jana Talent Agency
1923 1/2 Westwood Blvd #3
Los Angeles, CA 90025
(310) 441-2822

189

Lynne & Reilly Agency
10725 Vanowen St
North Hollywood, CA 91605
(323) 850-1984

[P] **Major Clients Agency**
345 North Maple Dr #395
Beverly Hills, CA 90210
(310) 205-5000

Maris Agency
17620 Sherman Way #213
Van Nuys, CA 91406
(818) 708-2493

[**] **Markwood Company, The**
1813 Victory Blvd
Glendale, CA 91201
(818) 401-3644

[L] **Media Artists Group/**
Capital Artists
8383 Wilshire Blvd #954
Beverly Hills, CA 90211
(323) 658-7434

[**,P] **Metropolitan Talent Agency**
190   4526 Wilshire Blvd
Los Angeles, CA 90010
(323) 857-4500

[L] **Miles, Marjorie & Harvey, Matt**
Literary Talent Agency
836 North La Cienega #358
Los Angeles, CA 90069
(213) 673-3717

[L] **Miller-Moore Talent Agency**
723 Ocean Front Walk
Venice, CA 90291
(310) 396-1549

[**] **Miller, Stuart M. Co., The**
11684 Ventura Blvd #225
Studio City, CA 91604
(818) 506-6067

[**] **Orange Grove Group, Inc., The**
12178 Ventura Blvd #205
Studio City, CA 91604
(818) 762-7498

Original Artists
417 South Beverly Dr #201
Beverly Hills, CA 90212
(310) 277-1251

[**] **Ostroff, Daniel Agency, The**
9200 Sunset Blvd #402
Los Angeles, CA 90069
(310) 278-2020

[*] **Panda Talent Agency**
3721 Hoen Ave
Santa Rosa, CA 95405
(707) 576-0711

[*] **Panettiere & Co.**
Talent Agency
1841 North Fuller Ave #206
Los Angeles, CA 90046
(323) 876-5984

[P] **Paradigm**
10100 Santa Monica Blvd #2500
Los Angeles, CA 90067
(310) 277-4400

[**,P] **Perelman, Barry Agency, The**
9200 Sunset Blvd #1201
Los Angeles, CA 90069
(310) 274-5999

[**,P] **Pleshette, Lynn**
Literary Agency
2700 North Beachwood Dr
Hollywood, CA 90068
(323) 465-0428

[**,P] **Preferred Artists**
16633 Ventura Blvd #1421
Encino, CA 91436
(818) 990-0305

[**,P] **Preminger, Jim Agency, The**
1650 Westwood Blvd #201
Los Angeles, CA 90024
(310) 475-9491

Price, Fred R. Literary Agency
14044 Ventura Blvd #201
Sherman Oaks, CA 91423
(818) 763-6365

[**] **Privilege Talent Agency**
9229 Sunset Blvd. #414
West Hollywood, CA 90069
(310) 858-5277

[**] **Production Arts Management**
1122 South Robertson Blvd #9
Los Angeles, CA 90035
(310) 276-8536

[**,P] Quillco Agency
3104 West Cumberland Ct
Westlake Village, CA 91362
(805) 495-8436

[L] Raine Agency, Inc., The
5225 Wilshire Blvd. #421
Los Angeles, CA 90036
(323) 932-0897

[**,P] Renaissance, A Literary/
Talent Agency, Inc.
9220 Sunset Blvd #302
Los Angeles, CA 90069
(310) 858-5365

[**] Richland Agency, The
2828 Donald Douglas Loop No.
Santa Monica, CA 90405
(310) 571-1833

[**] Roberts Company, The
10345 West Olympic Blvd
Penthouse
Los Angeles, CA 90064
(310) 552-7800

Rbins, Michael D & Associates
23241 Ventura Blvd. #300
Woodland Hills, CA 91364

Rogers, Stephanie & Associates
3575 Cahuenga Blvd, West #249
Los Angeles, CA 90068
(323) 851-5155

[**,P] Rothman Agency, The
9465 Wilshire Blvd #840
Beverly Hills, CA 90212
(310) 247-9898

[**] Sanford-Gross & Associates
1015 Gayley Ave #301
Los Angeles, CA 90024
(310) 208-2100

[**] Sarnoff Company, Inc., The
10 Universal City Plaza #2000
Universal City, CA 91608
(818) 754-3708

[**] Scagnetti, Jack
5118 Vineland Ave #102
North Hollywood, CA 91601
(818) 762-3871

[**,P] Schechter, Irv Company, The
9300 Wilshre Blvd #400
Beverly Hills, CA 90212
(310) 278-8070

[**] Schwartzman, Paul Office, The
3000 West Olympic Blvd
Santa Monica, CA 90404
(323) 651-5500

[**] Shafer & Associates
9000 Sunset Blvd #808
Los Angeles, CA 90069
(310) 888-1240

[P] Shapira, David & Assoc., Inc.
15301 Ventura Blvd #345
Sherman Oaks, CA 91403
(818) 906-0322

[**,P] Shapiro-Lichtman-Stein
8827 Bevelry Blvd
Los Angeles, CA 90048
(310) 859-8877

[**] Sherman, Ken & Associates
9507 Santa Monica Blvd #212
Beverly Hills, CA 90210
(310) 273-8840

Shumaker Artists
Talent Agency
6533 Hollywood Blvd #401
Hollywood, CA 90028
(323) 464-0745

Siegel, Jerome S. Associates
1680 North Vine St. #617
Hollywood, CA 90028
(323) 466-0185

[**] Sindell, Richard & Associates
8271 Melrose Ave #202
Los Angeles, CA 90046
(323) 653-5051

Smith, Gerald K. & Associates
(323) 849-5388

Smith, Susan & Associates
121 North San Vicente Blvd
Beverly Hills, CA 90211
(323) 852-4777

[**] Soloway, Grant, Kopaloff
& Associates
6399 Wilshire Blvd #414
Los Angeles, CA 90048
(323) 782-1854

[L] Sorice, Camille Talent Agency
13412 Moorpark St #C
Sherman Oaks, CA 91423
(818) 995-1775

[L] Starling, Caryn Talent Agency
619 N. Hollywood Way
Burbank, CA 91505
(818) 766-0436

Starwil Productions
6253 Hollywood Blvd #730
Hollywood, CA 90028
(323) 874-1239

[**] Stone Manners Agency, The
8436 W. 3rd Street #740
Los Angeles, CA 90048
(323) 655-1313

[L] Triumph Literary Agency
3000 West Olympic Blvd. #1362
Santa Monica, CA 90404
(310) 264-3959

[*] Turning Point Mgmt. Systems
6601 Center Drive West #500
Los Angeles, CA 90045
(310) 348-8171

[**] Turtle Agency, The
955 S. Carrillo Dr. #103
Los Angeles, CA 90048
(323) 954-4068

[**] Uffner, Beth & Associates
9242 Beverly Blvd #200
Beverly Hills, CA 90210
(310) 281-3400

[**,P] United Talent Agency
9560 Wilshire Blvd, 5th Floor
Beverly Hills, CA 90212
(310) 273-6700

[**] Universal Talent Agency
8306 Wilshire Blvd. #530
Beverly Hills, CA 90211
(310) 273-7721

Van Duren, Annette Agency
925 North Sweetzer Ave. #12
West Hollywood, CA 90069
(323) 650-3643

[**,P] Vision Art Management
9200 Sunset Blvd
Penthouse 1
Los Angeles, CA 90069
(310) 888-3288

[**] Wain, Erika Agency
1418 North Highland Ave #102
Hollywood, CA 90028
(323) 460-4224

[**] Wallerstein Company, Inc., The
6399 Wilshire Blvd #914
Los Angeles, CA 90048
(323) 782-0225

[**] Warden, White & Associates
8444 Wilshire Blvd., 4th Floor
Beverly Hills, CA 90211

[**,L] Wardlow & Associates
1501 Main Street #204
Venice, CA 90291
(310) 452-1292

[**] Webb, Ruth Enterprises, Inc.
10580 Des Moines Ave
Northridge, CA 91326
(818) 363-1993

[**] Wilson, Shirley & Associates
5410 Wilshire Blvd #227
Los Angeles, CA 90036
(323) 857-6977

[**] Working Artists Talent Agency
10914 Rathburn Ave
Northridge, CA 91326
(818) 368-8222

[**] Wright, Marion A. Agency
4317 Bluebell Ave
Studio City, CA 91604
(818) 766-7307

[P] Writers & Artists Agency (LA)
924 Westwood Blvd #900
Los Angeles, CA 90024
(310) 824-6300

COLORADO

Chardan Agency
5391 Cr 213
Durango, CO 81301

[**] **Hodges, Carolyn Agency**
1980 Glenwood Dr
Boulder, CO 80304
(303) 443-4636

[**] **Wendland, Jeffrey T. Agency**
265 South 38th St
Boulder, CO 80303
(303) 499-2018

[**] **Write Stuff Literary Agency, Ltd.**
3879 East 120th Ave #300
Thornton, CO 80233
(303) 252-9166

CONNECTICUT

[*] **Discovered Agency**
5 Craigmoor Rd
West Hartford, CT 06107

[**] **Tall Trees Development Group**
301 Old Westport Rd
Wilton, CT 06897
(203) 762-5748

WASHINGTON D.C.

[L] **Gabaldon, Theresa A. Literary Agent**
2020 Pennsylvania Ave, NW #222
Washington, DC 20006

[**] **Schecter, Leona P. Lit. Agency**
3748 Huntington St, NW
Washington, DC 20015
(202) 362-9040

FLORIDA

[**] **Berg Agency, Inc.**
12614 Twisted Oak Dr
Tampa, FL 33624
(813) 877-5533

[L] **Coconut Grove Talent Agency**
3525 Vista Ct
Coconut Grove, FL 33133
(305) 858-3002

[L] **Galleon Literary Agency, Inc.**
516 Southard St
Key West, FL 33040
(305) 294-6129

[**] **Garver, Hurt Talent, Inc.**
400 New York Ave, North #207
Winter Park, FL 32789
(407) 740-5700

[*] **Legacies**
501 Woodstork Circle, Perico Bay
Bradenton, FL 34209
(941) 792-9159

[L] **Mc Carthy, Cheryl Literary Agency**
7641 South Dixie Hwy #234
West Palm Beach, FL 33405
(561) 439-5181

Miami Consulting Group, Inc.
5735 San Vicente St
Coral Gables, FL 33146
(305) 661-4425

[**] **Pleeter, Louis J., Attorney At Law**
7615 Cinebar Drive #14
Boca Raton, FL 33433
(561) 391-7951

[L] **Reverie Literary Agency**
6822 22nd Ave, North #121
Saint Petersburg, FL 33710
(813) 864-2106

[**] **Salpeter Agency, The**
7461 West Country Club Dr
North #406
Sarasota, FL 34243
(941) 359-0568

[**] **Stafford, Glenda & Associates**
14953 Newport Rd #100
Clearwater, FL 33764
(813) 535-1374

[**] **Tel-Screen Int'l, Inc.**
2659 Carambola Circle North
Building A #404
Coconut Creek, FL 33066
(954) 372-8910

GEORGIA

[L] California Artists Agency
3053 Centerville Rosebud Rd
Snellville, GA 30039
(770) 982-1477

Genesis Agency, The
1465 Northside Dr #120
Atlanta, GA 30318
(404) 350-9212

K.T. Enterprises
2605 Ben Hill Rd
East Point, GA 30344
(404) 346-3191

[L] McBrayer Literary Agency
2483 Wawona Dr
Atlanta, GA 30319
(404) 634-1045

[*] Monroe-Pritchard-Monroe
722 Ridgecreek Dr
Clarkston, GA 30021
(404) 296-4000

[*] Talent Source
107 East Hall St
Savannah, GA 31401
(912) 232-9390

[**] Writerstore
2004 Rockledge Rd, NE
Atlanta, GA 30324
(404) 874-6260

IDAHO

[*] Author's Agency, The
3355 North Five Mile Rd #332
Boise, ID 83713-3925
(208) 376-5477

ILLINOIS

[*] Agency Chicago
601 South La Salle St #600-A
Chicago, IL 60605

[L] Aria Model & Talent
Management Ltd.
1017 W. Washington #2C
Chicago, IL 60607
(312) 243-9400

[*] Bryan, Marcus & Associates
3308 Commercial Ave.
Northbrook, IL 60062
(847) 579-0030

[*] Bulger, Kelvin C.,
Attorney At Law
11 East Adams #604
Chicago, IL 60603
(312) 280-2403

[**] For Writers Only
220 South State St #1320
Chicago, IL 60604
(773) 769-6350

[**] Hamilton, Shirley, Inc.
333 East Ontario Ave #302B
Chicago, IL 60611
(312) 787-4700

[L] Johnson, Susanne Talent
Agency, Ltd.
108 West Oak St
Chicago, IL 60610
(312) 943-8315

[L] K.P. Agency
10 East Ontario
Chicago, IL 60611
(312) 787-9888

[**,L] Orentas, Dalia Literary Agent
6128 North Damen Ave
Chicago, IL 60659
(312) 338-6392

[*] Rosenthal, Jason B.,
Law Offices, P.C.
20 North Clark St #444
Chicago, IL 60622-4111
(312) 345-0420

[L] Siegan & Weisman, Ltd.
200 West Adams #901
Chicago, IL 60606
(312) 782-1212

[L] Silver Screen Placements Inc.
602 65th St
Downers Grove, IL 60516
(708) 963-2124

[*]   **Stewart Talent Mgmt. Corp.**
58 West Huron
Chicago, IL 60610
(312) 943-3131

Universal Creative Artists
6829 North Lincoln #135
Lincolnwood, IL 60646
(847) 679-3916

[**]   **Whiskey Hill Entertainment**
1000 South Williams St
P O Box 606
Westmont, IL 60559-0606
(630) 852-5023

INDIANA
[L]   **International Leonards Corp**
3612 North Washington Blvd
Indianapolis, IN 46205

[L]   **Jez Enterprises**
227 Village Way
South Bend, IN 46619
(219) 233-3059

[**]   **Joint Venture Agency**
2927 Westbrook Dr #110B
Fort Wayne, IN 46805
(219) 484-1832

MARYLAND
**Nimbus Production Group,
Inc., The**
5519 Old New Market Road
New Market, MD 21774
(301) 831-3333

MASSACHUSETTS
[**,L] **Creative Career Management**
84 Spruce Run Dr
Brewster, MA 02631
(508) 896-9351

[*]   **Powley, M.A. Literary Agency**
56 Arrowhead Road
Weston, MA 02193
(781) 899-8386

MICHIGAN
[L]   **Grace Company, The**
829 Langdon Ct
Rochester Hills, MI 48307
(810) 650-9450

MINNESOTA
[*]   **Otitis Media**
1926 Dupont Ave, South
Minneapolis, MN 55403
(612) 377-4918

NORTH CAROLINA
[*,L]   **Artist Writings**
2250 Calloway Rd
Raeford, NC 28376
(910) 875-4344

NEW JERSEY
[L]   **Brown, Ellen Agency**
211 Clubhouse Dr
Middletown, NJ 07748
(201) 615-0310

[**,L] **Howard, Eddy Agency**
732 Coral Ave.
Lakewood, NJ 08701-5419
(732) 942-1023

Regency Literary Int'l Agency
285 Verona Ave
Newark, NJ 07104
(201) 485-2692

[L]   **Starflight Agency, The**
2450 Ogden Rd
P O Box 182
Union, NJ 07083
(201) 964-9292

NEW YORK
Adams, Bret Ltd.
448 West 44th St
New York, NY 10036
(212) 765-5630

[**,P] **Agency For The
Performing Arts**
888 7th Ave
New York, NY 10106
(212) 582-1500

195

[L] **Amron Development, Inc.**
77 Horton Pl
Syosset, NY 11791
(516) 364-0238

[L] **Amsterdam, Marcia Agency**
41 West 82nd St
New York, NY 10024-5613
(212) 873-4945

Artists Agency, Inc.
230 West 55th Street #29D
New York, NY 10019
(212) 245-6960

[**,L] **Berman, Boals & Flynn, Inc.**
208 West 30th Street, #401
New York, NY 10001
(212) 868-1068

[**] **Borchardt, Georges Inc.**
136 East 57th St
New York, NY 10022
(212) 753-5785

Brown, Curtis, Ltd.
10 Astor Pl
New York, NY 10003
(212) 473-5400

[L] **Browne, Pema, Ltd.**
Pine Rd, Hcr Box 104B
Neversink, NY 12765
(914) 985-2936

Buchwald, Don & Associates
10 East 44th St
New York, NY 10017
(212) 867-1070

[**] **Carasso, Joseph Martin, Esq.**
225 Lafayette St #708
New York, NY 10012
(212) 343-0700

[*] **Carry Company**
120 West 44th Street #17A
New York, NY 10036
(212) 768-2793

Carvainis, Maria Agency
235 West End Ave
New York, NY 10023
(212) 580-1559

[L] **Circle Of Confusion Limited**
666 5th Ave #303
New York, NY 10103
(212) 969-0653

[L] **Dee Mura Enterprises, Inc.**
269 West Shore Dr
Massapequa, NY 11758
(516) 795-1616

Donadio & Ashworth, Inc.
121 West 27th St
New York, NY 10001
(212) 691-8077

[**,L] **Earth Tracks Artists Agency**
4809 Ave, North #286
Brooklyn, NY 11234

[S] **Freedman, Robert A.
Dramatic Agency, Inc.**
1501 Broadway #2310
New York, NY 10036
(212) 840-5760

Gersh Agency, Inc., The
130 West 42nd St
New York, NY 10036
(212) 997-1818

[**,L] **Gurman, Susan Agency, The**
865 West End Ave #15A
New York, NY 10025
(212) 749-4618

[L] **Hashagen, Rick & Associates**
157 West 57th St
New York, NY 10019
(212) 315-3130

Hogenson, Barbara Agency, Inc.
165 West End Ave #19-C
New York, NY 10023
(212) 874-8084

[*,L] **Hudson Agency**
3 Travis Ln
Montrose, NY 10548
(914) 737-1475

[P] **International Creative Mgmt.**
40 West 57th St
New York, NY 10019
(212) 556-5600

[**,L] Jam Theatrical Agency, Inc.
445 West 45th Street #103
New York, NY 10036
(212) 290-7601

[L] Janson, Marilyn June
Literary Agency
4 Alder Ct
Selden, NY 11784
(516) 696-4661

[*] Kalliope Enterprises, Inc.
15 Larch Dr
New Hyde, NY 11040
(516) 248-2963

[**,L] Kerin-Goldberg Associates, Inc.
155 East 55th St
New York, NY 10022
(212) 838-7373

[L] Ketay, Joyce Agency, Inc., The
1501 Broadway #1908
New York, NY 10036
(212) 354-6825

King, Archer, Ltd.
10 Columbus Circle #1492
New York, NY 10019
(212) 765-3103

[L] Kingdom Industries Ltd.
118-11 195th St
P. O. Box 310
Saint Albans, NY 11412-0310
(718) 949-9804

[L] KMA Agency
11 Broadway, Suite 1101
New York, NY 10004
(212) 581-4610

Kozak, Otto Literary &
Motion Picture Agency
114 Coronado Street
Atlantic Beach, NY 11509

[**] Laserson Creative
358 13th St
Brooklyn, NY 11215
(718) 832-1785

[L] Literary Group Int'l, The
270 Lafayette St #1505
New York, NY 10012
(212) 274-1616

[**] Lord, Sterling Literistic, Inc.
65 Bleecker St
New York, NY 10012
(212) 780-6050

Markson, Elaine
Literary Agency
44 Greenwich Ave
New York, NY 10011
(212) 243-8480

[**] Matson, Harold, Co., Inc.
276 Fifth Ave
New York, NY 10001
(212) 679-4490

[L] McIntosh And Otis, Inc.
310 Madison Ave
New York, NY 10017
(212) 687-7400

[*] Meyers, Allan S. Agency
105 Court St
Brooklyn, NY 11201
(718) 596-2490

Milestone Literary Agency
247 West 26th St #3A
New York, NY 10001
(212) 691-0560

[P] Morris, Williams Agency, Inc.
1325 Ave Of The Americas
New York, NY 10019
(212) 586-5100

[*] Morrison, Henry, Inc.
105 South Bedford Rd #306-A
Mount Kisco, NY 10549
(914) 666-3500

[**,L] Omnibus Productions
184 Thompson St #1-G
New York, NY 10012
(212) 995-2941

Omnipop, Inc. Talent Agency
55 West Old Country Rd
Hicksville, NY 11801
(516) 937-6011

[**] Oscard, Fifi Agency, Inc.
24 West 40th St, 17th Floor
New York, NY 10018
(212) 764-1100

197

[**] Palmer, Dorothy Agency
235 West 56th St. #24K
New York, NY 10019
(212) 765-4280

Paramuse Artists Association
1414 Ave Of The Americas
New York, NY 10019
(212) 758-5055

Professional Artists Unltd.
321 West 44th Street #605
New York, NY 10036
(212) 247-8770

[S] Raines and Raines
71 Park Ave
New York, NY 10016
(212) 684-5160

Roberts, Flora, Inc.
157 West 57th St
New York, NY 10019
(212) 355-4165

[L] Sanders, Victoria
Literary Agency
241 6th Ave #11H
New York, NY 10014
(212) 633-8811

[*,L] Schulman, Susan
Literary Agency
454 West 44th St
New York, NY 10036
(212) 713-1633

[L] Schwartz, Laurens R., Esq.
5 East 22nd St #15D
New York, NY 10010-5315

[**] Seigel, Robert L
67-21F 193rd Ln
Fresh Meadows, NY 11365
(718) 454-7044

[**] Selman, Edythea Ginis
Literary Agent
14 Washington Pl
New York, NY 10003
(212) 473-1874

[*,L] Steele, Lyle & Company, Ltd.
511 East 73rd #7
New York, NY 10021
(212) 288-2981

Stern, Miriam, Esq.
303 East 83rd St
New York, NY 10028
(212) 794-1289

[*] Strata Spheres Inc.
205 Mulbarry Street #5F
New York, NY 10012
(212) 625-0365

[*] Sydra Techniques Corporation
481 8th Ave #E24
New York, NY 10001
(212) 631-0009

[*,L] Talent East
555 Main St #704
New York, NY 10044
(212) 838-1392

Talent Representatives, Inc.
20 East 53rd St
New York, NY 10022
(212) 752-1835

[L] Tantleff Office, The
375 Greenwich St #603
New York, NY 10013
(212) 941-3939

[S] Targ, Roslyn Literary Agency
105 West 13th St
New York, NY 10011
(212) 206-9390

Wright, Ann Representatives
165 West 46th St #1105
New York, NY 10036-2501
(212) 764-6770

[P] Writers & Artists Agency
19 West 44th St #1000
New York, NY 10036
(212) 391-1112

OHIO

[*] **A Picture Of You**
1176 Elizabeth Dr
Hamilton, OH 45013
(513) 863-1108

[*] **Amazing Entertainment Agency**
5723 Broadway Street
Cleveland, OH 44127
(216) 441-0647

[*,L] **Kick Entertainment**
1934 East 123rd St
Cleveland, OH 44106
(216) 791-2515

[*] **Le Modeln, Inc.**
7536 Market St
Boardman, OH 44512
(216) 758-4417

[**] **Tannery Hill Literary Agency**
6447 Hiram Ave
Ashtabula, OH 44004
(216) 997-1440

OREGON

[*] **Biggar, Lois & Associates**
8885 Southwest O'Mara St
Portland, OR 97223
(503) 639-3686

[*] **Qcorp Literary Agency**
4195 SW 185th Ave
Aloha, OR 97007
(503) 649-6038

[*] **Creative Communications**
6919 SE Holgate Blvd
Portland, OR 97007
(503) 323-4366

PENNSYLVANIA

[**] **Good Writers Agency, The**
113 Henry Hudson Dr
Delmont, PA 15626
(412) 468-0237

Sister Mania Productions, Inc.
916 Penn St
Brackenridge, PA 15014
(412) 226-2964

[*] **Winokur Agency, The**
5575 North Umberland St
Pittsburgh, PA 15217
(412) 421-9248

[*] **Wordsworth**
230 Cherry Lane Rd
East Stroudsburg, PA 18301
(717) 629-6542

RHODE ISLAND

[**] **Hanar Company**
34 Fairbanks Ave
Pascoag, RI 02859

[L] **Reynolds, Suzanne J. Agency**
167 Church St
Tiverton, RI 02878

TENNESSEE

[*] **Client First Agency**
2134 Fairfax Ave #A-3
Nashville, TN 37212
(615) 463-2388

[L] **Hayes, Gil & Associates**
5125 Barry Rd
Memphis, TN 38117
(901) 685-0272

[*] **Mirage Enterprises**
5050 Poplar Ave #2409
Memphis, TN 38157
(901) 761-9817

TEXAS

[L] **Adley, Philip Agency**
157 Tarmarack Dr
May, TX 76857-1649
(915) 784-6849

[L] **Bevy Creative Enterprises**
7139 Azalea
Dallas, TX 75230
(214) 363-5771

[L] **Boyle, Thomas D.**
1717 Main St #5400
Dallas, TX 75201
(214) 698-3117

[L] **Burnam, Carolyn Agency, The**
4207 Valleyfield St
San Antonio, TX 78222-3714
(210) 337-8268

**Stanton & Associates
Literary Agency**
4413 Clemson Dr
Garland TX 75042
(972) 276-5427

[L] **Star Quality Agency**
2634 Yorktown #412
Houston, TX 77056
(713) 961-2960

[*] **Tinsley, Robyn L.**
2935 Ferndale
Houston, TX 77098

UTAH
[*] **Lasting Impressions Modeling
& Talent Agency, Inc.**
62 West 940 North
Orem, UT 84058
(801) 224-1837

Opfar Literary Agency
1357 West 800 South
Orem, UT 84058
(801) 224-3836

[*] **Walker Talent Agency, Inc.**
10 West 300 South #616
Salt Lake City, UT 84101
(801) 363-6411

VIRGINIA
[L] **Deiter Literary Agency, The**
10707 Averett Drive
Fairfax, VA 22039
(703) 250-2367

[**,L] **Filmwriters Literary Agency**
105 Birch Cir
Manakin, VA 23103
(804) 784-3015

WASHINGTON
[**] **Aabaal Literary Associates**
1110 State Route 109
P.O. Box 482
Hoquiam, WA 98550
(360) 538-1251

[L] **Bliss, E. Thomas & Associates**
219 First Ave, South #420
Seattle, WA 98140
(206) 340-1875

[L] **Cano Agency, The**
8257 Latona Ave, Northeast
Seattle, WA 98115
(206) 522-5974

[**] **Cine/Lit Representation**
7415 181st Pl, Southwest
Edmonds, WA 98026
(425) 774-8214

WISCONSIN
[**] **Allan, Lee Agency**
7464 North 107th St
Milwaukee, WI 53224-3706
(414) 357-7708

Hawkins, A.J. Agency
3403 North 92nd St
Milwaukee, WI 53222
(414) 462-0635

CANADA
Kay, Charlene Agency
901 Beaudry St #6
Saint Jean/Richelieu, Quebec
J3A 1C6 Canada
(450) 348-5296

WHAT RON SUPPA'S STUDENTS ARE SAYING . . .

I was fortunate enough to attend the first course held by Ron Suppa in the UK. As a successful advertising copywriter, I must say it was undoubtedly the most interesting, informative and valuable course I have ever had the pleasure to attend. Consequently, I have no hesitation whatsoever in recommending Ron Suppa's course to anybody interested in developing a career in screenwriting.

The best way to describe the course is two days packed full of very positive personal experiences, frequently punctuated by priceless polished gems of advice and guidance. Even "produced" screenwriters would benefit enormously from Ron's knowledge. Aspiring screenwriters quite simply cannot afford to miss this opportunity.
—Doug Kissock

Your course was the best one I ever took at UCLA Extension. It was precise, insightful, and extremely useful in launching my career. My career in TV has taken off and I've just had my first screenplay optioned. Thanks for helping me. (Now can I have that "A"?)
—Ned West

The class in Chicago was great. In my case, you took a physician with absolutely no knowledge of screenwriting and transformed him into a physician who knows a lot about screenwriting, is motivated to learn more, and most importantly, is writing regularly. Just as you said, the rest is up to me. How you were able to do that for me, while doing the same for a group with such a wide range of background, experience, and talent, will have to remain your secret, because I have no idea.

So watch for me, Teach, I can't thank you enough for the introduction to a new mode of expression. I thank you, my wife thanks you, and my right brain thanks you.
—Roger Landry

Just a few lines to say what a gratifying experience your "Designing The Screenplay" weekend course was. At 35, I guess I'm a late starter in screenwriting, so I was particularly interested in new insights and angles on the profession and business. Well, I sure got it. Having completed a feature screenplay, I am revising aspects of it, based on what I learned, before submitting it to Hollywood.
—David A. Russell

ABOUT THE AUTHOR

Ron Suppa is a member of the Writers Guild of America, west, Inc. and a former entertainment lawyer. He is also a published author, a produced screenwriter, an international script consultant, and the producer of ten feature motion pictures. Mr. Suppa is also an instructor in the UCLA Extension Writer's Program, where he received the Outstanding Teacher Award for his courses and seminars in screenwriting. He lives in Los Angeles with his wife and son.